HOW TO SUCCEED IN CYBERSPACE

Colin Haynes

Routledge
Taylor & Francis Group
LONDON AND NEW YORK

 THE ASSOCIATION FOR INFORMATION MANAGEMENT

First published 1995 by Aslib
The Association for Information Management

Published 2015 by Routledge
2 Park Square, Milton Park, Abingdon, Oxon OX14 4RN
711 Third Avenue, New York, NY 10017, USA

Routledge is an imprint of the Taylor & Francis Group, an informa business

British Library Cataloguing in Publication Data
A catalogue record for this book is available from the British Library

ISBN 13: 978-0-85142-355-5 (pbk)

Dedication

"Nothing is so dangerous as being too modern. One is apt to grow old-fashioned quite suddenly."
Oscar Wilde

"The invention of the printing press is a small blip on the history of culture in comparison to what's happening now." Nicholas Negroponte, founder and director of the MIT Media Laboratory.

This book is dedicated to the high proportion of British managers that an Institute of Directors survey found to be uncomfortable with information technology. They may never risk the dangers of being considered too modern that Wilde warned about, and if they temper Luddite instincts with open minds and good sense, they will never become old-fashioned, and so can participate fully in the cultural revolution described by Negroponte.

The author

Colin Haynes has been a professional writer for over 40 years, an international marketing communications consultant specialising in the automotive and film industries, and a broadcaster. His previous books on business and technology have covered the virus phenomenon, public relations practices, industrial counterfeiting and other intellectual property rights issues, portable computing, paperless publishing, business travel stress, and the prevention of health problems resulting from computer usage. He has carried out assignments in 20 countries, made over 1,000 broadcasts, and spoken at leading conferences on the new Information Age technologies.

Contents

Preface

Pull on your asbestos underwear to protect yourself from the flames, watch out for the black holes and angry fruit salad, and stand by for a brain dump as we take a trip into the future for YOUR business or career in cyberspace.

Soon you can no longer be accused of being a burbling suit when you talk about the Information Superhighways. You will become familiar with the Brooks and Airplane Laws, brittle products, brochureware, firewalls, dinosaur pens, cretinous cross-posts and British big-endians.

In other words, the pages that follow should protect you from the risk of making gaffes in Internet etiquette that will result in strongly adverse reactions – flames – as you explore the enormous potential for doing business in the new media. "Angry fruit salad" describes flashy over-coloured screens that are uncomfortable to use. It is Internet jargon derived from the bright colours found in tinned fruit salad , vividly defining one of the many mistakes being made by big companies and individual entrepreneurs alike rushing to establish their presences on the World Wide Web.

Black holes are the places into which undelivered email disappears without trace, while cyberspace itself is a still evolving term that we use in this book to cover all the electronic media available to venturesome entrepreneurs. As I try to brain dump – share with you my research into entrepreneurship in cyberspace – you will no longer risk drawing contemptuous comments from hackers accusing you of burbling (as in Lewis Carroll's "Jabberwocky") because you are clueless about this new business environment.

Many of us are still suits, being required most of the time to wear uncomfortable business clothes, including the neckties which some of the young hackers we must deal with in the future believe are strangulation devices curbing our creativity and restricting the blood supply to our brains. (You will learn that the suit and necktie are optional in the virtual business world as we gain more freedoms to work how, when and where we wish.)

BRITAIN FIRST

Britain may have the world's first national interactive fibre-optic network. British Telecom has predicted that every home will have a fibre-optic access by 2005, possibly even by the turn of the century.

Cyberspace Naming

The name cyberspace – now widely adopted as defining the complex international web of computerised communications – was coined in 1985 by author William Gibson. He used it in his novel *Neuromancer* to describe what the players of video games perceived to be an imaginary place, an actual space, behind their screens.

Cyberspace is now a buzz word being misused to describe the physical connections – the telephone wires, fibre-optic cables and radio connections – which are more accurately dubbed The Information Superhighways (and motorways, streets and back roads). Cyberspace is perceived by the people actually functioning within it as describing a community and a place where human interaction is conducted thorough the medium of personal computers.

The Information Superhighways is the pop media term describing – often inaccurately – the complex links from your home, office, or mobile computer that provide the routes to reach any other location or individual anywhere in the world with similar access facilities. The Brooks and Airplane Laws are cyberspace versions of the management maxim that if you add more people and complexity to a project it risks being delayed even more. The first term is a tribute to Fred Brooks, an IBM manager who wrote *The mythical man month* (Addison-Wesley, 1975, ISBN 0-201-00650-2). The Airplane Law is based on the rule that complexity increases the possibility of failure – a plane with two propellers having twice the chance of engine problems. We will see that complexity can be a serious business mistake in cyberspace, but having power in reserve can prove extremely useful.

Brittle products are all too familiar in any form of business, and creating them is one of your biggest risks in cyberspace. One way we will try to avoid this is by following the familiar KISS Principle, keeping things as simple as possible, avoiding creeping featuritis so often afflicting marketroids who promise product features that cannot be delivered. Brochureware is one product of such dangerous management self-deceptions, worse than vapourware by indicating that the marketing department is actually selling mythical products, having gone to the expense of printing brochures for them. You may not intend to follow such disreputable business practices in cyberspace, but you need to know that your competitors may deploy brochureware and other new strategic weapons against you.

Firewalls are among the protective devices we will consider to keep crooks and competitors from damaging your premises and inventory in cyberspace, and we will see how the low cost and flexibility of new generations of personal computers are making redundant the complex and expensive dinosaur pens required to house mainframes. Cretinous cross-posts will need to be avoided at all costs as we deploy email and the other new media research and marketing tools.

This book will try to point out such pitfalls to you, but, in order to give a comprehensive overview of the opportunities for entrepreneurship in cyberspace, it will not be possible to go into great technical detail on any particular subject. That doesn't mean that you need to go out and buy lots of other books to fill in the gaps not covered by this one. Once we get you up and running online, you will find hosts of people within modem reach who are able and willing to give you sound, up-to-the-minute advice on almost every conceivable topic.

We will focus on essential information, basic principles and broad guidelines that you can adapt readily to your own particular business and career objectives.

Nearly half (49%) of white-collar workers admit to being "cyberphobic" or resistant to new technology, according to a 1995 Gallup Survey for MCI Telecommunications in the US. Women are more cyberphobic than men by 39% to 27%, and nearly 60% of all white-collar workers surveyed say they will only try technology after it is proven. However, 65 % use personal computers and 67% believe the Information Superhighways will give their companies competitive advantages.

Major fears – key human resources factors which need to be considered by organisations expanding into cyberspace – are:

≠ losing privacy	56%
≠ being overwhelmed by information	38%
≠ losing face-to-face contact with others	38%
≠ needing continually to learn new skills	35%
≠ being passed over for promotion	19%

Freud, in his *Interpretation of dreams*, defined an entrepreneur as someone who feels impelled to realise his ideas, but can do nothing without capital.

"He needs a capitalist who will defray the expense, and this capitalist, who contributes the psychic expenditure for the dream, is invariably and indisputably, whatever the nature of the waking thoughts, a wish from the unconscious," said Freud. It is important to emphasise that the entrepreneur venturing into cyberspace should not carry with him or her this dependency on a nurturing capitalist. Significant amounts of money need not be necessary to launch substantial business enterprises in cyberspace, but the entrepreneur may need at least to modify, and often abandon, traditional business models in this new environment.

The elimination of physical contact and the need to be concise and clear when communicating only with plain text have resulted in distinctive *new* styles of writing/speaking - *cybertalk*. The measures of human worth in cyberspace are in the quality of ideas and how effectively they are expressed. Eliminated are the physical appearance, accent, social status, body language and other complex socio-economic cues and inhibitions which play such important rules in conventional human contact.

Thanks largely to the transatlantic influence of *Monty Python's Flying Circus*, Americans in cyberspace tend to use the British pronunciation of 'cretin', but generally hacker jargon and the techspeak of computing are dominated by Americanisms. Consequently, some of the spellings in this book may be alien to some readers. I have avoided 'gotten' and other linguistic abominations, but program rather than programme is an example of a word that has a distinctive meaning in this context. Fortunately, the jargon – like everything else in cyberspace – is becoming more standardised.

The need for this is illustrated by British 'big-endians' (derived from Swift's *Gulliver's travels*), a legacy from the days before Internet email standards when the UK Joint Networking Team decided to put the name of the country before the name of the computer located in a particular national domain. There is *ad hoc* software to sort this out in most cases, but it is one of those little details that you will need to be well informed about.

Two centuries after the Industrial Revolution made possible by remarkable developments in transportation, we now are well into an information revolution in which fundamental changes to the national and international communications infrastructure are transforming the ways that we do business. Shorter product cycles and a multiplicity of niche markets illustrate some of the more tangible realities of this, but it is the changing of relationships between the elements of a business project and between than project and its customers that will be most significant. Already we are seeing the cyberspace equivalents of the Japanese *karietsu*, a web-like structure of companies and individuals that appear to be a single entity, but actually comprise myriad components coming together, perhaps temporarily, for a common objective. These are virtual corporations very different in structure from conventional business models, and they have an infinite variety – from the multi-billion pound consortia building the Information Superhighways, to the small enterprises setting up businesses alongside them.

The economic and social consequences of what is happening are enormous and will touch every business and every individual in the industrialised nations. The speed and scale of this information revolution are far greater than even the frenetic pace of the canal mania and the subsequent railway mania which transformed Britain, and much of Europe, in the 19th century.

The media hype about the Internet and Information Superhighways is but the tip of the iceberg. Even those of us trying to track the development of cyberspace are being overwhelmed by the daily – hourly – announcements of new projects, advances in technology, corporate realignments in the form of mergers and takeovers, and the thousands of individuals, small businesses, major corporations, government departments and organisations of many kinds entering what could be called "The Great Cyberspace Race".

The atmosphere is reminiscent of the rush for colonial possessions, land, and mining rights in earlier eras. But the pace and pattern are very different because the very fact that this is a communications, rather than transportation-based industrial revolution, makes everything happen faster and on an immediate global scale.

When building a canal or railway to link a town to the new industrial infrastructure, it was necessary to raise significant amounts of investment, obtain rights of way, negotiate and purchase land, move large quantities of workers and materials, and physically embark on a major financial, logistical and engineering venture with inherently great problems and risks.

But in the virtual environment of cyberspace, most of the physical problems are eliminated, yielding previously undreamed of opportunities for under-capitalised small companies and individual entrepreneurs to compete with major corporations. You can open a virtual office, consulting room, store or service on the World Wide Web, the fastest-growing sector of the Internet, for under £1,000 (often much, much less) and keep it open for under £20 a month. You can, with little technical knowledge, make your cyberspace premises more impressive and more efficient than those put up by some of the leading multinational corporations.

When the canals and railways came to town, our entrepreneurial forebears still had to cope with the problems of raising substantial investment capital or loans; buying, renting or building physical premises; hiring employees with all the hassles and commitments that implies; shipping in raw materials and moving out finished products; and advertising and deploying salespeople to generate orders for those products.

Of course, most businesses still have to meet some – or all – of these physically demanding requirements. But there is no business that cannot benefit from the information revolution by taking at least some of its activities into cyberspace to eliminate or find new solutions to problems. You can improve the efficiency of your procurement procedures, the hiring of both permanent and temporary staff, the research and development of your products and markets, the promotion of your products and services, and perhaps even make direct online international sales to end-users and distributors around the world.

All these activities can take place entirely in cyberspace for some products and services. Where it is necessary physically to deliver or implement them, then the new media can be deployed on specific tasks, such as market research and order processing. The nature of the product is almost immaterial – aircraft, flowers, books, live lobsters, medical services – these and many more figure already in cyberspace trading. New categories are being added every day.

While these are matters relevant to a greater or lesser degree to businesses of all kinds, the impact of this revolution is being felt particularly in the area of

CYBERPHOBIA RAMPANT

The Institute of Directors expressed its alarm in 1995 at the numbers of British managers failing to get to grips with the potential of cyberspace. As a result, the Institute published an instructional book - *A director's guide* - which emphasises the need for senior managers to take a lead, even if many of them will be among the least comfortable with the technology. (The guide costs £9.95 from Director Publications, Tel +44 (0) 171 730 6060.)

SECURITY FEARS
NO EXCUSE

Fears of security problems are being used as much as an excuse for delay as a justifiable rationale for not venturing into cyberspace. The real problems are rapidly being solved, and you will find in the following pages sources for information to help with any particular concerns that you may have. A good start, if you are not already online, is a call in the UK to +44 (0) 121 703 3020 for a free copy of a White Paper on Internet Security from the Firefox company. It also has a Web site at http://www.firefox.com.

small business and individual entrepreneurship. These are the categories that in virtually every nation are providing the main stimuli to growth. Never before in modern times have they had such opportunities to flourish.

As we move from an era of transportation development to communications enablement, we transform the ways in which a business can be launched or developed. Independent entrepreneurs can have, right on their desks, the power of traditional accounting, distribution, human resources and marketing departments. You can hire and fire from your keyboard, getting the best people for a particular task irrespective of where you are located, or where they may choose to live. You can deploy software programs that add the expertise and vastly enhance the performance of specialists in such areas as bookkeeping and order processing.

You may no longer need an advertising or direct mail agency to generate and disseminate your promotional materials because the word-of-mouth and hypermedia linking powers of the Net create new marketing communications media. Smart agent software that helps you to research your markets through cyberspace can be deployed also to go out and generate the publicity and locate the sales prospects. A craft business or florist's shop dependent on limited local and seasonal trade can expand its markets to a region, a nation, or the world with minimal cost. Many small businesses are already doing this, and we will look at some of them in detail later.

In the constantly changing environment of cyberspace, new opportunities are arising all the time, and we will examine also entrepreneurial activities not yet exploited in cyberspace. You may be surprised to find that your particular area of interest already has a presence on the Internet, or be able to identify an opening to stake your unique claim first.

But do bear in mind that cyberspace will never provide the appropriate facilities to research, market or deliver some types of business, product or services. You may still be able to use many of the opportunities that you will find described in the following pages, but you will need to blend them with more traditional ways of doing business. Just don't take a cursory look, decide that your needs cannot be met by the Information Superhighway facilities, and close your mind to them. What is not practical today, may well be – literally – possible tomorrow.

An example of this is the enormous progress being made in processing orders and payments online. Early in 1995, business and banking experts were sounding dire warnings that the Internet might never be a safe place for the processing of credit card payments. By mid-1995, many of those problems had already been solved and there is now a wide range of options for customers to pay for goods and services over the Net with at least as much security as they enjoy when writing cheques, or placing orders by mail and telephone.

Virtual shopping malls, town centres, online catalogs, employment agencies and other trading facilities are springing up all over cyberspace. When a need is demonstrated, there are hosts of entrepreneurs ready to leap in to seize the business opportunity to satisfy it. If you have a business need, cyberspace is the place to look for a solution, no matter whatever your need may be. In just one week, I found there an artist with a talent to draw angels for a book, air fares that beat everything that my local travel agent had offered, a brain surgeon with a great concept for a medical newsletter, new software that would cut by 75% my costs and workload for a difficult project, a solution to a personal medical problem, an overseas agent, and much, much more.

It is this enormous range of information, plus the expertise that transforms information into knowledge, and the sheer numbers of people that make cyberspace the place in which every business needs to have at least a presence. Even if you don't want actually to do business there, you need to visit regularly to know how our society, culture and ways of doing so many things are being transformed by this new element in our lives.

Take, for example, the impact on healthcare, one of the most important areas of personal concern and economic activity in every developed nation.

Doctors, surgeons and other medical professionals are using cyberspace in a host of ways. But it is how patients can communicate with each other online that is truly beginning to transform medicine. All over cyberspace there are groups of patients exchanging information about all kinds of diseases and other medical issues.

"It is," as cyberspace medical entrepreneur Dan Gardner of San Diego told me, "empowering patients in times when the quality of the care they receive may be threatened by managed healthcare programs and budgetary pressures on national health services. For example, patients can learn in detail about a

MANAGERS UNCOMFORTABLE WITH NEW TECHNOLOGY

The Science Museum in London, announcing its 1995 exhibition on cyberspace, quoted a survey undertaken by 3Com revealing that only 23% of British managers felt that they truly understood the term "information superhighway." The exhibition, sponsored by British Telecom (BT) and Oracle, posed the question whether the information superhighway "will transform our lives through developments such as virtual surgery and the arrival of the global office."

CYBERSPACE POPULATION 700 MILLION

Estimates of the growth of the cyberspace population vary enormously, but IBM probably has more information on which to make an intelligent guess than almost anyone else. John Patrick, IBM's vice-president for Internet applications, has gone on record predicting 700 million potential customers on the Net by the year 2000. IBM is doing some creative projects to help build that market, including sponsoring a Web page for the 1996 Olympic Games Committee at **http://www.atlanta.olympic.org**

new or alternative treatment from other online sufferers with the same complaint, and so be able to ask their doctors if it is appropriate for them. If they are denied the treatment for financial rather than medical reasons – it may not be approved by their insurers, or available through their health service – they can acquire online the knowledge aggressively to pursue their demand for such treatment".

Gardner, as we will learn in more detail later, is pioneering a number of important projects to help spread quality health information online. Such activities, even when motivated entirely to benefit patients, are not always welcomed by the medical establishment, hospital services and drug companies. The University of Pennsylvania in Philadelphia took over an information service started by one of its professors and began censoring the information being put online, including suppressing some reports already published in the print media. Online patient groups are proving very resistant to such tactics, and increasingly skilled at getting round them. An interactive forum might be established online by an organisation or company to serve its own needs, but actual control of it can be taken over quickly by its users in this most democratic of media.

Cyberspace communications in digital form can spread way beyond that environment into the physical world by powerful word of mouth when there is information circulating that people both on- and off-line have a real need to know. It is estimated that a third of the 30,000 Lou Gherig's Disease patients in America alone began taking a drug called Neurontin after reports of its beneficial effects circulated among the 1,000 online sufferers of this neurological disease. Although the distinguished British physicist Stephen Hawking survived ALS (amyotrophic lateral sclerosis) for many years, it is usually quickly fatal and so sufferers who use online services to mitigate their physical symptoms of immobility and difficulty in speaking roam cyberspace seeking any information that might help them. It is the same situation in the large numbers of online groups of cancer and AIDS patients.

When news started spreading that Neurontin, a drug for epilepsy and not approved as an ALS medication, had appeared to help some ALS patients, sufferers began dropping out of trials for other treatments. They exchanged information among themselves to discover if they might be part of a control group being given placebos. As a result, the whole basis for clinical trials of experimental drugs may have to be changed.

Some doctors fear that this "medical treatment through patient networks" may yield distorting psychological results. Both medical professionals and drug companies fear a loss of control as patients become better informed – or risk being misinformed and so not taking qualified medical advice.

The whole confidentiality basis of doctor-patient relationships may be changed as patients rush from the consulting room to the keyboard to pass around verbatim reports of what their doctors told them to seek comment from other sufferers. The recommendations – and criticisms – of doctors, surgeons and specialists is already a prominent feature of online self-help groups. Opportunities abound for an unscrupulous professional to seed cyberspace with spurious testimonials, or a drug company to start a wave of interest in a new drug, or for new uses of an older one. Millions can be made by such tactics. Many existing drugs could be given a commercial boost with a subtle online promotional campaign advocating their efficacy for diseases for which they have not been formally approved. This would be the black side of online entrepreneurship, with patients being manipulated online to expand the market for a drug by asking their doctors to prescribe that drug for conditions in which it has not been proved to be beneficial.

You can see how the ALS experience can extend to other non-medical situations because of the sheer power of the online word-of-mouth communications network. We will see it happening in, for example, the build-up to class action suits for product liability. The automobile manufacturer would be unable to control the spread of information and misinformation around the nation, or the world, when a vehicle proves to have a serious defect. Consumers – and lawyers – will find it easier to mobilise themselves to initiate legal actions in many territories, not just one, settlements could become even more difficult to negotiate, and the consequences could run into hundreds of millions of pounds. Such scenarios become more likely as cars, trucks and consumer and industrial products become more standardised and just one defect at source can have wide international repercussions.

An example of the potential was the problem the Japanese car manufacturers experienced in 1995 when problems were revealed with seat belts from the same source fitted to a variety of makes and models for world markets. Skilled public relations in the past have been able to mnimise the marketing consequence of such events, but will find it far more difficult to do so in the future

SNAIL MAIL IN DECLINE

European business-to-business postal communications (*snail mail* in cyberspeak) could decline by as much as 30% over the next few years if the growth of email, fax and electronic fund transfers matches that in the US.

as they swing away from more easily manipulated top-down print and broadcasting media, to distributed information in which every reader-consumer has the power to be a publisher also.

There are many pitfalls as well as rich strikes waiting in cyberspace. Consumers, agents, distributors and dealers who are able to compare notes readily with each other and be better informed on pricing, specifications and other issues will be able to change the way that many companies at present do business. An early consequence could be bringing down the price of computer hardware and software in Europe to be on a par with lower North American price structures.

Product life cycles are getting shorter also, and there will be little chance of getting away with versions of what in cyberspace hacker jargon is called crippleware. Although usually referring to demonstration versions of software products, there is also crippled hardware which the manufacturer deliberately makes inferior to a more expensive version. If the upgrade can be made by something as simple as moving a jumper lead, information about it will spread online like a bush fire, with a serious effect on sales and reputation.

There are numerous other examples of potentially positive and negative consequences of doing business in cyberspace. However you add the pros and cons together, you cannot ignore this new business environment. Even if you decide that it's not an arena in which you wish to participate, be sure that some of your competitors will be out there trying to make it work for them. At least you need to know what they may be up to.

Radiating Humans Online

Concern about the effects of radiation from Chernobyl could make a unique cyberspace resource an essential destination for European scientists, medical personnel, researchers and journalists. A digest of over three million cubic feet of US data on paper about the effects of radiation on about 9,000 people is now available on the Web at http://www.eh.doe.gov/ohre/home.htm.

1. What is cyberspace?

First steps into the online universe

Cyberspace is far more than the World Wide Web, or even the vast Internet that by now may have as many as 30 million inhabitants. There are numerous elements among tens of thousands of communications networks that comprise the global cyberspace environment, including islands of activity still operating in isolation. The information highways include many byways, back roads, private paths and other links which can be deployed to entrepreneurial advantage by large and small businesses. Here are the main categories.

PC-to-PC, LAN and WAN connections

The route that you create between your personal portable computer and your desktop system can by itself become a communications route vital to your business or professional operations. The connections you have with a few or many colleagues over a local area network (LAN) or a wide area network (WAN) can empower your operation with the shared knowledge and more efficient working that result.

Bulletin boards

That kind of closed circuit networking may be extended easily – and remarkably cheaply – by setting up a Bulletin Board System (BBS). This can be a private affair to which you carefully control access, or you can open it up as much as you wish to customers, dealers and others able to access it by direct telephone connections. Many BBSs operated by low cost older personal computer systems perform valuable services for corporate email, or customer ordering and technical support. Thousands are profitable in their own right, serving special interests and storing particular categories of information, or catering for local communities all within reach of it through local telephone calls.

GLOBAL INFORMATION STRUCTURE COULD CHANGE OUR LIVES

"The Global Information Structure is a world wide assembly of systems that integrate communications networks, information equipment, information resources, applications such as education, electronic commerce and digital libraries, and people of all skill levels and backgrounds. It has the resources, therefore, to have enormous beneficial impact on the citizens of our nations and people through the rest of the world."

So said Edward R. McCracken, chief executive officer of Silicon Graphics Inc. at the Group of Seven Ministerial Conference on the Information Society in Brussels in 1995. McCracken presented the business delegation's call to the governments of the industrial nations for open telecommunications and free competition because of the "new reality of extraordinary technological change".

"The Information Society, based on technology, has new and special requirements for creative freedom, private initiative and extraordinary risk-taking," he said. "The lightning speed of technological change makes a mockery of long-range, centralised planning and close supervision of creative talent. Computer power, relative to price, is increasing ten-fold every three-and-a-half years. Who is wise enough to predict and plan the future in that volatile technological environment?

"In my company, we tell young people who apply for jobs: 'If you will be uncomfortable having your desk moved every four months, you won't enjoy working for us'."

Any BBS may be visited by cyberspace explorers using only a modem and a telephone line.

Just one BBS may be, at this time, the only online business presence you need to set up, or cyberspace destination to visit. Later, a business or private BBS can be connected into the Internet in various ways.

Value-Added Networks

Even if you do want to travel much further afield through cyberspace, you may, as an individual or an organisation, still not need to set up a formal Internet connection. You can easily and economically connect to cyberspace through a value added commercial network (VAN) of which CompuServe, Delphi and the new Europe Online are among many examples.

A VAN is rather like an independent nation in the cyberspace world. For a few pounds a month you are provided with software and an access password to a community that, in the case of the biggest, CompuServe, is international with over three million members. It has been expanding in Britain, France and Germany at the rate of 100% annually.

A large VAN like this contains in microcosm many of the activities taking place on a larger scale over the Internet with perhaps ten times as many members. A VAN has forums, online marketing and other business facilities that may be all you need. It will send and receive your email to and from other VANs and Internet addresses, perhaps with some restrictions on length and the attachment of files, but still very easily and economically.

In an increasing number of urban centres you will be able to get access with a cheap local telephone call. (The fact that local calls are toll free in the United States has done much to stimulate the growth of email, the Internet and VANs there, while the different telephone billing structure in the UK and much of Europe has been an inhibiting factor.)

The software provided by VANs is becoming very sophisticated, yet easy to use with either a PC or Macintosh system. Although VANs may be perceived as mainly for home users, they are in fact powerful communications resources equally applicable to business use. What's more, to be competitive they have had to provide increasingly unrestricted gateways to the greater Internet universe beyond them. There may be restrictions in reaching and using different parts of the Internet, but a VAN gateway may be all you need at this time, or for the immediate future. Many entrepreneurs join two or three of these VANs so that, as members, they can research and trade within them, as well as venture further into cyberspace.

The Internet

The Internet itself is composed of many elements and you may wish to use just one or two, or all of them. There are thousands of services, special interest groups and other resources that you can reach by computer and modem, some of which may be more specific and appropriate for your information needs.

The network began in the 1970s as a communications experiment by the US Defense Department, then grew in size and range of uses to serve universities, research organisations, and now a rapidly increasing number of individual and business users around the world. It is still very informal and largely unregulated, but the use of major parts of the Internet by business is somewhat restricted in key respects.

The routes and vehicles by which you reach the different places in cyberspace will vary according to which of the commercial services you use, or how your Internet and other network access facilities are organised. Things are changing all the time, so the following must be general guidelines. In particular, the commercial VANs are developing their Internet facilities in a business environment of very keen competition, so that you may find that through them you have more user-friendly interfaces and routing to many online destinations than a specialist Internet service provider can offer.

For the time being, let's do a quick overview of what is available to you. We can explore the alternatives in more depth as we look at their different roles in specific aspects of doing business in cyberspace – research, marketing, email, etc.

Bulletin boards

These can be set up for just a few hundred pounds – you may already have a redundant PC or Mac that is suitable. It can become a BBS with just the addition of a modem and low cost software, some available online for free evaluation as shareware.

WHERE TO GET MOSAIC

Mosaic is the universal point-and-click browser program that, in its standard and enhanced commercial versions, is driving the popularity of the World Wide Web for commercial purposes. *Mosaic* runs under *Windows* 3.1 on a system with *Winsocket* compatible TCP/IP software, 6MB of RAM and a hard disk. For the Macintosh, *System 7*, TCP/IP software, 4MB of RAM and a hard disk are required.

You get the necessary software from your VAN or other Internet service provider. If not, it can be obtained via FTP from **ftp.ncsa.uiuc.edu**.

3

The usual BBS address is just a telephone number, but many are accessible through what is called a "packet network". FidoNet is an example of a network that links thousands of individual bulletin boards, and offers many local access numbers so that users in these areas can pay a monthly fee and get to other more remote elements of the network without incurring the expense of long distance telephone charges. If you intend to make extensive use of a board that involves a long distance call, you should check whether it has acquired packet network access – this information may well be displayed on the screen that greets you when you dial up the direct number for the first time.

ALL THE WORDS IN A LIBRARY TRANSFERRED EVERY SECOND

The functional power that the Internet is acquiring to transmit information is becoming too great to be ignored by business. In 1994, typical business-to-business transactions transported data over the Net at speeds equivalent to a typed page or two every second. In 1995, new systems were developed which would transmit the equivalent of all the texts in a town library every second.

Email

Millions of online individuals, organisations and resources can be reached by ordinary electronic mail – email. You will recognise these because they include the "@" symbol in their addresses. You exchange email as you do conventional "snail mail", except that it is much cheaper and faster. Basic email is the single most powerful force making cyberspace the engine to drive so many social and economic changes. It can free us from the restraints of time and physical location in ways not made possible by the telephone and fax machine. Millions of business people now regard email as their most important communications tool.

The cost of sending and receiving email is very low – usually falling within the few pounds a month for your monthly subscription to a VAN, bulletin board, or Internet service provider.

Some services accessible by email require you to subscribe, either free of charge or on payment of a fee. When you establish contact you will probably be either stepped through a series of questions, or asked to send a short message requesting to become a subscriber. If you want to subscribe, make sure that the key word "SUBSCRIBE" is prominent in your message. (If you no longer want to be a subscriber, you can send another message later which prominently features the key word "UNSUBSCRIBE".)

Some of these mail list resources function as "list servers". You can make requests for information or files, and they will reply to you through your own return email address. Although you do not interact in real time as you might with a discussion group, forum, or other online resource, mail servers are very useful research and communications tools.

Mailing lists can save you a lot of time and money in telephone and connect charges, because the communications take place without your computer needing to be hooked up directly with the other computer. This also makes it less demanding in time – you can make your contact at any time convenient to you, and should get a response without having to wait online, so that you can access (or download if it is a file) at your convenience.

You should know if your message has not been delivered, because it will be "bounced back" to you with an explanation.

How email addresses are compiled

An email address is constructed from this formula:

username@domain.top-domain

The username is the name of the addressee – one of my email addresses is a combination of my initials and surname to give **cfhaynes@aol.com**.

The "@" sign and first part of the address that follows it indicates where I am located, i.e. the "domain" for my email. It is America Online, a VAN, abbreviated to "**aol**", which functions rather like the name of the city and postal code, except the domain name directs my email to a particular computer system operated by the company America Online. When communicating with other AOL members, I need only give my username because my email does not go outside the AOL network.

The second part of the address, separated from the first by a full point, is the "top-level domain name", which categorises what kind of organisation is supplying the email service. Mine is "**.com**" because I am using America Online, which is a COMmercial organisation. You will find addresses that include "**edu**", because they are EDUcational institutions, "**gov**", because they are GOVernmental, "**net**" because they are NETwork resources, "**org**" indicating ORGanisations, including charities, and you may encounter also the top-level domain "**mil**", representing MILitary addresses.

Top-level domain names are used also to identify geographic locations – "**ca**" for California, for example. International Internet mail usually incorporates a national address – for Britain, the geographic location will be identified by "**uk**".

NETWORKING GROWTH

Revenues from commercial Internet access services were expected to near $500-million (over £300-million) during 1995, and global revenues for LAN and WAN networking products and services grow by about 18% for the second year running to exceed $57-billion, according to *Data Comm*. International revenues for ISDN telecommunications – a low cost way of providing much better data links than ordinary telephone services – were expected to increase by 45% in 1995, with the music industry becoming a significant ISDN user to network recording studio facilities.

VIRTUAL LANs

There is a new way of working of potential value to many organisations that creates a localised, self-contained version of the massive brain power sharing of the Internet. Called Virtual LANs, these are workgroups that can be brought together electronically for specific projects or other purposes without the need to juggle with the hardware of the corporate network. All the connections between group members can be set up through LAN software, and changed easily at any time as the group needs to acquire or shed members. The procedure varies, but the virtual LAN facilities are usually readily available from the suppliers of the switching hub or internetworking products your organisation uses.

You can arrange to have an overseas address if it will be of help in your business, or is financially advantageous. We'll explain that later also. International Internet sites use two-letter identifiers that tend to be the same as those displayed on road vehicles when they are used outside their country of registration – "**fr**" for FRance, "**dk**" for DenmarK, etc. It usually does not matter if you use capital or lower case letters, or mix them up. But it's generally easier to stick to lower case.

Signatures add impact to email

Make your email work for you as a promotional business tool by creating an attention-grabbing, informative signature file for all your messages. These "sigs" should be no more than four or five lines long, otherwise they may be resented by recipients, particularly those who have to pay for their incoming email and will not welcome anything that makes messages more expensive to receive. You can use the sig file as just a bald statement of how to contact you, or include in it a message or ASCII text graphical representation of a logo or other image. Here is a simple but effective signature file from Jonathan Schull, president of SoftLock Services, which gives his physical and email address, as well as the Web sites where he is active.

```
==============================================================
  Jonathan Schull, Ph.D.,        President, SoftLock Services
  Inc. Schull@SoftLock.com,       36 Brunswick St., Rochester,
  716-242-0348 (voice/fax)        NY 14607-2307,

  City Planner,                   Philosopher King
  Downtown Anywhere               Rochester Anywhere
  http://www.awa.com/             http://www.servtech.com/re/
==============================================================
```

Unless you stay within your VAN, most of the cyberspace addresses that you encounter will be Internet addresses. The route to them may differ according to who provides your Internet access, but the basic address rules remain the same, following the Domain Name System convention of **user_name@the_address** defined to varying degrees of specificity.

Telnet

One of the longest-established ways of connecting to other computers over the Internet is to use *Telnet*. Although other options are gaining ground, there may be important resources for you that can still only be accessed via the

Telnet program. It is software – a program, not a network of itself – which enables you to connect over the Internet with other computers using *Telnet*.

Usually, you will find the *Telnet* program in the main menu of the computer or service that you use to access the Internet. You start *Telnet* with a click of the mouse or a simple keyboard instruction, then usually get to a prompt line on which you type **OPEN**, followed by the **TELNET ADDRESS** that you wish to reach.

FTP

FTP – for File Transfer Protocol – is another program also frequently found on the Internet access provider's main menu. You use it in a similar way to *Telnet* to reach another computer from which you want to download a file. It goes beyond *Telnet* by allowing you to transfer copies of files from the distant machine to your own. FTP enables you to obtain files of information or programming that may have been created on a Macintosh on the other side of the world, transported over a predominantly Unix network, and which can be captured on your desktop PC.

Most of the addresses that you access with FTP are in the "anonymous FTP" category. You do not need to have an account on that distant computer to access it, and can log in by typing "anonymous" or any other name that you wish. However, it is part of Internet etiquette when using such resources to give them your own full email address, just as you should identify who you are when making a telephone call.

Usenet

The Usenet network contains many useful resources for entrepreneurs. Some of the newsgroups found through Usenet are predominantly media for announcements of importance in the subjects that they cover, others are more for discussion of those subjects. Each newsgroup is divided into "topics" in which "articles" or messages are "posted".

You can reach USENET newsgroups through Internet links using News Transfer Protocol software and programs called "news readers". Again, these facilities should be available through your Internet access provider.

REGISTERING DOMAIN NAMES

A major problem arising as a result of the rapid growth of the Web for business purposes is the registering of domain names, or URLs (Uniform Resource Locators), which act as Internet addresses. Usually it is best to leave this to your service provider. You have considerable scope in choosing a name, and the supplier will set up the procedures necessary to route calls to the individual user addresses within your organisation. If you intend to operate your own server, check with your suppliers or other expert sources for the latest procedures.

Domain name registration used to be quick and easy through the Internet Network Information Center, but it was getting overwhelmed as this book went to press. For more information, email **mailserver@rs.internic.net** and **hostmaster@rs. internic.net**. EUnet has been handling commercial registrations in the UK. Call +44 1227 266466, or email to **sales@Britain.EU.net** for information

Usenet addresses follow a similar structure to the standard Internet addresses, but instead of indicating locations, reflect the hierarchy, or different levels of specialty – of the subjects they cover. For example, many of the newsgroups of most interest to writers and creative artists include the abbreviation "rec" for recreational and arts topics, "soc" for social issues, "alt" for alternative discussions, and "misc" for miscellaneous topics.

Gopher

Plain text predominates in the areas of the Internet that we have looked at so far, with the exception of the most popular VANs which are becoming increasingly graphical in the screens that they display. *Gopher* is the most popular software tool for exploring these textual areas of cyberspace. It is more than just a program, a complete way of communicating very efficiently between your computer and the thousands of *Gopher* "server" resources available online.

BEWARE BANDWIDTH RESTRICTIONS

Despite all the hype, the Internet has problems looming as the pressure on existing networks – particularly the increase in graphical and video content – mounts. Already there are frequent delays and difficulties accessing some of the most popular sites on the Web because of the increased bandwidth and switching capacity requirements posed by the additional traffic. New solutions take time for service providers to implement. As an entrepreneur in cyberspace monitor these issues carefully – they can be as damaging to your business as having the road dug up outside your shop!

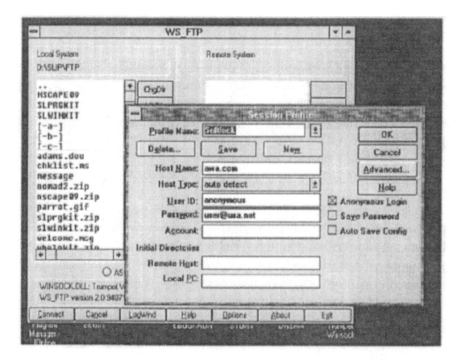

Figure 1.1 – FTP is the cyberspace way to download files directly from computers that may be the other side of the world.

When you load *Gopher* – again usually through your Internet access provider – it will present you with a variety of multi-level directories leading to *Gopher* "server" addresses located at thousands of universities and other information resources. Once at your cyberspace destination, *Gopher* helps you to navigate further to specific sources within that server organisation.

It does this very efficiently, opening and closing connections without you needing formally to log in and out, as you do with BBS connections. This saves you connection costs, and makes efficient use of network resources.

Despite the enormous growth of the World Wide Web, the number of *Gopher* servers is increasing, so this could be your first choice in some research and marketing assignments. *Gopher* economises in the time and money you need to spend online. It can establish connections and enable you to download files, without keeping a physical connection going between computers when this is not necessary.

The World Wide Web

This is the area of the Internet most appropriate to most business needs, so we will be concentrating a great deal of attention on it. The *Mosaic* program – and derivatives of it – function on the Web in a similar way to *Gopher* in enabling you, as a "client" seeking information, to establish contact with a "server" who has the information that you need.

A Web browser should be available on your Internet access menu. If not, type "www"', and it may appear and link you up to the world's largest hypertext system, with many graphical and other multimedia features available.

The most popular way to create a business presence in cyberspace is by getting a Web address and setting up a page there with pictures and text that you can create quite easily with a variety of programs. All you may need to do to create those pages is to convert – with a few mouse clicks or keyboard instructions – a text generated by a word processor into the HTML (Hypertext Mark-up Language) that is the *lingua franca* of the Web.

WAIS

The Wide Area Information Service (*WAIS*) is similar to the World Wide Web in some respects and enables you to do specific keyword searches of hundreds of databases accessible over the Internet.

WEB STANDARDS

There are three prime standards that make the World Wide Web work as a place to do business.

1. **HTML** – the Hypertext Mark-up Language, that standardises the way that Web sites or pages are created. New software enables you to create HTML documents without any programming knowledge.

2. **HTTP** – the Hypertext Transfer Protocol – is the very flexible and fast standard for linking documents around the Web, enabling computers to connect, exchange information, and disconnect very quickly.

3. **URLs** – Uniform Resource Locators form the standard method of addressing to enable networking computers to locate each other and make possible the hypertext linking from one site to another.

MANUFACTURING LEADS THE WAY

A survey of 350 medium- and large-sized companies in 1995 revealed that manufacturing was the business sector most active on the Internet, followed by government, finance and trade.

You may have WWW and *WAIS* client programs already on the computer you use to access the Internet, otherwise you can *Telnet* to a public computer that will permit you to use its client software. A public WWW browser is, for example, available at the New York Internet address of **fatty.law.cornell.edu**, or in Europe at **info.cern.ch** in Switzerland. You can also download a browser by FTP from **info.cern.ch**.

Up-to-date versions of the software for accessing most of the cyberspace addresses you will find in this book and exploring their resources are available online as shareware from several places, including by FTP from **ftp.info.cern.ch**, and **ftp.ncsa.uiuc.edu**. (Remember, it's largely irrelevant where in the world a resource is located because you are not being charged by distance to travel through cyberspace. However, following a long and complicated route from one computer to another can result in delays and technical problems.)

2. Marketing and communicating around the world

The inter-linking web of computer networks growing so rapidly provides a completely new medium for the marketing of products and services, and meeting other business needs. The aim should be not only to reach the estimated up to 30 million people active online already, but through them physically to penetrate national and international markets and research and production resources. You can, for example, use online services to locate agents, distributors, wholesalers and retailers for the physical distribution of your products in territories it was impossible for you to exploit before.

However, cyberspace, big as it is and growing so quickly, is still more of an *opportunity* for entrepreneurship than a *developed marketplace* ready for exploitation. It is essential not to think of it as primarily a place for the direct selling of goods, but more as a whole range of marketing and other business support services which you must evaluate carefully before identifying which could be attractive propositions for your particular business activities.

This is particularly the case in Europe, where in some respects the impact on business could be less, and in others even greater than it is proving to be in North America. Some of the enhanced opportunities for European business people are illustrated in a 1995 report from the McKinsey Global Institute. It found that European employment in the service industries of banking, retailing and film-television-video grew at only about a fifth of the rate of the United States during the decade up to 1992. McKinsey attributed this to what it called "product market barriers", including restricted retailing hours and zoning laws which inhibit where, how and when business can be conducted.

Frustrated European entrepreneurs will find few such restrictions in cyberspace and, as they seek to develop both national and international markets, will discover many ways to circumvent bureaucracy, outdated legislation, and even some taxation. This could be a time to dust off business plans that have been thwarted by such factors in the past, to see if they can be adapted to this new business environment.

TAKING YOUR FIRST CYBERSPACE TRIP?

When making your first excursion through the Web, here are three useful sites to visit first:

1. *The Global Network Navigator* at **http://neearnet.gnn/gnn.html** for an over view of what is available

2. **http://www.tig.com/IBC/index.html**, where *The Internet Business Center* is located.

3. **http://www.mecklerweb.com** – the home of Mecklermedia, leading publishers on Internet topics.

The main thrust, however, will come from using cyberspace to help existing businesses to grow more efficiently, and to enable start-ups to improve their at present lamentably low success rate. The opportunities are particularly good for small firms, which in some sectors account for 90% of British business.

Let's look at some basic reasons why *you* should be considering moving into this still undeveloped new business environment.

Low capital and operating costs

Don't accept some of the high prices being quoted. You may have been discouraged when you obtained a quote for setting up a site on the World Wide Web, perhaps just for promotional purposes, or actually to sell from in the form of an online catalogue or store. £1,000 a Web page, or £10,000 or more for even quite a basic site are not unusual quotes – and that's enough to cause problems getting budgetary approval, or in raising enough start-up capital. Even in the US, $25,000 has been the kind of price quoted by some contractors to put together a Web site which might comprise comparatively few pages of text and graphics with little interactivity or hypertext link building to other sites to generate the traffic necessary to make the venture worthwhile. High rates continue to be quoted on both sides of the Atlantic for maintaining as well as originating Web sites.

The good news that emerged during 1995 is that prices are falling everywhere, except those obtained through large consultancies or for cyberspace ventures set up by advertising agencies and other consultants who tend both to use facilities carrying high overheads and put large markups on to creative time. There is now no need to pay an outside contractor at all, unless you wish to go that route. Easy-to-use software has been introduced that will run on ordinary Macs and PCs to enable businesses or individuals to do all the creative work themselves without needing special professional skills. (Some of these programs you can get online for nothing. There are more details in Chapter 6 and Appendix I.)

You may not be able to match a professional artist or programmer in the visual sophistication or the slickness of interactivity that they may be able to create. But by observing a few commonsense rules and taking advantage of the vast selection of templates, clip art and royalty free photographs now available, almost anyone with basic keyboard skills and business nous can put

The Ideal Business PC

What would be the optimum specification for a business desktop PC in 1996? The respected *Byte* magazine surveyed the options and recommended an Intel P6 processor of 250MIPS or better, between 32 and 64MB of RAM, at least a one-gigabyte hard drive, full multimedia capabilities, voice navigation, and video conferencing capabilities. However, you can use the Net quite efficiently with a 386 with 100MB hard disk and only 4MB of RAM – even a lower specification if you use a text-based browser.

together a Web site that will communicate effectively, perform smoothly and attract prospects. Do it well, and it can appear as substantial and impressive as a site created by an enterprise a thousand times your size.

In addition to saving money, there are other benefits to be derived from the time investment in learning the basic skills necessary. Having these skills in-house makes it easier for you constantly to keep freshening up your site and attracting repeat business – better than paying out most of your budget to a contractor, and then not being able to keep your Web site evolving in such a way that you will encourage repeat visits. That would be like a magazine which expends its annual budget on the January issue, and then is forced to leave it on the newsstand and expect to go on making sales in April.

However, if you do adopt the D.I.Y. approach, it's worth getting someone with technical skills to test your site comprehensively before it is opened for business. You can recruit someone online for this task, if a suitable person is not available locally, but be careful not to give anyone an opportunity to compromise any security procedures that may be necessary to protect your site from hacker – or competitor – attack.

If you don't need to create a marketing presence, and want to use the Internet only for research and communications tasks, your costs for doing so can be trifling. Many big corporations are saving enormous sums without appearing to be very active in cyberspace. They are discreetly using the Net for such tasks as email and data transfer, often behind security firewalls. Banks and financial services are among these leading players who deliberately do not draw attention to their cyberspace activities. The analysis of traffic patterns indicates that a massive amount of research is going on online, with some of the big corporations pulling in a lot more data than they are sending out.

There are many routine tasks for which cyberspace offers practical, cost-saving solutions. If you have significant expenditure on courier services for documents, then large savings might be achieved by moving that traffic online. Documents can be scanned very efficiently these days to turn them into digital files, or to be faxed directly from your computers to the computers at their destinations, or to conventional fax machines. Online fax services are expanding rapidly, and can result in great improvements in efficiency at both ends.

SIGN ON ONLINE

Even the unemployed are within reach of new interactive online technologies. PIN (personal information numbers) are issued to unemployed workers in the US state of Oregon and they sign on for benefits over the telephone. Callers using a touch tone phone are stepped by interactive voice response through prerecorded questions to supply the information about their unemployment status that they would normally give in person at the office. They verify everything with their PINs, which are regarded as being as secure as handwritten signatures on claim forms. Substantial savings have been made by the system, which enables benefits payments to be made weekly instead of every two weeks as before.

The same principles can be applied to online communications for other purposes, but there are concerns about the security of PINs communicated in this way.

If you have substantial international and long distance telephone bills, then there should be no problem in justifying a move to email. Convinced email users now much prefer to do most of their communications this way than put up with the extra time and disruptions caused by voice calls which could be more efficiently handled as email messages. Telephone tag is eliminated, as are the problems caused by communicating across time zones. If you want to conduct real-time live discussions, there are ways to do this economically on the Internet also, with Internet Relay Chat sessions just one possibility.

Research and development

One bright person with a computer may find out much more valuable information for product development than a whole team of researchers with clipboards on the street – and do so far quicker and at a fraction of the cost. Cyberspace is packed with people exchanging information about topics that can contribute greatly to market research and product development. You can participate in, or eavesdrop on, discussions yielding information which you can convert into knowledge that will give you competitive advantages.

Online research has special advantages if you are in a high tech business and need to keep up to date with what is happening in specialist areas. You can pick up information well ahead of the technical and industry print journals and newsletters. Indeed, you can go straight to sources that they may not have developed.

Problem solving

The small venture with limited resources can score greatly by having access to online expertise and information to help solve a whole range of business and technical problems. In many situations, advice and experience is shared freely, while for sensitive problem-solving tasks, you can use cyberspace resources to track down just the expert you need to recruit for more confidential consultancy work. I know of one company that got immediate payback for all its hardware and software costs to get into cyberspace with just one quick answer to a manufacturing problem it was having with adhesives.

Training

The Internet contains a wealth of low-cost training materials for learning about cyberspace itself, computer software, and many other things also. You

WHERE THE TRUE COSTS LIE

Surveys have shown that purchasing the hardware and software to establish a network is often significantly less than the cost of managing and supporting it over five years.

THE INTERNET SOCIETY

The Internet Society is an international organisation devoted to furthering the development of the Net. It manages the establishment of standards, arranges conferences, and has many other activities. If you are interested in joining, send an email to **ISOC@nri.reson.va.us**

can download interactive tutorials, manuals, specifications , simulations, video sequences, and other training aids that are almost certainly cheaper and more up to date than print materials for similar tasks.

Cathay Pacific executives in Hong Kong attend an MBA degree course conducted by a professor at the University of Michigan business school using a teleconferencing system set up by British Telecomm and AT&T. Universities, with their considerable experience of the Internet, offer hosts of entrepreneurial opportunities to market their resources to the world. Faculty members who may not perform well in full-scale video conferencing like the Cathay Pacific venture, may well realise their potential by shining in other forms of online interaction. The interpersonal skills that have been so important to some careers are changing, and we look at such important human resources issues in more depth later.

Recruitment

If you are seeking to hire – or looking for a job – cyberspace can bring vacancies and candidates together very efficiently. I know one entrepreneur who launched a very successful business by recruiting all his specialist staff online, briefing them by email from his home computer, and getting them to deliver their work in digital form by modem. He has never even met some members of the small team who helped him on the way to his first million!

Collaboration

There are many examples of online collaboration within and between enterprises. You can bring together a team in cyberspace for many projects that previously required expensive, time-consuming transportation of the people involved to a fixed location and special facilities. Now, even if a powerful computer needs to be operated by team members in scattered locations, they can use it remotely with the new software available.

Online communications can be used to great effect after a merger, or when two firms come together for a particular assignment, as is happening increasingly. In addition to data exchange – text, drawings, databases, etc. – there can be real-time face-to-face or group conferences using email, various forms of discussion groups, and full-scale video conferencing.

April Fool's Day Opportunities

April the First is an annual entrepreneurial opportunity you might be able to use to generate some exposure for a product or service without getting flamed. One year I fell for an offer of what proved to be a hoax *ScentMaster* card to add nose-bending special effects to multimedia presentations. Pull a creatively clever prank targeted to the right audience, and you might at least generate some useful email addresses.

Valentine's Day is another annual opportunity – there are lots of appropriate groups online.

PCs Pass TVs

Sales of personal computers for the home were larger than sales of standard colour television sets for the first time in the US in 1995.

Customer support and technical services

There is a strong trend among those familiar with online procedures to prefer to get support information from a bulletin board, Web site, user group or similar facility than by voice phone, even if the supplier has a toll-free number for this purpose. Usually at just the times when you want your support to be prompt and efficient, voice facilities get swamped and there are not enough lines or staff to cope with the demand. At other times, the demand for support is comparatively slack and your expensive facilities may be under-utilised.

But provide support online and customers can almost always get faster and better responses. A single problem may generate hundreds, even thousands of inquiries. You need only to create one detailed response – perhaps well illustrated with diagrams – post it to your online support bulletin board or Internet or VAN site, and it is available there round the clock for anyone who needs it. This is the way such high cost support services as automotive service "fixes" will be communicated to dealers and their service personnel in the future.

The best technical expertise you can apply to a service problem can be made available to customers all over the world whenever they need it. The savings are enormous, and customer satisfaction greatly enhanced. It's a straight win-win.

Promotion and publicity

Journalists are using online services increasingly to research stories, and many prefer to get statements and media releases in electronic form because they are easier to process than conventional printed copies. (However, don't blanket email to journalists with your publicity releases as you might have tended to do through the postal service. Establish first whether key journalists on your lists are receptive to email releases, otherwise you might provoke a negative hostile reaction.)

Extend your use of electronic media even when holding conventional press conferences, or mailing out hard copy media kits. Texts and illustrations – including full colour photographs and video sequences – can be distributed far more economically on floppy or CD-ROM disks than in their normal visual form. The days of the 8x10 glossy print are seriously numbered. It has now become routine for the press kits for a movie release to include a selection of publicity stills on a CD disk.

Lost Someone?

An example of an entrepreneurial venture that can be started from scratch or extended from an existing small business is an American cyberspace bureau called Find A Friend located on the Web at **http://www.ais.net/findafriend**. It looks through a large collection of databases to track people down, and if it fails you do not get billed for the standard charge of about £12. There are specific legal procedures to follow if setting up such a service in the UK.

You can also use *Gopher* and other agent software to seek out groups and individuals to whom you can target promotional materials online. (However, note the warnings elsewhere about the need for very soft sells to avoid flaming.)

Well-conceived publicity can also draw journalists and your sales prospects to your online "premises" where you can make available to them words, pictures, demonstrations and other promotional materials. Such a facility, once established, will keep working for you day and night, perhaps generating opportunities for you in markets you never even considered servicing before. You don't actually have to *sell* anything on line – although this is possible. You may meet your objectives by sparking enough interest to get prospects to fill in a form while they are linked to your online facilities, which you can follow up in the usual way with printed brochures, sales calls, or whatever else is appropriate.

Annual reports, shareholder notices, merger documents, etc.

A wide range of corporate documents can be distributed or made available online. There are obvious opportunities to increase readership of expensively produced annual reports or special publications that mark such events as new product launches or plant openings.

Years ago I wrote the text for an expensively illustrated and printed book in English and French to mark the opening of Ford's transmission plant in Bordeaux. It was sad to see that a large and expensive effort was limited in life and reach only by the cost of printing. Now such an informative promotional publication could be scanned, turned into an interactive HTML Web document and be offered online for downloading by the many people around the world who would be interested in it. Such a venture could become a profit centre in its own right. In this case, the opportunity for global exposure for Bordeaux should prise some funds out of the city's coffers, as well as pull in advertising or sponsorship from local businesses. Selling wine, Bordeaux's most famous product, is already a well-founded Internet activity. (See Appendix II.)

Motor manufacturers have been enterprising in making promotional materials such as driving simulations and demos of new models available online, but few companies realise what valuable resources they can tap by turning existing printed material into attractive cyberspace promotional vehicles.

HEADHUNTERS ON THE PROWL

Headhunters are prowling cyberspace looking for news of mergers, redundancies, hirings and firings. They get a competitive advantage over agencies waiting for such intelligence to be published in print.

CYBERSURFING PRIESTS

The Internet is getting religion. There is a Confession Booth staffed by a Digital Priest at **http://anther.learning.cs.cmu.edu/priest.html** on the Web.

Over 40,000 Web Sites

Businesses are so keen to get hooked up to the Internet that over 50% of corporate network managers in the US surveyed by *Network World* said that they planned to switch in 1995 to the Net's TCP/IP protocol standard. There may be over 40,000 Web sites operating by the end of 1995.

Knitting in Cyberspace

The potential to help refugees and other victims through cyberspace is still only barely tapped. However, churches, voluntary groups and aid organisations are all getting online. One initial success was using the Net to establish contacts with knitters and weavers to get contributions of yarn for Bosnian and Croatian women.

Telecommuting

The Industrial Revolution changed our lives by leading to the introduction of the time clock and the daily transportation of millions of people every working day from their places of residence to and from their places of employment. Now the rapid development of cyberspace facilities is driving clock-free flexible time and *tele*commuting forward from small-scale experimentation to large-scale implementation.

Although telecommuting has been slow to take off in Europe, an indication of what is going to happen here is that there are already nearly seven million telecommuters in the United States, and their numbers are increasing by some 20% annually. Over half are men, many at management level. The Pacific Bell telephone company alone has some 2,000 managers telecommuting at least once or twice a week, and reports that productivity has increased by up to 40%.

A six-month trial in Phoenix, Arizona, quantified just some of the personal savings possible from telecommuting. The 134 workers involved saved themselves 3,705 hours of stressful driving, and the 97,078 fewer miles that they put on their cars also avoided dumping nearly two tons of pollutants into the air they breathe.

As online bandwidth makes possible more sophisticated telecommuting services, such as economical video conferencing, many of the human problems – particularly a sense of lack of social contact – arising from telecommuting are being reduced. The growth of the ISDN (Integrated Services Digital Network) in Britain will have a big impact on the spread of telecommuting. It enables an ordinary telephone line to provide full high-speed video and digital communications to and from anywhere at relatively low cost.

Those British telecottages run by true entrepreneurs rather than just administrators can be expected to flourish if they step boldly into cyberspace to take advantage of these opportunities. Indeed, a well-run and equipped telecottage could become the single most important strategic resource in many of our small towns and villages.

POWERFUL RESEARCH TOOLS AND SERVICES

Specialist research facilities are becoming available to provide the detail analysis of online traffic patterns of the kind that advertisers regard as essential tools for their print budget allocations. A range of these services is available from WebTrack, including their *World Wide Web Marketing Directory*.

To analyse what is happening on your own Web sites, they have proprietary software that installs on your own Web server to collect data on such key aspects as overall traffic patterns, user analysis, the hot – most frequently read – pages, site traffic timing distribution, and peer group traffic benchmarks so that you can compare the performance of your site against competitors. More information from **info@webtrack.com**.

Freeform text databases are good at doing this, with among the most flexible and Internet compatible being the British *Idealist* Information Manager, and the American *askSam*. There is a *Mac* as well as *Windows* version of *Idealist*. Both programs function rather like word processors and are quite easy to learn. You do not, as with most databases, have to put your information into fixed fields or structure it in other ways. Just dumping the information you gather from the Internet into them converts a rapidly-growing pool of information into the equivalent of a database with efficient search facilities.

Both these programs have executable run-time modules so that you can distribute your research as a functioning database to colleagues and others. However, you need to negotiate a licence to use the run-time programming to create a commercial product, so they are not necessarily the best solution for electronic publishing tasks. These licensing policies may change as the brightest future seems to lie with products that make it as easy as possible for users to publish electronically with them. This is an important point to consider when making the crucial decision which data management programs to select for your projects.

Idealist comes in Macintosh, DOS and *Windows* versions for single or multiuser purposes. It boasts impressive institutional users, including the British Library, London Business School, and the Motor Industry Research Association, as well as several universities. More information and demonstration disks in the UK are available from Blackwell Software +44 (0) 1865 206206. *askSam* is a favourite tool of lawyers and journalists in the US, and more information about its DOS and *Windows* versions can be obtained by email to **70401.1415@compuserve.com**.

You can find out what mailing lists are available from various directories and online sources, but finding specific individuals, organisations and groups on the Net can still be a challenge. There are various commercial services springing up, such as InfoSeek Search which can be contacted by email to **info@infoseek.com**. Try also the free *Lycos* search facility on the Web at **http://lycos.cs.cmu.edu/**. The Knowbot Information Service and Four11 Online User Directory are bringing millions of addresses into their databases, and you can find out more about them by email to **is@cnri.reston.va** and **info@four11.com** respectively.

Your VAN probably guides you to more search sources at the opening screen for its Internet gateway.

As new lists are created, they tend to get publicised online and in newspaper and magazine articles, particular by the trade mags that serve your particular area of interest. You should use a similar media mix if you start your own list and wish to publicise it.

Some mailing lists are highly automated, so that when you send an email message asking to join you must be very specific about who you are and what you want. The repeater lists tend to be the most automated and blast out information to all subscribers as it is received. This can result in several messages to you every day. In contrast, the digest and moderated lists contain compiled information which may benefit from intelligent human editing.

Lists launched with high hopes tend, like newsletters, to have a high casualty rate as the initiators realise the full extent of the workload involved. Consequently, the following examples may not all be still around as you read this, but they represent good starting places to find out what is happening in the way of marketing on the Internet.

MARKET-L

This *Marketing Discussion List* comes from Charlie Hofacker (**chofack@cob.fsu.edu**). It is a forum for the discussion of topics of interest to marketing practitioners, students and educators. Typical topics covered include pricing tactics, distribution, promotion and advertising, surveys, service quality, marketing planning for non-profits, positioning, exporting, market models, product design, marketing information systems and decision support, channel structure, relationship marketing, database marketing, ethics, branding, and salesforce compensation.

To subscribe, send email to **LISTSERV@nervm.nerdc.ufl.edu**. In the body of the message, type **SUBSCRIBE MARKET-L** followed by your real name. (Many lists ask for your real name, and you should supply it. Do not use your email address, but your actual name.)

Your application might read: **SUBSCRIBE MARKET-L John Thomas**.

If you decide you do not want to continue as subscriber, you send the command **UNSUBSCRIBE MARKET-L** in an email message to **LISTSERV@nervm.nerdc.ufl.edu**.

Be wary of traffic data that only refers to "hits" or accesses, which can be very misleading. You need to know far more than just how many people arrived at your site, or passed through *en route* to somewhere else. The traffic needs quantifying to be meaningful.

PLAY BINGO

Bingo is a gambling game that can be set up in various ways to work online. The concept has been used by the music industry to promote new record releases, and could be tied in with promotional activities through the physical as well as virtual media, and through retail outlets.

If you need assistance, send the command HELP, or any other commands related to the list to **LISTSERV@nervm.nerdc.ufl.edu**. A different address is needed because the subscription one is automated and cannot deal with various queries that may arise. If you do not make your message intelligible to the system, it will be bounced back to you.

You can use many lists like this for your own promotional purposes, providing that you supply information that will be of value to other subscribers. The cardinal Internet rule is to give as well as receive. Address any article submissions to **MARKET-L@nervm.nerdc.ufl.edu**.

MARKET-L is a one of those lists that can be supplied as a digest, a periodic collection of articles. To order the digest, after receiving your subscription confirmation, send the command **SET MARKET-L DIGEST** to **LISTSERV@nervm.nerdc.ufl.edu**.

This is also one of those lists that maintains archives. To obtain a list of these, send the command **INDEX MARKET-L** to **LISTSERV@nervm.nerdc.ufl.edu**. (Archives are available via *Gopher* at **gopher://cob.fsu.edu:4070/11/other/serials/ml/**.) You can also get an FAQ (frequently asked questions) summary over the World Wide Web at **http://nsns.com/MouseTracks/Market-L.FAQ.txt**.

INET-MARKETING

The Internet Marketing Discussion List from Glen Fleishman (**fleglei@connected.com**) covers the discussion of marketing goods and services in ways that are appropriate on the Internet. To subscribe, send email to **LISTPROC@einet.net**. Include in the body of the message **SUBSCRIBE INET-MARKETING**, then your real name and that of your organisation. For example, **SUBSCRIBE INET-MARKETING John Thomas London Nuts & Bolts**.

To unsubscribe, send the command **UNSUBSCRIBE INET-MARKETING** in an email message to **LISTPROC@einet.net**. Send the command **HELP** and any other list-related commands to **LISTPROC@einet.net**. Your contributions go to **INET-MARKETING@einet.net**.

RAPID EXPANSION

Active Internet usage has been growing at a rate of 160,000 per month, according to The Internet Society, which estimated a total of between 20 and 30 million active users by the end of 1994.

To receive a digest after becoming a subscriber, send the command **SET INET-MARKETING DIGEST** to **LISTPROC@einet.net**. As this mailing is edited, submissions are reviewed before being approved for distribution. The list is moderated also, so that some discipline is imposed. In any case, even with highly automated unmoderated lists that do not impose such controls, be succinct and stick to the main topics covered by that list or risk offending other subscribers. In the case of the *Internet Marketing Discussion List*, the topics include how to reach consumers/end-users/purchasers, advertise and market appropriately, forums for marketing, CommerceNet's attempts to unify the business of doing business on the Net, commercial Internet publishers and shopping malls, ordering and credit card purchasing.

RITIM-L

The *Telecommunications and Information Marketing Discussion List* covers such topics as technology in the household, the future of cyberspace, the cable industry, telecommunications and public policy, home shopping, etc. It is sponsored by the Research Institute for Telecommunications and Information to provide a forum for scholars and managers to exchange ideas and experiences in technology and marketing. The list also serves to distribute RITIM working papers.

To subscribe, email to **LISTSERV@uriacc.uri.edu**. In the body of the message, type **SUBSCRIBE RITIM-L** followed by your real name. To end your subscription, email the command **UNSUBSCRIBE RITIM-L** to **LISTSERV@uriacc.uri.edu**. **HELP** and all other list-related commands go to **LISTSERV@uriacc.uri.edu**. Send articles to **RITIM-L@uriacc.uri.edu**.

Marketing and communications professionals have responsibilities in such areas as advertising, public relations, trade shows, sales support, and strategic and tactical marketing communications.

The following lists – HTMNEWS and HTMARCOM – are primarily for marketing communications professionals handling high technology products such as software, peripherals, semiconductors, board-level products, cards, data communications, systems, and other computer and electronics technologies. Others, such as editors, service providers, publishers, analysts, academics or students may also subscribe. Such lists can be invaluable to keep your finger on the pulse of the technology.

HTMNEWS

High-Tech Marketing Resources and Tools News is a one-directional list – you only receive information – from Kim M. Bayne (**owner-htmnews@ bayne.com**). It distributes *HTM*, an online monthly newsletter of marketing.

To subscribe, send email to **LISTPROC@usa.net**, with **SUBSCRIBE HTMNEWS** followed by your real name. in the body of the message. To unsubscribe, send **UNSUBSCRIBE HTMNEWS** in email to **LISTPROC @usa.net**. Send **HELP** and other list-related commands to **LISTPROC @usa.net**. Send all other list-related commands to **LISTSERV@uriacc.uri.edu**.

HTMARCOM

The *High Tech Marketing Communicator* from Kim Miklofsky Bayne (**kimmik@bayne.com**) is the full interactive list from which the *High-Tech Marketing Resources and Tools News* is compiled. Subscribers can share information and solve problems about different aspects of marketing communications. All subscribers receive the newsletter in the first week of each month, and resource lists and past newsletters are archived and retrievable.

To subscribe, send email to **LISTSERV@cscns.com**, including **SUBSCRIBE HTMARCOM** followed by your real name in the body of the message. To unsubscribe, email **UNSUBSCRIBE HTMARCOM** to **LISTSERV @cscns.com**. Send **HELP** and other list-related commands to **LISTSERV @cscns.com**. Contributions go to **HTMARCOM@cscns.com**. To get the digest, after receiving your subscription confirmation, send the command **SET HTMARCOM DIGEST** to **LISTSERV@cscns.com**.

Newsgroup lists

The newsgroups on Usenet bring together literally millions of people around the world. You do not subscribe to a newsgroup in the same way as a conventional mailing list. They are really forums which you visit through your Internet service provider. Delphi and most of the VANs have a Usenet option or icon on the menu which leads you to a reader enabling you to tailor how you interface with the newsgroups you wish to visit.

Finding Auntie on the net

The BBC has been a cyberspace pioneer through its BBC Networking Club. You can find Auntie on the Net at **http://www.bbc.org.uk**

When you arrive at a newsgroup, you tap into an ongoing exchange of messages called "posts", which are numbered in the order in which they were received. Consequently, the subject line for each posting is very important to identify the topic. When a topic generates responses, these posts develop into a "thread" referring back to the original subject.

There is so much traffic – so many words! – in newsgroups that to use them as a research tool, and when you want to disseminate information, there are some basic rules that must be followed. These tips will prove helpful – they are a summary of guidelines originally compiled by "Net citizens Chuq Von Rospach and Gene Spafford", which apply particularly to newsgroups, but help also when compiling email or participating in other areas of cyberspace:

1. Never forget that the person on the other side is a human being

Avoid personal attacks. Don't speak (type) hastily – try not to say anything to others that you would not say to them face-to-face in public.

2. Be brief

Newsgroups generate lots of words. Stay on the topic – and being succinct will have greater impact. Don't post the same message on more than one newsgroup unless you are sure it is appropriate.

3. Remember that your messages reflect on you (and your organisation)

Most people online will only know you by what you say, and how well you say it. Make sure your messages are easy to read and understand.

4. Use descriptive subject headings in your messages

The subject line of your message is there to help people decide whether or not they want to read it. Use the subject line to tell people what your message is about. For example, if you are sending a message to an Automobiles Newsgroup, a subject like "66 MG Midget for Sale " is much more informative than "Car for Sale."

5. Consider your audience

Stay on the topic. Post your messages in the appropriate newsgroup. By reading a number of the messages before sending one yourself, you will be able to get a sense of the ongoing conventions and themes of a newsgroup.

400+ Banks on the Web

About 400 American banks had posted home pages on the Web when the banking industry's first conference on the Internet convened in April 1995.

MAKE LIFE EASIER

Online life can get a lot easier if you have one comprehensive and easy program to handle all your communications tasks. There is an increasing choice of *Windows* software that will do this better than even the improved facilities in *Windows '95*. Some, like *HyperACCESS*, remove the need to type in many commands, so that most tasks can be accomplished with a mouse click or two. *HyperACCESS* also greatly speeds up file transfers in its Windows, DOS and OS/2 versions, and screens for viruses. More details can be found from **info@hilgraeve. com** or **GO HILGRAEVE** on CompuServe.

6. Be careful with humour and sarcasm

Without the voice inflections and body language of personal communications, it is easy for a remark meant to be funny to be misinterpreted. You can convey the emotions that words alone cannot express by using such online conventions as "smileys" e.g. **:)**

7. Summarise what you are following up

When you are making a follow-up comment to a message, be sure to summarise the parts of that message to which you are responding. This is best done by including appropriate quotes from the original message. Don't include the entire message, because this unnecessarily increases the volume and could be irritating – and expensive in online time – for people who have already read it. A standard way of indicating that you are quoting a previous message is to precede that section of text with a greater than sign like this >.

8. Give back to the community

If a message you send to a newsgroup requesting information generates many responses, it is a courtesy to prepare an edited message compiling the responses to the newsgroup where you originally posted your question. Take the time to strip headers, combine duplicate information, and write a short summary. Credit the information to the people who sent it to you.

Be a "giver" as well as a "taker" in this online community. If you have good and valuable information to share, do so in the appropriate newsgroups.

9. Try not to repeat what has been said already

Read responses to messages before you chime in, so that you are not needlessly repetitive. Make sure your responses have substance – answers like "OK " and "I agree" won't be appreciated.

10. Cite appropriate references

If you are using facts to support an argument or information, state the source.

Among the many newsgroups of interest to entrepreneurs are:

> **alt.business.misc** for general discussions about business start-ups and management

> **alt.business.multi-level** for multi-level marketing topics

> **misc.entrepreneurs** for general business management issues.

Look for "**biz**" and "**com**" in Internet addresses to steer you towards discussions of business topics.

FAQs

If you don't want to spend a lot of time online initially exploring such research resources as newsgroups and mailing lists, you can access CD-ROM collections of FAQs, or make quick excursions into cyberspace to collect the FAQs of most interest to you. FAQs – Frequently Asked Questions – are archives that give you a good overview of what topics a group or list covers. Many contain very useful information. You can get a list of FAQs by sending a HELP email message to **mail-server@rtfm.mit.edu**.

There are several "lists of lists" . One accessible by email is at **listserv@vm1.nodak.edu**. Type the message **get listoflists**.

If you want to start your own list or newsgroup you will need software to act as a list server. As a first step contact your Internet service provider to check on the latest facilities being offered. There is a good introduction to Britain's *Mailbase* system obtainable by emailing to **mailbase@uk.ac.mailbase**, with **send mailbase user-guide** as the message. Details of other information about *Mailbase* available online is obtained by the message **index mailbase** to the same address.

Telnet

The most powerful tool for detailed research in cyberspace is software called *Telnet* – and it could be important in selecting your service provider to check that it has *Telnet* software available to you. If you are already online, it may be just a click or the command **telnet** away. When your system and another Internet location with which you connect have *Telnet* operating, you can effectively operate the remote computer to do searches. In addition to searching databases, you can also run programs at the remote location – accessing games is a popular *Telnet* pastime, and interactive demonstrations are becoming an important marketing tool.

There are an increasing number of alternatives to researching with *Telnet* becoming available, including *Gopher*, *WAIS* and the sophisticated browsers for the World Wide Web allowing you to get into information resources that previously were available only through *Telnet*. One of the best tools for using

Telnet is the program *NCSA Telnet*, and there is a lot of information documentation available with it. You can get both the program and the information about using *Telnet* by what is called an "anonymous ftp" call to **ftp.ncsa.uicc.edu**.

FTP

The File Transfer Protocol – FTP – is a standard way to transfer files across the Internet. These files can be complete programs, databases, texts, publications, graphics, music, videos – whatever. It is a particularly useful way to get updates and bug fixes for software.

A high proportion of the files available online are compressed so that they become small and self-contained. The transfer takes place quickly and, on receipt in your system, a single "zipped" file can be exploded into all the individual files and documentation.

VANs are now providing software free to subscribers that will handle this downloading and decompression automatically. Otherwise there is a marvellous shareware program called *WinZip* that will both decompress the files that you receive, or compress those that you wish to distribute. You'll find details of it in Chapter 9.

FTP has another useful business application in addition to research in that it can be equipped with protective passwords and customised for corporate use to transfer files – and consequently anything that can be turned into a computer file – for fast and reasonably secure transmission between locations.

Most FTP sites open to the public allow anonymous FTP so that you use them without being a subscriber. When you log in to such sites, you give "anonymous" as your username, and then – although it may not be demanded – give your email address as the password. You can remain anonymous, but it's not good Internet etiquette.

FTP modules are available from many online sources, and incorporated in communications programs. Check first what is available in the communications software that you are using, and from your Internet service provider or VAN. If you draw a blank and want the latest and one of the best selections of such software for the PC, you can find most of what you are likely to need at the University of Michigan archives, accessible by anonymous ftp to **archive.umich.edu.his**.

PRETTY PICTURES

Use a slow shutter speed to take colour slides or prints of your online efforts for publicity purposes or to feature them in presentations. Faster speeds than 1/25th of a second risk only capturing part of the image. You need to shoot at about 1/8th or 1/15th with the camera on a tripod to be sure of getting several scans superimposed to create a complete image. To capture screen images digitally, look out in shareware libraries for the graphics program *Paint Shop Pro*. It includes a very easy screen capture utility.

Another approach if you do not want to venture beyond your email resources, is to use an intermediary through FTP mail. You email your request for a file to an FTP mail server, which will go and fetch it and then email it back to you. However, it is becoming more practical to do it yourself directly through the FTP program that most Internet service providers make available.

Gopher

Much online research, particularly for business purposes, may start out being unfocussed. You may want first to surf through cyberspace much as you browse the shelves of a supermarket, sussing out generally what is on offer before you narrow your search down to the equivalent of buying decisions. *Gopher* is the tool for this. Named after a small burrowing rodent that is the mascot for the University of Minnesota, where the original program was written, it burrows – ferrets would be an appropriate English expression – around the Internet looking for the categories of information, or types of files, that are of particular interest to you. It is in some respects the predecessor of the smart agent software capable of very sophisticated and automated Internet searches that we will get to in a moment.

There are more sites that will allow you access through *Gopher* than using *Telnet* because *Gopher* is very smart at not wasting time and resources. It makes the connection to the site, passes on your request for information or a file, then breaks the connection until that host site is ready to respond.

Veronica – Very Easy Rodent-Orientated Net-Wide Index to Computerised Archives – is a utility that works with *Gopher* to facilitate keyword searches. If you already know the name of the file that you are seeking, then *Archie* may be your preferred Internet search tool. You can use it in conjunction with *Gopher* to track down the location of the file that you want and download it into your system.

WAIS

The Wide Area Information Service is another searching utility that is good at finding files or documents by subject and key words. But it is limiting in that it will only allow you to search files that are in the *WAIS* format and you need to point it in the right direction towards appropriate sites.

WWW

The World Wide Web is becoming the major business online research resource because it is so easy to use and attracting a lot of information of particular use for business, rather than academic or scientific, purposes. The Web is an enormous international collection of hypertext documents. The Web browser software that you acquire when your Internet or VAN account is set up enables you to hypertext link around the world through words, phrases or pictures that connect with other sources of related information.

If you have a PC running *Windows*, or a Mac, you can get the idea by navigating around the Help files – except that on the Web the hypertext links seem to go on for infinity, enabling you to move from one place to another in a search for related and supplementary information that never seems to end, so vast are the resources available.

We'll get to the Web in more detail in Chapter 5 when we look at setting up your own Web site. That information will suggest the various ways that the Web can be used for marketing and other entrepreneurial business research.

Smart agents

The future in online business researching lies with smart agent software, the cyberspace robots that will tirelessly roam around the networks seeking information that they think will be useful for you. They'll get steadily better as they learn what you accept and reject, and will become more like super-efficient secretaries as you give them more responsibility to handle your email, your appointments diary, and even your travel arrangements.

Some of the commercial forces behind the development of smart agents are giving them animated personalities to help make it easier for us to relate to these artificially intelligent cyberspace slaves. Rupert Murdoch's *News Electronic Data* has been developing one called *Oliver* that is personified on screen as a faithful Labrador retriever.

Smart agents that can help sort your mail, whittling out the junk and assigning priorities as they learn more and more about the sources and content you regard as being most important will soon become essential business tools for overloaded entrepreneurs. The information gathering agents primarily used as business research tools are already threatening to become so numerous that they may clog up the information highways with virtual traffic jams. These web crawlers can be selfish roadhogs, or discreet and considerate of the needs of other Net users. If you pick one that behaves badly, or instruct it carelessly, the antagonism that it generates towards you from other Net users could be more damaging to your cyberspace business image than the information it collects.

The smart agent field is developing at amazing speed. To keep up with the technology and the entrepreneurial opportunities it offers, check in with the British software company Nexor's list of Web agents at **http://web.nexor.co.uk/mak/doc/robots/robots.html**.

Of course you may not need an agent at all because your prime needs may be just to zero in on a particular source for a specific project, or to make periodic checks on what's happening in a special interest group or two. So a mail list or contact with a newsgroup or a single bulletin board or Internet site may be all you need. Even in this restricted fashion, researching in cyberspace can be very beneficial. There are, for example, a few really good patent databases which can save firms tens of thousands of pounds a year in legal fees – and potentially many millions in bringing products to market.

Electronic clipping services

If you want to keep everything simple and comparatively painless – but potentially expensive – subscribe to a clipping service that will monitor both printed and online information resources. These are proliferating and vary greatly in their charges and efficiency. The usual arrangement is that you list the topics of main interest to you and will be sent by fax or email every day a summary of, say, 20 headings of relevant articles. Then, for a further fee, you can order through an automated system the full texts of any items of particular interest.

Some of these services are expensive – thousands of pounds a year and often a hefty additional fee for each full text that you request. Others are very affordable – the cost isn't always directly proportional to the quality of service they provide. Most will offer a free trial to see if your needs match what the service can supply. Two recommendations for which you can email for more information are **newshound-support@sjmercury.com**, and Individual Incorporated's *HeadsUp* service – **info@individual.com**, or call them in the UK at +44 (0) 1491 638 123.

Expect to see a growing selection of clippings services available through the VANs, which are themselves becoming enormous databases of information. The *Journalist* program, for example, enables you to assemble and desktop publish in newspaper-style format the categories of information you instruct it to collect from CompuServe. It helps you to set up a basic layout, then roams around CompuServe retrieving information and formatting it into a professional looking document.

The interaction with CompuServe is fully automated and this *Windows* program could be a real research boon to any size of company, or as a service of perceived high cost and value to be supplied to clients by a PR or other consultancy. There are, of course, copyright restrictions on how you use the information that *Journalist* tracks down for you from places like the Associated Press news wire.

On-disk resources

You don't need actually to go online to tap into a lot of Internet research resources. Many are being collected on to floppy and CD-ROM disks, although because of the time lag in producing and distributing them, these are mainly archival materials and not the latest information available by travelling yourself through cyberspace to their resources. If you are a Mac user, there is a very large collection on CD-ROM of Macintosh programs and files collected by Stanford University. Email to **711175.3152@compuserve.com** for information. A CD with 600MB of Usenet news comes out monthly from Sterling Software at **cdnews@sterling.com**.

If you are a glutton for statistics, McGraw-Hill's *Encyclopaedia of world economies* on CD-ROM will satiate you and runs well – if not very entertainingly – on a plain DOS system. Great bargains if you are researching mailing lists are the CD-ROM compilations of telephone numbers and addresses. They have got a lot cheaper, come out more quickly, so are among the most current mailing lists that you can find, are easy to use, and the tendency is not to cripple them any more to restrict their ability to print out unlimited mailing lists which you can use without fees. The *PhoneDisc* CD of businesses in the United States is one of the best – and runs under DOS, *Windows*, or Macintosh to give access to address and telephone numbers of over 9.5 million business listings, for a street price of around £50.

Incidentally, some of the data capture for telephone and other American directories on disk is done in China – an example of international business made possible by the Internet. The Chinese are forging ahead at great speed into cyberspace, in some respects moving further and faster than Europe in developing Information Superhighway routes to entrepreneurial opportunities around the world.

4. Where to locate your business

In both cyberspace and the real world

Although theoretically location is largely irrelevant in cyberspace, when you move to do business in this virtual world you must give careful consideration to the best neighbourhood, city and nation as the physical base for your enterprise. There could be significant legal and taxation implications.

Attention must be paid also to the virtual address. There is now a rush for prime addresses on the Web, and even big corporations risk missing the boat to maintain well co-ordinated marketing imagery between their physical addresses and telephone numbers and those of their cyberspace operations. McDonalds, for example, might be fast with food but they were really slow in registering the company name for inclusion in their cyberspace address. When a journalist discovered this and could not get a satisfactory explanation from any corporate spokespeople, he went ahead and registered it himself.

McDonalds, which goes to great lengths to protect its name in the physical world, agreed to equip a New York school with an Internet connection before the journalist relinquished his rights to use McDonalds as the domain name part of an Internet address.

There will be lots of cases like that over the next few years as people who have realised the opportunities for a little corporate arm twisting have been securing potentially lucrative addresses, mainly in America where the rush by businesses to get on to the World Wide Web has created delays in approving and allocating addresses.

This is most likely to be a potential problem if you are setting up your own Internet Web domain – having your own computer system as the direct access to the Net. The computer system operating the domain is identified by the names that follow the @ in the address, and there are good business reasons for making this section of the address easily remembered and readily identifiable with who you are, or what you do.

If you use an Internet service provider for your gateway to cyberspace, then you will have to incorporate your name with the provider's name in your Internet address. You get to choose the username that comes before the @ – unless someone using the same domain has secured it first. You don't get any choice over the last part of the address, which is called the top-level domain name and is separated from the domain name by a full point.

Top-level domain names follow a standard practice across the Net of incorporating a three letter abbreviation of the type of domain involved – **com** for businesses, **gov** for government, etc. – and a two-letter abbreviation to indicate the country from which the domain is operating – **uk** for United Kingdom, **fr** for France, **jp** for Japan, **de** for Germany, **it** for Italy, and so on.

The Americans don't have to include **us** as they were the only people on the Net when they started and funded, initially as a strategic resource to keep communications flowing in time of war and for exchanging military research. Only subsequently did it grow to become an international business network also. However, you will find some American organisations using their addresses to identify where they are, with abbreviations such as **sf**, for San Francisco, **ny**, for New York, and **ca** for California. This form of geographical identification can make business sense. You are more likely to follow through with enquiries about placing an order for high tech equipment if the address incorporates **sf.ca** than **bz** (for Belize).

The Internet address is just one part of helping to ensure that your business and products/services will be visible in cyberspace, but there are many other considerations.

Taxation implications

Still unresolved is how you define locations for virtual businesses in cyberspace in order to regulate and tax them. So you should not rush into getting a New York address rather than one in, say, Wigan, because you think it will add prestige to your international online activities and look good on the business cards and letterhead. There are very serious moves afoot in the US – and other countries – to use the domain or server as the best identification of a physical location which can be made the controlling factor in taxing and applying legal requirements.

FREE INFORMATION FROM EUROPEAN STUDY

The European Commission's IMPACT programme (Information Market Policy Actions) has carried out a strategic study on New Opportunities for Publishers in the Information Services Market. Free copies of the Executive Summary can be obtained from Aslib - email **aslib@aslib.co.uk**.

The study indicates that most European publishers are not anywhere near as aware of the opportunities of the new media as those in the USA and Japan. It urges the better exploitation of the European ability to supply content. It estimates that the European market for new media publishing will reach 12,000 million ECU or more by the year 2000.

Beware the lawyers

Bear in mind that, whatever your actual intentions, when you publish in cyberspace you publish to the world. That could expose you to litigation over defamation, product liability, and other types of action on which American lawyers particularly feed voraciously. The most improbable legal cases which would never even get started in Europe, are routine in the US because lawyers there are virtually uncontrolled in the way that they tout for business and take cases on contingency. Often it is the lawyer, not the perceived victim, who will be the biggest winner if a case succeeds in court, or is settled early to avoid the high cost of business disruption. Most such settlements are not publicised for fear they will stimulate still more litigation fever.

Canada is an example of a country with very strict obscenity and child pornography laws. Material published online that might be within the laws of Britain, the European Union, and the United States could cause serious legal repercussions elsewhere.

Intellectual property rights

The picture gets even more complex when you start considering intellectual property rights and licensing situations that could arise – where do cyberspace's ambulance chasing lawyers go to sue if an issue of product liability or copyright or patent infringement arises?

Despite the fact that there has been far-reaching international rationalising of copyright and other intellectual property rights legislation, cyberspace poses many risks in this respect. In the US in particular, there have been numerous conflicting interpretations of rights of fair use, public domain, and to what extent creative concepts in virtual forms can be protected.

Big companies are becoming increasingly aggressive in trying to preserve their rights, and it is virtually impossible to win against them unless you have a very deep pocket to pursue a case through the courts.

One of the most disturbing developments in 1995 was the giant Unisys Corporation starting to enforce its rights over the GIF (graphic interchange format), the most popular standard for graphics files online. Although the Unisys patent does not apply to GIF images, it does affect many products that incor-

A virtual convention can cost little to set up and, with the right online promotion, could attract very large audiences. Leveraging the profit out of such a venture need not be difficult, with opportunities to sell books, videos, music, T-shirts and other merchandise which has been properly licensed. Often large inventories of quality licensed merchandise are left over after a major movie's first release, can be picked up at big discounts, and might find new markets this way.

There is an official Paramount Pictures Web site for Trekkies at **http://voyager.paramount.com,** and an independent unofficial one at **http://www.umich.edu/~gmbrown,** with an email address for information on a Trekkie mailing list from **trekchatter~request@umich.edu**

UK COPYRIGHT COALITION

The Creators' Copyright Coalition is a not-for-profit organisation dedicated to protecting creators' rights in the electronic media. You may already be involved with it through one or more of the member organisations, which include: the Association of Authors' Agents; Association of Illustrators; Association of Photographers; Authors' Licensing and Collecting Society (ALCS); British Association of Picture Libraries and Agencies (BAPLA); British Copyright Council; the Broadcasting, Entertainment, Cinematograph and Theatre Union (BECTU); the Chartered Institute of Journalists; the Chartered Society of Designers' and Artists' Collecting Society (DACS); Graphical, Paper and Media Union (GPMU); National Association of Press Agencies; National Union of Journalists (NUJ); Outdoor Writers' Guild; the Society of Authors; and the Writers' Guild.

porate the read and write programming for the images that Unisys claims to be covered by its patent. CompuServe introduced GIF as its standard in 1987, and has already capitulated and done a licensing deal with Unisys.

That case has given the biggest boost yet to a new cyberspace speciality of developing work-arounds for patentable and copyrightable products.

In another legal offensive against cyberspace publishing that could set some dangerous precedents, the powerful Church of Scientology has been using its copyright and trademark claims to suppress online criticism of the sect's activities.

It is already impossible to define exactly where many Internet transactions take place and the serious entrepreneurs are looking around for the best low-tax, low-cost, legally friendly physical locations to position their virtual businesses.

Staffing such businesses presents intriguing issues also. You could be based in Central London, yet have all your employees and contract workers in China putting together products that are sold back to British clients. Minimum wages, import controls, customs duties, work permits and similar traditional business issues have to be rethought completely. It will take years for the Brussels bureaucrats to catch up with the reality of the changes taking place very rapidly.

Finding Good Traffic Locations

Another consideration involved in settling your cyberspace business location is making sure that you will get the traffic that could be the deciding factor in your success or failure. Even if you have the wherewithal to set up your own distinct domain – and this is getting easier and cheaper all the time – you could find yourself sitting there in splendid isolation with no paying customers coming through the door.

There is a very real need to consider giving your online business presence a location that reflects the physical world's justifications for paying higher rents and accepting more restrictive trading requirements by locating near a sales generating anchor tenant in a shopping centre or mall. The VANs, as well as some significant new online vending ventures, are positioning themselves aggressively to be the equivalents of the supermarkets, department stores and major catalogue companies in cyberspace. You may want to hang on to their coattails for at least your first entrepreneurial ventures into cyberspace to take advantage of their strong market images and name recognition, security, billing services, friendly user interfaces, and high traffic rates.

They are adding off-line activities also in which you may need to participate, such as catalogues of their online offerings compiled into CD-ROM disks which can get massive market coverage when distributed with consumer magazines or via large direct mail lists.

Expect the VANs to offer increasingly sophisticated software and access to expert help in setting up a cyberspace business that fits into the marketing mix they are building to attract subscribers – and to keep those subscribers online within their own cyberspace territories. You may save a lot of cost and even more hassles by letting Big Brother help you to set up and operate your business.

There is much misinformation circulating in business circles about the enormous potential of cyberspace for free independent trading, without due consideration being given to how this evolving market is fragmenting, and to very different demographic patterns emerging in the individual VANs and on the Internet as whole.

Some big companies risk being steered in potentially dangerous directions because their cyberspace policies are unduly influenced by information professionals who are insensitive to the great difficulty most consumers face in trying to make what is to them the very difficult process of an Internet connection. Internet software is become more user-friendly, but still it is the consumer and home user orientated commercial VAN that makes ease of use its prime concern to attract new subscribers. They are moving fast to exploit such elements as interactive multimedia to add the necessary sizzle to the online steak, so they may well be doing much of the essential groundwork to bring your market within reach.

From the typical consumers' viewpoint, venturing beyond their familiar VAN environments into the perceived hostile atmosphere of cyberspace can be an adventure they are reluctant to repeat. It's not just that making the connections can be difficult. Actual antagonism may be experienced from net surfers who declare online how they despise novice explorers unfamiliar with the subtleties of the Net and who are identified as inexperienced newcomers both

The express aim is to secure fair contracts for freelancers, who will produce much of the commercial information disseminated in cyberspace. The coalition and its member organisations are particularly concerned about publishers claiming the right to unlimited electronic exploitation of creators' work without further payment. Email enquiries to **mike.holderness @mcr1.poptel.org.uk**.

39

by their behaviour and email addresses. There are virtual gangs out there verbally beating up novice non-members in a way that can have strong negative effects and send consumers scuttling back to the security of their familiar point and click icon-rich VAN online environments.

There is surprising ignorance of such things among would-be cyberspace entrepreneurs, and even when these realities are pointed out many tend to show a reluctance to temper the dreams that the Internet hype has inspired by accepting that they might find their best markets with a popular VAN rather than establishing their own premises in the exciting frontiers of cyberspace.

That said, most business projects still need to establish at least part of their cyberspace enterprises as distinct entities on the World Wide Web. It has long passed critical mass to continue surging forward as the inevitable leading way of distributing information and conducting business online. In 1995, software became available for the first time that will – for as little as £100 – enable any high-specification PC or Macintosh to function as a fully featured Web server that does not require great technical expertise to operate. This breakthrough brings within easy reach the ability to create interactive Web pages on your desktop, set up a site and operate it so that it can accommodate, depending on the level of connection, up to about sixty users at any one time.

With the appropriate telephone connection, you are into business without needing to go through any network server or other intermediary. You are directly part of the Net. This brings enormous power to small businesses, the departments within larger concerns, and to individuals.

However, balance that independence against the benefits resulting from the competition among the commercial Internet service providers who in 1995 were subletting really meaningful space and facilities on their sites for as low as £60 a month. At such rates, it can be still be more cost-efficient to do the cyberspace equivalent of leasing rather than buying – but make sure that your service provider is sound and efficient or you risk losing much of the equity in your Web premises if you are forced to change your address later.

In most cases, it will pay to put together a combination of business facilities that include a Web site, representation in the leading VANs, activity in the portable physical media of CD-ROM and floppy disks, and participation in the predominantly text-based Internet environments of the mailing lists, newsgroups, etc.

Bulletin board attractions

Don't forget bulletin boards either – those fixed locations in cyberspace where a modest computer at the end of a telephone line can perform many valid business tasks. The BBS emerged in the late 1970s mainly as a forum for hobbyist activities, but the majority of software packages being sold now by market leaders Mustang and Galacticomm are to businesses. It is estimated that there are nearly 100,000 active bulletin boards in operation around the world, and they may have approaching 20 million users – more than all the VANs put together and close to real world estimates of actual Internet usage.

Although they are tending to be regarded as old hat, the well-conceived BBS can still be the cheapest and most practical form of interactive online service to set up and operate. It can be a completely isolated facility that enables a select few – such as the employees in a company or department – to exchange information among themselves. You might, for example, set up a BBS just to support a small-scale departmental or small company move towards telecommuting.

Users of Mustang's Wildcat, the most popular BBS system for business users, range from the Salvation Army having one for communications between field offices to a wholesale distributor of natural foods using its BBS as a round-the-clock ordering system at the end of a toll-free telephone line, to a furniture sales and distribution company that has a catalogue of 3,000 items on its BBS with images that customers and interior decorators can download, and to a charity that set up a BBS to provide the logistical communications support for its annual 350-mile bicycling event.

An accountant deals with his clients' tax questions through his own BBS, while a small travel agency uses a BBS to extend its market by offering an online database of over 1,000 leisure travel packages. As many as 1,500 clients in a month download from this one source a wealth of information that would be difficult, or impossible, for even an experienced agent to assemble for an individual customer. The facility generates a lot of repeat business.

Estate agents can put a BBS to particularly good use as a way of exchanging data and illustrations of listed residential property with prospective buyers and other agents, particularly overseas clients. A pioneer in this field is Jeff Tucker of North Carolina, who recalls a typical case in which an out-of-state client did all the initial discussions over the BBS, evaluating online the details of 80 available properties, then narrowing his search down to ten which he actually visited before making a decision.

"Online services like electronic bulletin boards are the future of real estate," maintains Jeff Tucker. If you are in the property business, or considering some similar BBS application, it could be worth the call to Jeff's board on +(1) 704 531 7375 to see what can be achieved.

British companies and individual entrepreneurs who have not considered bulletin boards previously as viable vehicles for providing technical and other forms of customer support should rethink in the light of the explosion in modem sales and the ease with which a BBS can be set up to provide friendly, efficient 24-hour services.

"If you have a business and your computer system does not allow you to communicate with the outside world, it is a real handicap," the industry's "Mr. BBS", Mustang president Jim Harrer comments. "If you are not online today, you will have to be online tomorrow, and a BBS provides one of the best ways to achieve that communications link."

5. Setting up your cyberspace business

To approach cyberspace as if it is just another advertising medium is an exercise in futility. Unless you are blessed with sensitive, flexible and well-informed staff or consultants, expect indifferent results at best if you throw the task at your in-house or agency advertising people.

Below-the-line experts with track records of coping with challenging PR assignments could be a good choice, particularly if they have a background in journalism, or habitually use journalists to ensure that their media materials are content-rich. My dream team for a corporation setting up its first marketing communications effort in cyberspace could comprise a veteran executive or line manager between assignments or close to retirement, a young software engineer and Internet enthusiast drawn from the information services department, and a contract writer from outside the company who is experienced in generating human interest stories.

The senior manager would have deep knowledge about the company and, hopefully, be motivated to want to communicate the qualities of the company's products and services to a wider audience without needing to shout about them aggressively. He or she might well be out of the mainstream of corporate marketing tactics and be seen to be old-fashioned because he or she does not relate to the contemporary hard sell, in-your-face, type of advertising in both print and electronic media.

The young software engineer would have – or could easily acquire – all the technical knowledge necessary to set up bulletin boards, create Web sites, and similar tasks. Equally important, he or she would be tuned in to Net etiquette and be sensitive to what is acceptable behaviour in cyberspace.

The writer from outside the corporation – probably a successful freelance journalist capable of selling to both the tabloids and the trades – would be trained to see the general human interest – as well as niche market technical – angles. He or she would write tightly in straightforward direct prose and realise that if you don't hit target readers right between the eyes with the hook in your heading and first paragraph, they'll move right on. The virtual round file in cyberspace is the inevitable repository of verbose, unfocussed material, and freelance journalists have practical experience in avoiding that fate.

Difficult as it might be for management to accept, the key member of the team is the journalist. He or she can tap into the company or outside sources for the other skills and knowledge, but nothing can substitute for the ability to communicate in an entertaining and effective way, driven by a sensitivity to meeting the needs of the target readers. The journalist must be able to stand up to corporate pressures about the content of the cyberspace presence. However, he or she should, of course, be open to second opinions. An essential step is to test the resulting Web site or other cyberspace venture against a representative cross-section of the target audience.

What is sadly lacking amid all the hype and information flooding us about cyberspace is that the new media with all their fascinating technologies do not negate the basic marketing communications premise that **Content is King**. Those are the most important three words amid the 65,000 or so in this book. I hope that by now you are sharing my enthusiasm for the new media and a vision is starting to emerge of how you can put them to good use. But before we move on to the practical details of setting up your business presence in cyberspace, we must pause for a moment to become aware of the basic principles necessary to create the content of what you need to disseminate.

Many companies, after spending inordinately large sums, are learning that the Web sites they have created are not being visited to anywhere the degree they had expected. Even when accessed in significant numbers, visitors tend to move on quickly. A particularly common mistake has been failing to realise that your material should work without relying on fancy graphics or interactive features. At the present state of the technology affordable and available to your target audiences, the inherent quality of the content of the text is paramount. Indeed, many of your targets may, for a considerable time to come, actually see what you offer on screen only as plain text. They do not have the hardware, software or Internet connections to play back your efforts in the way you intended.

PR Agencies Online

Public relations and advertising agencies are rushing into cyberspace – and often it is the PR specialists who do a better job because they are more geared to the long-term nurturing of relations with a client's various publics, than a typical advertising agency's focus on short-term merchandising or sales.

The first of the big PR consultancies to establish a presence on the Web was Edelman Public Relations Worldwide, and you can see what they are up to at **http://www.edelman.com**.

Others, with systems and Internet access able to display large beautiful graphics, run videos and animations, or play music and other sound files, may move on without exploring sophisticated multimedia features because they play so slowly. What looks great in the board room demonstration using a high speed Pentium system displaying millions of colours on a large high quality screen may drive the end users mad as it slowly, painfully – and probably expensively – reaches them through the clogged narrow bandwidth arteries of cyberspace and is far too rich for their typical £1,000 system.

Fleishman Hillard is at **http://www.frleish. com.** Ketchum Public Relations helped to set up the Miller's Brewery site at **http://www. mgdtaproom.com**, and to see how a real PR challenge is being handled, go to **http:// www.joeboxer.com**, the first cyberspace site for underwear.

Sometimes a small PR agency can outperform a big consultancy by searching through cyberspace for journalists with particular interests, then emailing specific material directly to them.

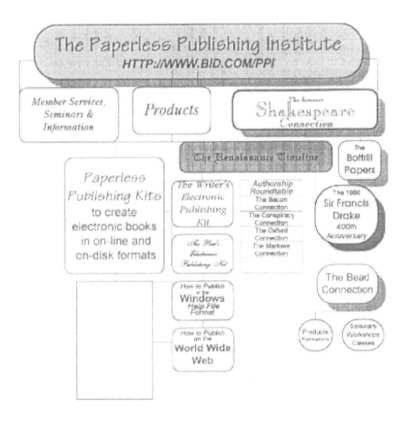

Figure 5.1 Planning a Web site is easier if you draw a flow chart or diagram of its elements

45

Cast Away Yesterday's Wisdom

"Nothing is harder than casting aside the thinking, strategies, and biases that propelled a business to its current successes. Companies need to learn how to unlearn, to slough off yesterday's wisdom."

So said Eckhard Pfeiffer, president of Compaq Computers, quoted in *Euromoney* after leading his company to becoming the world's No. 1 PC vendor. Compaq sold 4.8 million PCs in 1994, compared to about four million each for IBM and Apple. Pfeiffer, who continually demonstrates how he dares to be different, aims to triple sales by the end of the decade, and forecasts that China could become the world's biggest PC market.

There is a simple test. Even in this digital age, if a summary of the content of your cyberspace project is not a turn-on when written out double-spaced in 12pt Courier on a single sheet of white paper, tear it up and try again.

It is important to understand this before getting into the detail of setting up a Web site if you are managing a corporate project, or putting your own money and effort into an entrepreneurial cyberspace venture. The underlying marketing communications concepts are not new and unproved, but seem too often to be forgotten these days. The PR kits distributed to over 1,000 journalists every spring at Comdex in Las Vegas – the world's largest industry exhibition – would fill a ten-ton truck. In fact, most of it ends up in garbage trucks heading for the Nevada refuse disposal dumps. The fancy folders, the full colour brochures, the corporate letter headings all look great but, with the exception of technical details, most of the content is boring and deploys hype to compensate for lack of substance. As a working journalist with non-technical readers you search with increasing despair at Comdex for good stories and pictures that will entertain and inform. I found much the same situation when I visited all the main computer shows in Britain.

We were communicating better 30 years ago at Ford of Europe, after Public Affairs Vice President Walter Hayes moved from Fleet Street to help change the corporation's stodgy image. In what is still not properly appreciated as one of the most brilliant examples of successful marketing support communications, Walter and key team members such as present vice-president John Southgate and Ford of Britain Public Affairs Director John Waddell used every human interest angle from saving village ponds to winning Grand Prix races to associate Ford products with innovation, excitement, and fun. My role was to roam around the company to find the stories and create the pictures that would reach our different publics because of the content.

The sell in each case could be as soft as I liked to make it to ensure that the story or the pictures would bypass the editorial round file and make it into the papers on the strength of the content. When winter came, I had monkeys warming themselves around the fire that keepers had lit for them in Woburn Park. A family in a Cortina wagon parked in the background looked on. I wrote an article about preparing the family car for holiday trips with former World Champion Jackie Stewart bending down to point out the dangers of tyre under-inflation and his wife Helen packing suitcases into the first of the hatchback Capris. The story only got published around the world because of the quality of the content – the value of the advice Jackie had for family car owners. A small Ford logo on the hub cap near Jackie's ear, and the implied message in the picture of Helen that the Capri now had greater luggage capacity were sufficient pay-offs.

When Ford engined cars scored 100 Grand Prix victories we vastly increased our media coverage by putting 100 Corgi diecast models of racing cars on the grid at Brands Hatch, setting up a trick photo to make them look real, and then telling how it was done, using a Granada saloon in the background to illustrate the scale. The coverage in the *Daily Express* alone covered my salary and that of photographer Ken Denyer for a year, not counting the magazine front cover in Italy and the pictures and stories published in over a hundred newspapers and magazines around the world.

When Ford sponsored a campaign to restore Britain's thousands of neglected village ponds they achieved enormous corporate image, product exposure, and dealer traffic benefits from a very low key approach. The campaign's logo did not even feature Ford – but the duck inside an oval of the same dimensions as the Ford trademark got the point across in a whisper that was heard by everybody. Giving corporately substantial cash and support services to save butterflies, bullfrogs and wildflowers helped Ford of Britain to achieve record sales and a much better image as an environmentally aware, responsible part of the British community.

That campaign illustrates the three basic rules that apply to cyberspace marketing communications : (1) content; (2) content; (3) content. In cyberspace, you cannot get away with the type of television advertising that is so lacking in content. You must set out to inform and entertain without the commercial hype. The predictions of continued rapid growth in Internet usage are based on the premise that large numbers of consumers are seeking richer content than television provides. They want information and, contrary to what some marketing communications specialists seem to believe, they are not beguiled by complex pretty pictures that are slow to load. The computer is being switched on and pointed to cyberspace for information and interactivity as a preferred alternative to passively watching images on a television screen.

Another maxim in setting up your cyberspace business presence is that it will surely be more blessed if you try to give before expecting to receive. This is a business environment in which most of what is on offer is free information,

SIMULATE THE INTERNET

Even if your organisation does not plan an immediate project on the Web, you can still save money and enhance productivity by simulating the Web on your own LAN. By using the Web's Hypertext Transport Protocol and *Mosaic* browser you can create what is, in effect, a mini-Web within your organisation which has cost-saving and other attributes making this a viable alternative to such information-sharing software as *Lotus Notes*. Advantages include not having to distribute databases, and being able to link Unix, Macintosh, and Windows systems.

47

and value standards are set by the quality of the content of that information.

Often what you have to offer on-line will be information that you have already gathered and deployed to benefit your business. Blend it with the expertise at your disposal and abstract the knowledge that will be of interest and benefit to the people using the online services. Don't be miserly in holding back material of the kind that traditionally has been regarded as confidential. If it had potential importance to competitors, they probably know about it already, and if you only disseminate online ra-ra positive information, your site and services will soon lose credibility. Your attempts to promote your enterprise among discussion groups and areas where overt commerce is frowned on will be flamed out, seriously reducing your chances of success.

LEGAL REPORTORIAL HAZARDS

Among many legal issues posed by online publishing is the rapidly increasing email traffic between individual journalists and readers. Management need to keep editorial staff alert to the fact that a defamatory email comment from a reporter may be construed as a publication in the legal sense. Powerful pressure groups, such as anti-abortionists and Fascists, are using email to reach editorial staff, and this is contributing to the risk of defamatory messages being exchanged.

You might do best, as in the Ford village pond promotion, to work through a charity or good cause. Provide online services in which you are associated with a popular cause or organisation, as Ford did with the British Waterfowl Association, and you will be welcomed into the cyberspace community rather than greeted with suspicion, if not outright hostility.

Identify projects that offer tangible benefits directly to your end users. If you are in banking or other financial services, give them the opportunity to download software that will help them to build their savings, do their tax returns, find markets, negotiate loans, etc. If you are in health care, supply them with quality information about medical problems and their solutions. If you are in transport, give them maps, route guides, practical tips, technical services and the like. If you are in publishing, give them generous extracts and support services relating to the hard copy or digital books, magazines, and newsletters that you want them to buy. Too many good online publishing projects are still-born because of a lack of generosity in making available substantial extracts and over concern about copyright infringements.

If you are in foods and beverages, give them recipes and expert dietary and culinary advice. There are references elsewhere to successes in selling wine, coffee and live lobsters, and promoting restaurants in cyberspace in which a wealth of information is offered in soft sell formats. Great chefs are scoring more by sharing their recipe secrets than by hoarding them.

For example, cyberspace offers a unique opportunity to promote internationally the merits of British regional cheeses because of the rich information content it is possible to create about them. I am involved in a project using cyberspace to promote foreign tourist and business use of Britain's inland waterways which hinges around this basic premise of disseminating quality information that will entertain as well as educate.

Let your imagination loose on imaginative promotions. An electronic shopping centre has staged the first Easter egg hunt in cyberspace, and tying in with actual real-life sea voyages and other adventures can pull in large audiences. Even the most way-out ideas can be considered for viable online promotions.

Many negative stories are circulating about entrepreneurial failures in cyberspace. The first florist online, for example, has been followed by others who have not generated traffic or sales. It is not just because they were not first, but primarily because they did not offer enough. Only a few had inappropriate products.

What is an appropriate product? There really are not too many limitations. Cars are being sold increasingly through the dissemination of online information about the wheels and the deals available. Herbal medicines have great opportunities because they can so easily be delivered by mail with orders placed online from shoppers who are offered a wealth of information about the different options available. A large multinational manufacturer of DIY products is getting a boost by sponsoring a bulletin board run from their home by the husband and wife authors of DIY household repair books. The list of possibilities is enormous.

I hope I have convinced you that, before we get down to the specific practical and technical aspects of getting online, your planning in these respects should be driven by the *content* of what you are going to offer. You should make the medium fit the message and its audience. In most cases that means you will set up facilities on one of the VANs and/or on the Internet's World Wide Web.

Creating a business presence on a VAN

VANs differ widely in their demographics, and in what they allow you to do on their networks, as well as how you do it. This whole section of the online industry was in a great state of flux in Britain during 1995, particularly as a result of America Online, the fastest-growing of the American VANs, linking up with the Bertelmans AG German publishing giant to launch a European

Email is proving also to be an effective source for tips – particularly whistle-blowing by disgruntled employees – and this poses hazards also that go beyond defamation to issues of trade secrecy and the like. Reporters eavesdropping on the thousands of Usenet newsgroups looking for stories risk provoking a hostile reaction, and many have been flamed when their identities have been discovered.

Driving in Cyberspace

There was a more than 2-1 response in favour of floppy disks over video tapes when Nissan Motor Company tested the pulling power of the new media in the USA. Nissan offered a free video tape or an interactive floppy disk promoting its *Altima* model in advertisements on cable television and in motoring magazines. Only 15% of respondents ordered the video tape alone, 40% ordered the disks only, and 43% asked for both.

service. A British publisher, Pearsons, heads a consortium setting up Europe Online, and the telecommunications multinational MCI – in which British Telecomm has a substantial stake – is pumping massive sums into its increasingly wide range of facilities.

Delphi and CompuServe were among other major players going through big changes, and we have smaller enterprising VANs such as the one started by the BBC to increase further the many choices available. Microsoft and Apple are building their own international VANs, which inevitably will be forces to reckon with because they are geared for particularly easy access by users of the world's most popular operating systems. Network access is actually built into *Windows 95*, giving Microsoft what its competitors claim is an unfair advantage that Bill Gates will no doubt exploit. He has a vision of communications satellites around the world that could bring a billion people online in one way or another within a decade. Most of them will be using his operating systems.

Access details and information about these developments are covered particularly well by *The Guardian* in its weekly electronics pull-out, and *The Sunday Times* has a technology section that often comes up with stories the others miss. Address details, special rate offers and other information can also be found in the glossy magazines about the Internet to be found on all major newstands. They tend to focus – sometimes obsessively – on the tastes of young males, and the graphics can be gruesomely unattractive to anyone over 25, but they do help to give you a feel of what is going on for the younger sector of the market.

The best way to evaluate how and what you can do in the way of business on a VAN is to take advantage of their introductory offers and get free usage for as much as 10 hours in the first month. Roam around, explore the forums and special interest groups. You may find many opportunities to adopt a soft sell approach to get your messages to your target publics through a combination of VANs.

Check out what commercial activities are taking place in the virtual malls and, if they are relevant to your business, such member areas as travel services, hobbies, and technical support. If I was marketing products related to real beer, adventure holidays, genealogical books and research services, or alternative medicine and self-help, I'd turn to the VANs first because they have finely defined special interest groups catering for these topics. There are scores of other examples and you may be surprised to find how well your target markets are represented on these commercial networks.

Do your homework and you might well be able very quickly and effectively to open up a significant business presence without needing any technical help, special software, the creation of interfaces, and at no significant cost. If you are seriously selling software, it is becoming almost essential that you have a support facility on-line, and the VANs can be the easiest, cheapest and most effective way of setting these up. They are getting particularly good at processing email promptly, cheaply and efficiently, which is why even serious Net surfers who do not need their pretty point and click graphics are using them.

The VANs are offering also some of the best electronic payment processing schemes. Many consumers feel more comfortable dealing in that environment when it comes to such key decision points in the purchasing process as typing in a credit card number.

You can, in their commercial areas, blatantly make a hard sell pitch, but again think carefully whether this is the right tactic in this environment. It might work better if you are targeting consumers in North America, but remember how slow the television shopping channels have been to catch on in Europe whereas in the US they have become a major marketing medium. The hard sell is not as successful in the UK , where we prefer to be guided rather than pushed towards making buying decisions.

Much of the information that the Europeans are being fed about the commercial potential of cyberspace comes from the other side of the Atlantic, and what works there is not necessarily applicable to different nationalities and cultures. There is a really imaginative American online wine merchandising scheme described in detail elsewhere, but I doubt if would be viable in Britain for a few years, and perhaps in France never! However, the arrival on this side of the Atlantic of the major American VANs must inevitably exert a strong influence on future patterns of online merchandising and your marketing mix may include elements of more aggressive selling in certain VAN environments, and more subtle tactics in areas of the Net that are important to you.

BARCLAYCARD FIRST

Barclaycard's Netlink was the first British financial institution Internet service. The Web address is **http://www. barclaycard.co.uk**

Connecting to the Web

Hooking up a bulletin board or venturing into cyberspace through a well-organised, user-friendly VAN requires little knowledge and probably only the addition of a modem to your existing PC or Mac. Going on to the Web can be significantly far more difficult, and the claims for various packages offering to get you there in a few minutes are deceptive. However, this is the business place to be, with the number of Web server computers exploding from less than a thousand to over 10,000 in only about a year.

By early 1995, the numbers of people actually using the Web on a regular basis was probably around two million. You will have heard much bigger figures, but they tend to reflect hopeful expectations rather than actual reality. Also, those who were on the Web were not really buying anything in significant quantities.

Then, as the 1995 winter in the Northern hemisphere ended, new software and better telecommunications facilities burst forth like blossom in spring. We moved, in the space of a few months, from clunky programs which made it difficult to create Web sites, and a limited range of options in ways of actually connecting to the Web, to a whole new set of tools that made all Web tasks much easier, as well as major developments in the facilities offered by Web service providers and an increase in the quality of the telephone lines and radio links necessary to travel along the Information Superhighways.

Now, if the facilities are not available through your company or organisation, you can put together quickly the essential tools for going to the Web and doing business there. Excluding the modem, budget to spend between £100 and £500 in software and fees actually to get on to the Web. You may already have everything you need and not know it.

If you are part of a corporate LAN, then all the facilities may be in place for that network to provide direct access to the Internet. Check with your network administrator. If you are going it alone, then you require a modem – as fast a one as you can afford, with 14,4000 bps data transfer a practical minimum. (Make sure this is the rating for *DATA* transfer, many advertisements and packagings are misleading in this respect; the speed rating that grabs your attention may be only for fax transmissions, not the data transfer rates necessary for acceptably speedy cyberspace data transportation.)

You will need also software for TCP/IP (Transmission Control Protocol/Internet Protocol) and either SLIP (Serial Line Internet Protocol) or PPP (Point-to-Point Protocol).

TCP/IP is the Internet's standard way of handling communications. Increasingly this programming is built into the software package that comes with your computer's operating system or the "dial-up" account that you open with an Internet service provider. (A dial-up account, sometimes called a shell account, connects you to the Net through a service provider who has the actual computer running as a host on the Net. Your system is a bit like an annexe to that host and, although it may be transparent to the user, it is the host and not your computer that is actually a permanent part of the Net.)

There can be considerable advantages in establishing your cyberspace operations through a dial-up service, even for large businesses. In addition to providing your connection, the service provider may offer also attractive deals for helping you to create a business presence on its host computer which is accessible by your customers and contacts from anywhere else on the Net. This is in contrast to the facilities on a VAN, which can be accessed only by other subscribers to the VAN.

You can use almost any computer to run your dial-up account for most functions, including most of the research and file transfer tasks we discussed earlier. The power necessary for travelling through cyberspace is provided mainly by the host computer, pulling your system along with it rather like a trailer.

If you need a more independent set-up, and access to the Web using a graphical interface browser like *Mosaic* and its derivatives, the next step up in Internet connectivity is SLIP or PPP. You still connect over standard telephone lines to a service provider, but SLIP or PPP software programs enable your own computer or LAN to take over many of the online tasks. You need a more powerful computer – a Mac Quadra or a 486 will suffice – but for a comparatively modest outlay you can effectively have an independent Net site that will cope with high traffic volumes, greater interactivity for customer form-filling and ordering, and full access to the Internet's hottest area for business activity, the Web, when you want to tweak or change it.

The downside is that installation and monthly charges may be many times those for a basic dial-up account, and getting the elements of the software to work well together can be tricky. You are entering the area where considerable

7. What software do you supply? For a shell account, do I get at least a recent competitive version of a *Mosaic*-based Web browser, full email manager, FTP, *Gopher*, *Archie* and *Veronica* programs?

8. What is your policy on technical support? What help will you give me to set up my system? Is there prompt voice telephone help available whenever I need it?

9. Can my cyberspace activities grow with you? Do you have special services to help me create and maintain Web pages and pursue other business activities? How much do they cost?

10. Will you give me names and addresses of your existing clients prepared to answer my questions about their satisfaction or otherwise with your service?

Be particularly careful in contracting with small, new providers offering very attractive discounts – they are likely to be the first casualties as the service provider side of the industry settles down into a viable pricing structure.

MODEL RAILWAYS

An example of how a manufacturer catering for a particular special interest hobby can generate good will by giving information away free is the Web site for model railways at **http://www.atlasrr.com/atlasrr**. To get in touch with model railway enthusiasts world-wide, you can also go to the newsgroup rec.models.railroad, with its frequently asked questions file obtainable by FTP to **ftp.rfm.mit.edu/pub/usenet-by-group/rec.models.railroad**.

Hobbyists online may well be more receptive to commercial approaches than other newsgroups, but the pitch still needs to be subtle and offer at least good information along with the hook to generate business.

technical knowledge may be needed to get you up and running, although there are new packages that make it much simpler and it is still possible to get everything installed and working properly quite painlessly.

If you only want to get on to the Web to roam and research, then the VANs are coming up in their aggressively competitive sectors of the market with Web access facilities which may be all you need. Even if you want to have your own distinctive business presence, it is becoming easier to do this through specialist subsidiaries and associates working with your VAN, or a number of commercial service providers to whom you can send the contents of your virtual store or whatever, and they will integrate it with the other trading and promotional activities taking place at their Web host sites. There is also some neat electronic sleight-of-hand offered by some dial-up servers so that you can use their hosts, but appear to have your own independent node with its distinctive separate domain name address. There are few functional advantages in this, but it can look good and be deployed effectively in marketing.

(The way in which domain names are obtained and registered varies from country to country and the procedures were in a state of flux as this book went to press. Normally, your service provider will do this for you, and should charge no more than a nominal fee for doing so.)

Emerging also is in an increasing variety of choice in very reasonable deals available to display an electronic publication or other product on the Web at an appropriate site, with you processing orders for it, or having the fulfilment done in some cases by the owners of the site. Prices are coming down to under £100 a year. So you can create one or more Web pages using the HTML authoring tools described in Chapter 6, send your compilation to the host service and hope that the revenues start flowing. But be warned – the orders won't come in unless you also put the requisite marketing effort into both motivating customers to want your book or other product, and knowing where to find it in cyberspace.

You might discover that you have to put as much effort into promoting the virtual store as you do into publicising your own product in it, and that investment of time, effort and money might yield better long-term returns if you build and promote your own Internet node. That way you'll own the store, can push other products and services through it, and build up equity in your own virtual property. The difference is between advertising and improving a shop on which you have a short and uncertain lease, to the additional security and much larger potential returns from building a business in your own premises.

You can go further into becoming a major cyberspace player by enhancing a SLIP connection so that your own computer takes on the major tasks and becomes an Internet host or node. This is becoming easier and cheaper also. The dedicated leased lines to supply the necessary transmission quality and band width used to be very expensive. Now ISDN connections are becoming available at low cost to turn ordinary telephone lines into powerful data transmission trunk routes so that affordable quality cyberspace access can be brought directly into the small office and home through a modified SLIP connection or a full node.

ISDN is an example of a technology that has been looking for an application. Indeed, for a time it was dubbed Innovation that Subscribers Don't Need. Now they do need it to get the most efficient access to the superhighways and ISDN services have become much cheaper and easier to get in both Europe and North America. In some places the set up and monthly charges are not much more than a standard telephone line, and by the beginning of 1995 British Telecom had reduced its standard ISDN installation charge to £300.

Some forecasts say that ISDN usage in Europe will grow by 40% a year for the rest of this decade, with costs falling as more subscribers plug in. Consequently, creating and operating your own Internet node will become increasingly attractive, giving even small concerns affordable opportunities to create powerful Internet presences capable of dealing with almost a limitless volume of visitors.

ISDN will greatly increase telecommuting also because it removes the main physical barriers preventing a home worker from accessing a company network and interacting with distant computers as if they were on his or her desk. Video conferencing to and from home offices becomes possible also, bringing back the face-to-face communications that are not possible now.

The options becoming available may seem bewildering and with the regulatory changes taking place in the telecommunications business and the increased competition you need both to make your choices carefully, and try to keep your options open. There could, for example, be serious repercussions if

AUTOMATE TECHNICAL SUPPORT

A particularly profitable cyberspace business over the next few years will be providing services to companies needing to improve their technical support for customers. Hundreds of companies around the world are using bulletin boards, VANs, and the Internet for this purpose already, but many more still need to do so and will prefer to use consultants and outside contractors rather than do the work in house.

The basic principle is to capture all the relevant information and knowledge within the company and collect it in a relational database with an efficient search engine. This resource can be set up for easy online access by customers. In some cases, it might be practical also – or alternatively – to put all that information onto a floppy with a search module and give the disk away to customers. In a basic, near universal format, this could be done with an ebook compiling program such as Writer's Dream, Dart or BigText, all readily available from shareware sources and costing very little to license for such uses.

you are locked into an Internet address which you promote heavily both on-line and in traditional media, then are forced to make a change. There are various ways to redirect connections to other addresses, but this also can pose problems. That alone is one reason why big corporations are rushing to secure their own distinctive Internet addresses which they control absolutely by having their own nodes on the Net. If that is not practicable for you, then your best tactics would be to do deals with one or more of the main VAN operators. They are all substantial, evolving rapidly, and compelled by market forces to keep improving their facilities and making their prices competitive.

This is a good point to send up a flare to cyberspace neophytes who, as they delve deeper into the technology, become more familiar with the jargons and more confident in exploring some of the many options. Don't move too far ahead of your target markets and audiences and be guided by what facilities they will have and what areas of cyberspace they will be populating.

Unless you have some particular business operations that make it, for example, appropriate to set up your catalogue at an anonymous FTP site, or concentrate on Usenet and discussion groups, remember that the main growth in cyberspace activity by most consumers and businesses will be on the Web and the VANs. They have passed critical mass and should keep on growing rapidly. What's more, they are the easiest to use.

6. The new languages of cyberspace

How to build your business site on the Web

There is a cultural revolution taking place linked to the impact that cyberspace is having on many ways that we conduct business. Words and pictures are moving off paper into virtual documentation of different forms at a rapidly accelerating rate. We may already, according to some estimates, have more textual information available in digital formats than has ever been committed to print. Vast amounts of data now never get on to paper at all – particularly in the business world, where products such as aircraft, vehicles, ships and engineering equipment may need literally tons of paper with instructions just to operate them, let alone create them.

This trend is being given much greater momentum with the growth of online communications, and so we are starting to see cyberspace influences creeping into the content, structure and visual appearance of nearly all forms of written information. It is a pervasive cultural shifting process that affects the printed books, magazines, newspapers, manuals, letters and other documents that we read.

In some areas the results are more obvious than others. Books about computing, for example, tend more and more to follow the pattern in editorial style and typographical formatting of the printed manuals that accompany software, which were in turn heavily influenced by the screen displays of the online Help documentation standardised in the Macintosh and *Windows* graphical interfaces.

Web publications – which will be of prime concern for you in any cyberspace entrepreneurial venture – are drawing on these antecedents to establish a distinctive style which is exerting its influence in particular on newspapers and magazines, and the design of much corporate documentation, such as manuals, specification sheets, sales literature, signage, even letter head design.

Storyboard Techniques

Planning what and how you want to communicate in your cyberspace project can be helped immensely by creating a storyboard using similar techniques to those used to plan the shots in a feature film or a television advertisement. Various types of software can help you to do this, including the large selection of business presentation and graphical programs that permit storyboard creation by using their facilities for assembling a sequence of text and graphical displays, e.g. for a slide show. Several multimedia authoring programs use the storyboard metaphor also.

But you can use an ordinary word processor. Set the page layout to landscape (horizontal) and put the text that you wish to communicate in a column on the left or right, leaving the rest of the page for graphics, which can be imported if you already have them in digital form, or sketched or pasted on to the hard copy.

The ways that we read are changing also. For centuries, most reading has been essentially a linear process, with one word leading on to the next in a sequence dictated by the author and editor. That will continue to be the way that most fiction is compiled, but not with much non-fiction – both in print and online – which is essentially for information or reference. We scan and dip into these documents online, and do so increasingly in print. Consequently they need to be constructed in very different ways from conventional linear publications.

To compete with paper, online documentation must exploit its unique strengths of being so dynamic, offering immediate links to other material within the same publication, or making hypertext links to another publication from the same source, or across the world to related information stored in a completely different system.

Hypertext – or, more correctly, hypermedia because the links can be graphical as well as textual – is an important new business research and marketing tool. Cyberspace entrepreneurs must have at least a basic understanding of its strengths and weaknesses, and preferably play an active role in creating publications for the Web, the world's largest hypertext system. The hypertext links that you either create yourself, or exploit when they have been created by others, possibly your competitors, could determine your success or failure.

The way in which you use pictures in business is changing also. They are not optional accessories, but essential elements in a Web publication. Visuals play vital roles in how Web sites perform, and there are technical and business objectives as well as design and creative criteria to satisfy.

In many printed books, the illustrations tend still to be grouped into sections because of the mechanical and cost considerations inherent in the mechanics of the printing and binding processes. In contrast, there is much more freedom in cyberspace publishing because augmenting plain text with full colour illustrations incurs few cost penalties. The graphical elements can be integral with the text and perform many more roles than providing supplementary information to the words, or adding visual appeal. Now the graphics can be tools for the reader, such as the buttons and icons which trigger software actions.

Writers – particularly technical writers – must learn new lessons about when it is necessary to abandon the words that have always been their exclusive raw material and use pictures, sound, animation, video, or interactive procedures such as training sequences. Writers must learn new styles also, communicating with shorter active sentences and paragraphs and modified vocabularies. Artists must learn to use colour and line in different ways. Often they must temper their enthusiasm about the power the new media gives them to the reality that large complex images can display painfully slowly online, and that the sparkling 16 million colours in which they create illustrations may be reduced to a limited range of muddy tones if they do not take account of the technical limitations of software and hardware used by their readers.

Insert a page break command between each page, which you rough out to represent a screen of information.

Sort the pages into the linear sequence you wish to follow, starting with your home page. Then create other pages in the same way containing supplementary information, or representing the addresses of hypertext links which you wish to create to other sources. Working on a large table or the floor, shuffle the pages around as you make decisions, or as suggestions are made at planning meetings. Of course, if one screen is designed to scroll down linearly to others, then you have a stack of pages, with the first screen at the top.

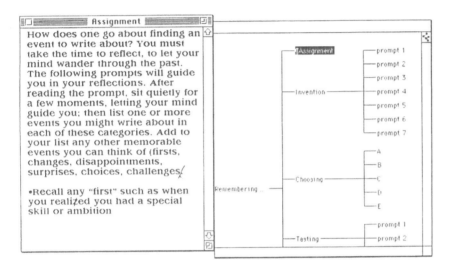

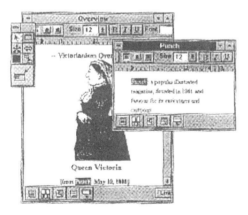

Figure 6.1 Creating the hypertext links in a Storyspace project

This very low-tech approach can be helpful at the beginning to give a sense of physical reality to what is being created for the virtual environment. It can be developed in many ways. For example, the pages can be stuck on to the front of file folders into which can be assembled the reference materials needed to create the text and graphics for that particular section of your site.

Any drawing program – particularly one like *Visio* which has special features for creating organisation and flow charts – can also be adapted to create storyboards. But if your source material is coming from paper, it can still be beneficial to spread it all out and get a physical feel for the hypertext structure that you wish to create. It is a particularly appropriate approach for a group project.

These are not detail technical or academic matters, but are worthy of your serious consideration as an entrepreneur, business or professional person because they can have a direct impact on the success of your cyberspace ventures and on the bottom line of other business activities. You may, for example, be able to save enormous amounts of time and money when an organisation makes that often painful and expensive move from a paper-based corporate culture to one that exists in various virtual forms on LANs, WANs, disks, tapes, bulletin boards and cyberspace. Much of the trauma inherent in the transition may be avoided if you do not succumb to the powerful commercial pressures to use software systems and professional services that give undue attention to preserving the visual appearance of printed documentation when it is moved into electronic forms.

When material is prepared for reading text from a screen it must take into account that this is a very different process from reading from printed pages. For a start, the off screen reading rate – even when the monitor is of good quality – may be 30% slower than from an equivalent print document. It is also inherently more tiring – both physically on the eyes and mentally in comprehending the information being conveyed.

The reading differences between the two media increase with the age of the readers. In some studies, middle-aged readers – who may make up the vast majority of your target audience on some projects – may read off screen at only a tenth of the speed of the young software engineers who you contracted to compile your documentation into Web pages.

Consider notebooks

A typical business situation is the creation of online documentation that will primarily be read on notebook computer screens, e.g. service information for technicians in the field. The documentation will almost certainly be created on a desktop system with a quality colour monitor. Unless it is tested under real-life field conditions, it may be markedly inferior to a printed version. Informed management control is required to monitor such considerations in a cyberspace project.

Even if great pains are taken to ensure that the on screen document is written and designed to compensate for the reading problems inherent in the new electronic medium, the electronic document may still be at a disadvantage in these respects. Consequently, it makes little sense – except for archival purposes – to put significant cost and effort into converting paper documentation into electronic forms that preserve the typefaces, line lengths, column widths, bold facing, italics, underlining, headings and other features of the original. I am at a loss to understand why the business community is being persuaded to invest so heavily in carrying over hard copy print concepts into the electronic media, particularly when the battles to establish standards for this in the marketplace are causing such confusion and incompatibilities. It just makes no sense.

We are being misled in so many ways. Word processor manuals still introduce novices moving from paper to screens to view a digital document as a long roll of paper that scrolls up and down. In fact, even those using computers every day still relate each screen display to being a single page – a page only about a third the size of a typical printed one and of completely different landscape rather than portrait orientation. That gives more emphasis to the "golden rectangle" concepts used in art teaching as well as print publication design to define the areas of maximum impact. The more we read in cyberspace, the more that golden rectangle formed by the proportions of our monitor screens will influence design in the physical world.

Very few communications people yet have adequate understanding of all these factors involved with the new media. You may not need to study them in depth, just be aware of them and use your entrepreneurial instincts and careful testing to ensure that you get your online communications materials as effective as you can make them.

Now let's get down to the detail of how Web pages are authored. Remember, this is not just creating a catalogue, brochure or annual report. What you publish to the Web is your front office, your shop front, your showroom, your telephone system, your letter heading – a combination of elements from the many traditional interfaces that an organisation has with its publics.

Our tool for doing this is the Hypertext Mark-up Language – HTML. In addition to converting texts into a form that is attractive and dynamic on the Web, HTML plays also some of the roles in cyberspace of desktop publishing, multimedia authoring and database programs.

When you have got your planning finalised, it can be helpful to create a wall chart showing the layout of your hypertext document, perhaps cross-referenced to files of the hard copy and digital resources on which you are drawing.

You will find that your storyboards done this way evolve into web-like structures that are becoming the models also for organising many types of businesses. The classic top-down hierarchical business structure is evolving – thanks largely to the influences of the information age – into more natural web formations. Some management experts liken this to a move from an unnaturally imposed organisation model to one based on the structure of a natural biological organism.

The increasing popularity of web-like peer-to-peer networks where server-based networks used to be considered the best option reflects this new business culture.

VIRTUAL RESPONSE CARDS

To generate returns from information you provide online, try using the electronic equivalent of the response cards that many print magazines now provide as a way for readers to get further information from their advertisers. These can work in various ways, either to meet a request with mailed printed information, by fax or voice phone, or by the faster, cheaper and more efficient online response capabilities. The form-filling capabilities of the Web can be deployed to capture an enquiry, and a *Gopher* server or other automated system used to zap back email responses within seconds of receipt. Many email handling programs have a built-in automatic response capability, and will capture all enquiries so that you can build up a mailing list.

It goes far further than "merely" being able to combine graphics and text into Web page documents that are displayed on the monitors of visitors to your site. HTML is a tool for generating multimedia and multidimensional presentations on the Web, exploiting the interactivity and hypermedia potential of this global medium. HTML is the language that enables you to function throughout this information sharing, publishing and business environment. You can use HTML to create a virtual showroom or store for a business, an Internet presence for an organisation, or just a simple way of posting media releases or service bulletins into cyberspace.

Fortunately, this new language is not difficult to learn and there are powerful new tools becoming available that will automatically translate your word processor files into Web documents. The same basic techniques will work for a novel, a catalogue, an electronic magazine, or any other type of publication that you may want to distribute on the Web. With just basic knowledge, you will be able to create good-looking online materials, but they still demand further attention to make them work efficiently as business tools.

Your Web site toolkit

The tools you need are:

> 1. an *HTML editor* or authoring program – the Internet's equivalent of a word processor that enables you to create a Web site and pages that *Mosaic* and other Web browsers can read. It enables you to incorporate the special codes that make texts and graphics display properly on virtually any computer connected to the Web.

> 2. *Mosaic* or other software based on this universal standard for Web browsers.

> 3. a communications program that enables you to run the Web browser to test HTML files as you create them. This will enable the *Mosaic* software to act as if you are actually on the Internet.

You have the choice of putting this package of software together independently – or getting it prepacked in a nice box, all integrated into a complete Web business building toolkit. If you decide to go the independent – and cheapest – route, all the necessary software is available online as either freeware or shareware that you can try before you register. These programs are evolving rapidly, and you can get the latest versions over the Internet directly from the US, where most of the development work is being done.

You will find copies also on the leading VANs and many bulletin boards. Look out particularly for add-ons to popular word processors such as *Microsoft Word* and *WordPerfect* which enable the files from these word processors to be converted automatically into HTML documents. These are freely available online also, either from resources maintained by the word processor publishers, or in software libraries and user groups. You can, for example, easily get free copies of the *Internet Assistant* for *Microsoft Word*. One source is Microsoft's own FTP site at **ftp.microsoft.com**.

If you are serious about doing business on the Web, I suggest you make the investment in one of the specialised HTML authoring programs. *HoTMetal PRO* from Canada is particularly powerful and versatile. It is a self-contained *Windows* word processor with templates that make creating a Web home page a straightforward routine. A Mac version of this program becomes available during 1995 also.

HoTMetal PRO had a comprehensive tutorial incorporated with it soon after its initial release. This provides a great way of becoming familiar quickly with the key aspects of HTML authoring. This software could be a core resource for you if your business plans envisage extensive electronic publishing, e.g. to meet government and corporate tendering and contract requirements.

While *HotMetal PRO* is a stand-alone Web authoring tool, it is also part of a suite of programs for creating SGML(Standardised General Markup Language) documents to the international standard. So you can develop your business with it into other electronic media in addition to the Web.

You can contact the publishers, SoftQuad, by email to **hotmetal@sq.com**. There is a freeware version available online at **http://gatekeeper.dec.com:/pub/net/infosys/NCSA/Web/htm/hot-metal**, but it has limited features.

Another freeware HTML authoring program worth considering is *HTML Assistant*, from **http://cs.dal.ca/ftp/htmlasst/htmlafaq.html**.

Among the easiest HTML programs to use is Quarterdeck's *WebAuthor*. Although not as powerful as *HotMetal PRO*, it neatly automates the process of

LIBRARIANS CAN SCORE

Many librarians feel threatened by the new technology, but examples are building rapidly of enhanced careers and much better salaries for librarians who adapt to cyberspace. There are also opportunities for researchers with online knowledge to be able to move into newly created corporate positions, or set up as independent consultants, to be the guides to the electronic libraries of cyberspace.

Companies are learning fast how cost-effective – even priceless – cyberspace research can be for marketing, manufacturing, credit checking, and myriad other tasks. Even when research leads to a conventional printed source, the corporate benefits can be significant. An American company needed a book written in the late 1930s in Nazi Germany to resolve a multi-million-dollar patent. The company librarian did an online search and found a copy at an air force base, apparently captured as war material. The book, which had never been checked out before, proved to be worth millions of dollars to the company.

generating Web documents from within the *Word for Windows* word processor. You see the Web layout as you go along without needing to load a separate browser, and the program's *Anchor Manager* simplifies creating links. To find out more, email to **info@qdeck.com**, or visit the Web site **http://www.qdeck.com**.

A significant development in 1995 was SoftQuad's introduction of the first SGML viewer for the Web, which could have long-term implications on business use of the Internet. This *Panorama* program enables companies and publishers to put their SGML files on to the Net with many more powerful features than HTML supports. Publishers now have the opportunity to have just one set of source documents for their HTML, SGML. CD-ROM, Braille, print and other versions.

A free version of *Panorama* is being included by the US National Center for Supercomputing Applications with *Mosaic* versions that can be downloaded from the Net. When *Mosaic* encounters an SGML document, it automatically launches *Panorama*. To take full advantage of SGML to publish to the Net, you need *Panorama Pro*, which runs on *Windows 3.1* or *Sun Open Windows 3.x, X11R5*. Email **panorama@sq.com** for details.

Of course, most of the Internet still functions using plain ASCII text files that any Mac or PC can both create and read. But as soon as you see the way that HTML can make text and graphics display and perform you realise why it is making the Web the most attractive place to be in cyberspace for most business purposes.

HTML started as a subset of SGML which is becoming the preferred method of creating many sophisticated electronic documents, like those now being demanded of its suppliers by the military all over the world when compiling the manuals for advanced military equipment. A war ship may carry up to 40 tonnes of paper documentation which could be whittled down to a few kilos in digital form – and searched and updated far more efficiently.

Other government departments, publishers, and aircraft and motor manufacturers are among the sectors using SGML as their industry standards for digital publishing.

Even if you do not have one of the commercial software packages mentioned above, the more basic HTML versions of SGML are- you will be pleased to hear!- easy to use. There are just a few codes that you can learn quickly and then apply in your favourite word processor to turn any text into an HTML document that can be displayed effectively on the Web.

Even a basic text editor like *Notepad* in *Windows* can be used to generate HTML documents, and it will not take much time to step you through the basic procedures.

HTML is essentially a collection of styles which are marked in your text (and any graphic elements you include) by means of what are called mark-up tag codes. These tags define different parts of your publication – the headings, the paragraphs, the hypertext links, etc. – to create the components of a Web document. They are similar to the format commands that tell the printer to justify, align, make bold or italic, and use particular fonts in a printed document.

HTML establishes the basic structure for a document, creating the ground rules for how that document will appear. But it goes further in making the words – and pictures, if there are any – truly dynamic so that the publication can perform in the many different ways in which it may be used. It may be read linearly, for example, searched for general or specific information, or provide many layers of information that cater to the differing knowledge and needs of a variety of readers.

The hypertext linking that HTML makes possible means that readers can no longer be expected to move through a publication from start to finish, but will chart their different ways through the text depending on individual inclination and need at the time of reading. The structure that you create for the hypertext paths may help to guide your readers in the directions that you wish them to follow, but you cannot be certain of the routes that they will actually take.

You, or your editor or graphic designer, can never know exactly how your texts and pictures will appear on the screens of your readers. HTML does not create a fixed formatting on a document, only a general styling structure. So different browsers and different monitors will display an HTML document in a wide variety of fonts, type sizes, colours and line lengths. Some end users have only text browsers and will not see the pictures. Your Web document may not be displayed at all, but converted to speech for the visually handicapped.

DON'T OVERDO THE GRAPHICS

Although there is rapidly increasing use of higher speed modems and browsers that will display graphics more effectively, pictures in most Web documents should still be used mainly to accent text and be kept as simple and compact as possible. Consider your target audience, particularly if you want to appeal to consumers entering the Web through gateways provided by the VANs. Their systems may display Web graphics painfully slowly – and at significant connect time expense – for many people, who risk becoming resentful and move on to less demanding sites. One trick the VANs are usingto get their own graphics to display quickly on their subscribers' monitors is to transfer frequently used graphics to the user's hard disk so that they do not need to be downloaded each time.

Creative Cross-Platform Hypertext

Some of the most creative hypertext work – including interesting experiments with fiction – is being done in the *Storyspace* program. *Storyspace* is available in both *Windows* and *Macintosh* versions, and works created in one format can be moved across to the other, as well as exported to the Web.

The publishers, Eastgate Systems, are true pioneers in the way that they have worked with writers to get experimental hypertext works published, including complex poetry. Looking at their indepth hypertextual examinations of the works of Tennyson and Dickens are interactive voyages into the future for cyberspace fiction.

Consequently, you must take even greater care to ensure that the *content* of your writing communicates effectively without relying on typographical props. HTML will help by creating basic structures such as headings in various levels, bold type and paragraph breaks, but don't expect any fancy formatting or graphic elements such as drop letters, tables and bullets to get to your readers' screens in the format that they left you.

Indeed, many of your readers will use browsers or viewers that will not display any but the most basic HTML features. This is either because the readers' systems are not sufficiently powerful to cope with the demands of more sophisticated displays, or that they don't want to waste time and money waiting for graphical elements to travel comparatively slowly over telephone lines. Research indicates that users are not inclined to wait more than 15-20 seconds for a Web document to display on their screens unless they are really keen to access it.

Despite all the hype that *Mosaic* is receiving, there are text-only browsers being used on the Web that will not display graphics at all. Or some of your readers may have low resolution or monochrome monitors. Consequently, when authoring for the Web, you cannot become too dependent on graphics unless you know that your target markets want them, and can cope with their system demands. Even if you follow the ground rules and standardise on small .GIF files within your HTML document, don't expect all your readers to see your visuals as you created them – or at all.

So the prime requirement in any writing in the past continues into the future in these new electronic media – Content is the King. Acquiring the skill to use HTML will not ensure an effective publication unless you have something worthwhile to communicate. However, if your content is good, then HTML is the electronic publishing tool to present your words and pictures most effectively in attractive documents for a rapidly increasing audience able to read them.

The first steps

Here is a short introduction on the actual steps required to create an HTML *Mosaic* document. The final result will look similar to a *Windows* Help file. A reader on the Web with a Mac or *Windows Mosaic*-based browser will see a clean, attractive display in whatever default font he or she is using, and incorporating basic formatting of paragraphs, headings, bold type, etc.

That display effect, together with the hypermedia features, is achieved by adding HTML tags to code specific sections of the text so that they will display on any screen in a predictable and attractive way. Even if you use software that can automate the adding of these tags, it is beneficial to step through how they are created manually. Another reason for doing this is that if, while exploring cyberspace, you see a Web page that appeals to you, you can download the source file and study the tags to see how it was compiled.

Step 1. Identify your publication as an HTML document

Do this by typing an **<html>** tag at its very beginning and another **</html>** at the very end.

(Note that the code word or instruction within the tag to identify the beginning and end of the formatted text is enclosed within angled brackets. These are the brackets over the full stop and comma at the bottom right of the keyboard which are intended primarily for use as mathematical greater than and less than symbols.)

The end of the tagged section is marked by placing a back slash before the tag code. You don't always need to mark the end, but it's a good habit to get into because HTML versions are being developed with commands that will make it more important always to have tags in pairs, so that they act as what are called *containers* for sections of text

Step 2. Create a title line

Place tags at the beginning and end, like this:

<TITLE>How to Publish on the World Wide Web**</TITLE>**

Note that the *title* is not the headline for your document, but an identifier for it. Usually readers will not see it on the first page that opens up, but in the title bar of a display window – the place where in *Windows*, or on the Macintosh, you are used to seeing the names of the program that you are running, and the name of the current file which is open.

This title is used by many browsers for identification purposes, so you should make it descriptive, but not any longer than a single line that will fit into a typical title bar.

If you want seriously to keep near the cutting edge of the creative uses of hypertext, get *The Eastgate Quarterly Review of Hypertext*, which costs about £40 for an annual subscription for four on-disk issues mailed to Europe. You can see the system demonstrated on the Web at **http://www.eastgate.com/~eastgate**, and order or get more information through Net email to **info@eastgate.com**. The chief scientist there, Mark Epstein, has a rare vision of the cultural as well as practical aspects of hypertext publishing.

Step 3. Tag the body text of your document

You define the areas of body text with the tag containers **<BODY>** and **</BODY>** at the beginning and end respectively.

You cannot govern the lengths of the lines that will be displayed. The word wrapping at the end of each line will depend on the browser being used by your reader, influenced by such factors as the size and type of display and the font being used.

But you do need to define the paragraphs, otherwise the text will run without any breaks or white space to aid readability. Your readers' browsers will ignore any carriage returns that you put in to mark paragraphs or blank lines.

Step 4. Tag your heading

To format the actual heading material that will appear at the top of your document when it is displayed, you need to tag that text with the codes **<HEAD>** and **</HEAD>.**

To give different levels to lines or blocks within your introductory section, and in the main text, you use **<H>** tags. You might want to repeat the title that appears at the very top of the screen display so that it is viewed as part of the document. In that case, you would tag it like this:

<H1>*How to Publish on the World Wide Web*</H1>

Then you might want to give prominence to a sub-title, or the names of the author, or the source, like this:

<H2>**A Paperless Publishing Institute Publication**</H2>

Note that there are no spaces between the tag commands and the text section they contain, and they are not case sensitive, so you can use capitals or lower case letters.

You can use up to six levels of headings and sub-headings, but try to stick to four – <H1>, <H2>, <H3> and <H4>. Most Web browsers will have no trouble giving distinctive weight and styles to up to four levels of headings, but many will not cope effectively with more than four.

Anyway, a document that depends on multiple levels of headings probably needs editing and splitting up with hypertext links to make it communicate more effectively. Don't expect your readers to keep on scrolling through long slabs of text or subtle degrees of headings, which probably won't work on screen, even if they do in hard copy print.

Step 5. Define your paragraphs

In the earlier versions of HTML, the tag <P> is all that is required to end a paragraph and put in a line of "white" space, or to indicate where the next paragraph starts. You must put in these <P> tags to create a blank line, as any blanks in the document not marked in this way will not be displayed by the browser. Tabs and taps on the spacebar used to try to create blank spaces will be ignored also by browsers.

Later versions of HTML require paragraphs to be contained with a <P> at the beginning, and a </P> at the end of each.

Creating lists

HTML has simple and effective ways to create lists. Adding <OL> and </OL> creates an ordered list, with each individual item in the list being contained by the <LI> tag. (As with the <P> tag, you don't need an </LI> tag in earlier version of HTML to end a list item.)

A browser will automatically put the numbers sequentially against the individual items in an ordered list, which makes it easy to update an HTML document.

If you create an unordered list by the tags <UL> and </UL>, the browser will display the list with its own particular default form of bullet symbol for each list item.

Creating links

You create hypertext or graphical links in a very similar way to how you insert tags. The links that you insert can be either to related text or to an image in the same file, in another file within the same directory or computer system, or to resources on a distant computer somewhere else on the Web.

When a sophisticated Internet site is being created, there will be many links between text and graphic files on its own server computer, and reaching round the world to other computers on the Web. These links are hidden, so that readers are not readily aware whether they are still at the same Web site, or reading information contained on a university computer thousands of miles away. The BookZone project described later involved creating over 1,000 such links. The number and quality of links should be a key factor when evaluating quotes to set up a Web site.

You create HTML links as follows:

Step 1: Tag the starting point of the link

You tag with an ANCHOR code the section of your text, or the graphic image such as a button or icon, that offers readers the opportunity to link to something else. You embed in your HTML document the commands that will ensure that your reader's browser will highlight that area in some way to show that it is a link. *Mosaic*, for example, will display the text with a distinctive colour and underlining.

You must ANCHOR this hypertext-related section of your document with an <A> tag, which includes the address where the end of the link is to be found. The anchor tag is constructed by having first <A, followed by a space, then the code HREF= (which is an acronym for Hyptertext Reference equals). Then, within double quotes, type the location and file name to which you are linking. Following the closing quote after the file name, close the tag with a > bracket.

Then follows the section of your main text that identifies the hypertext link. Finish by tagging the end of the anchor with </A>.

For example, if we wanted to put a link between the words What is hypertext? in this document, to a detailed explanation of what hypertext is contained in a file called hyper.txt in the same directory as this file, we would create the follow anchor and link:

```
<A HREF="hyper.txt">What is hypertext?</A>
```

If you want to create a link to a more distant resource, then you put in the full address of that resource. (There are many details and examples of doing this in the HTML primer and sampler files that you can obtain from the National Center for Supercomputing Applications at **pubs@ncsa.uiuc.edu**.)

The same anchoring techniques can create links to a specific section of another document, or between different parts of the same document.

Address tags

There are other HTML tags with specific purposes. For example, the <ADDRESS> tag is a useful way to get people to contact you as the author of a Web document, or the operator of the business being promoted, as in this way of contacting me:

```
<ADDRESS>cfhaynes@aol.com</ADDRESS>
```

When you want to link to postal or physical addresses, you need to use Forced Line Breaks.

Marking lines

To create horizontal lines, a very useful formatting device for Web pages, you use the <HR> tag which will draw a line right across the window displayed by the browser.

Graphics

You will probably want to use in-line images, which are graphics displayed alongside the text. They must be used sparingly because they will slow down the display rate, and may not be brought up at all by some browsers. Again, consult the primer for details of how to do this. You can also create text to substitute for visuals that will be displayed by browsers which cannot bring up graphical images.

Sound and animation

Other HTML options include links that will give the reader the choice to activate sound or animation files, or large images that, for practical reasons, are not incorporated in the main document.

Response forms

Businesses using the Web will need to know about fill-out forms, which allow readers to respond with orders or information. These are described in the primer's *Fill-out Forms Overview* and in the documentation that accompanies the commercial software programs I suggested earlier.

7. Collecting the money

The Internet is acquiring abilities to transform banking services, the foreign exchange markets, and even our traditional concepts about money. Cyberspace is becoming an enormous international virtual economy with remarkable new opportunities for both legitimate business and fraudulent operations.

Conservative bankers have been predicting that the Net could never realise its potential of a giant global market place because of the presence of hackers who could intercept electronic cash and credit transfers and pose risks that financial institutions just will not tolerate. In fact, many of those problems have been solved already. There are several schemes which, safely and efficiently, allow you to authorise payments from a current account, or by means of a credit or debit card, with security commensurate with writing a cheque or placing a credit card order by telephone in the physical environment.

I have sold books and software this way with no problems for some time. The challenge has not been collecting the money, but generating the orders!

In many business situations – particularly if selling information products online which involve nominal per unit "manufacturing" and distribution costs – it is an acceptable risk to fulfil orders without first doing significant credit checking. It may be better to swallow quite a high proportion of payment defaults than not operate the easiest possible system to facilitate impulse purchases. I became convinced of this while observing the high proportion of cancelled orders in an electronic cash transfer scheme in which buyers were asked by email to confirm their orders.

The scheme itself works very well. The seller opens an account with First Virtual Holdings, a pioneering online bank, and in his cyberspace store encourages customers to do the same so that they can make purchases with any of the growing number of suppliers participating in the programme. The customer responds, hopefully, by filling in a simple form online and receiving a virtual bank account number by email.

THE EIGHT PRINCIPLES

The guidelines crucial to future business in cyberspace were agreed in March 1995 at the Group of Seven meeting in Brussels between government leaders from Canada, France, Germany, Italy, Japan, UK, and the United States, and over 40 telecommunications business executives. It was the first time private sector roundtables were held at a Group of Seven meeting.

They approved eight basic principles for the development of a global information infrastructure:

≠ promoting dynamic competition

≠ encouraging private investment

≠ defining an adaptable regulatory framework

≠ providing open access to networks

≠ ensuring universal provision of – and access to – services

≠ promoting equality of opportunity for all citizens

Whenever a purchase is made, the customer gives this number to the supplier, who passes it on to the bankers and processes the order in a similar way to a conventional credit card transaction. A significant difference is that, to cope with customer demands for speed and efficiency in cyberspace, the supplier's automated fulfilment service may have delivered the product before the customer has checked his email and responded to a message from the bank to confirm the charge to his account. If the buyer changes his mind, the product may already have been delivered online, or a password provided to unlock it if it was in encrypted form, as is becoming increasingly popular for information productions made available on CD-ROMs as well as online marketing facilities.

(You receive a catalogue of such products on a CD and can freely browse the descriptions and run the demonstrations. If you decide you want a program, a database, or some examples of clip art, you can immediately get the complete product off the disk by telephoning or going online to make payment and receive an unlocking code.)

The extra step – the buyer confirming the transaction by email – removes the instant gratification for both parties from the transaction and so is a limiting way of handling orders except for a somewhat restricted range of products. However, it can be very attractive for certain business-to-business transactions, and a great boon to small business suppliers having their cash flow ruined by slow payers.

Better for most general transactions are the many schemes emerging from the joint projects being developed by banks and credit card companies who have formed alliances with specialists in online technology. Netscape Communications and BankAmerica launched one of the first of these which you can try by getting the necessary software through an FTP call to **ftp.mcom.com**. The software encrypts the customer's credit card number before it travels through cyberspace. So even the seller does not know the true number, but passes the encrypted version straight on to the bank for approval. When confirmation is received, the order is processed in the normal way with the bank taking any risks of default.

Visa and Microsoft were developing a similar scheme as this book went to press, and there are many others emerging. This type of process – payment through a third-party financial institution protecting both buyers and sellers from fraud – seems to be the brightest future for commerce in cyberspace, but it may not be much help to the small start-up entrepreneur unable to get credit card merchant status, particularly if the bulk of his or her transactions will be online and not from what the banks have perceived in the past as the much safer walk-in business when the plastic is physically produced and, in theory, the purchaser's signature and authenticity verified.

There are some interesting alternatives. The Mondex smart card system from the National Westminster Bank subsidiary has potential online, and the other High Street banks all have programmes under development. There is much international interest in the Dutch DigiCash and the American DigiCash concepts which are similar to the advance purchase of tokens or cards for making telephone calls or trips on the Underground.

In these schemes, a customer turns conventional cash or credit into an electronic token which has sophisticated cryptographic and tracking features to again ensure in theory that each of the units making up the value of the virtual token can be spent only once online. This could be a very effective way to process a large number of small payments – a prime online commerce need.

I have, for example, large information resources resulting from my two books on fakes, forgeries, industrial counterfeiting and intellectual property rights issues. These can be converted into a viable online business when there is an efficient way of setting them up as an evolving database. I must be able to charge antique and art collectors, auction houses, lawyers and others who need to know specific facts from the database a small amount for each access that they make. My research indicates that the project is not viable if I seek up front the necessarily large subscriptions for unlimited access. Like many other entrepreneurial ventures in both the real and virtual worlds, I need to prove the value of the service I am offering before expecting clients to make substantial commitments to it.

Many entrepreneurs can build information resources like this online when ways of charging small sums for limited access become more practical. It is a particularly appropriate concept for software or research resources that a client needs only occasionally, and so does not want to pay a substantial amount to buy outright or subscribe to.

The broader bandwidth and faster communications that ISDN makes possible could eventually lead to widespread renting of time on distant computers to

≠ promoting diversity of content, both cultural and linguistic

≠ recognising the necessity of co-operating on projects to ensure that underdeveloped countries also can tap into and benefit.

It was further agreed to adopt policies designed to:

≠ promote interconnectivity and interoperability

≠ develop global markets for networks, services, and applications

≠ protect intellectual property rights

≠ allow for co-operative research and development ventures

≠ monitor the social and societal implications of the information society.

Information on just how well these objectives are being met in the European context can be found at Welcome to Euro*Gopher* on the Web at **http://www.sunet. se/eurogopher/eg. html**

do specific tasks that are charged for so much per project or on a time basis, much as you can take your dirty washing to the launderette and pay per load to get it clean, and per minute to have it dried. Some newsletters may do better distributing a free summary and charging for access on demand to individual items, with the whole process automated through secure passwords and electronic payments.

The technology to make electronic tokens feasible has other professional and entrepreneurial applications also. One area of expected growth is in online notarial services so documents that at present need to be taken physically to a public notary or Commisioner of Oaths are verified online with digital signatures and time stamps.

Your selection of one or more of the different payment processing services becoming available could be influenced by the contribution, if any, they might make to your marketing efforts. Some services offer online facilities for supplier clients to promote their own businesses – the bank or other fianncial institution sets up a virtual mall at its high exposure online premises where you can promote your own products and services for a reasonable fee. You need, however, to make sure that it is a cost effective deal all round. Check if the online site really does attract large numbers of your potential customers, and whether you benefit in credibility and the services offered by being there.

One such prospect worth exploring has been set up by ex-IBMers – there are lots of them venturing into cyberspace since they were no longer guaranteed jobs for life! PeachWeb Corporation combines expertise in online security with a talent for creating attractive and functional Web pages. They will put up four screens of promotional material at their Web site for about £150 and a monthly fee of about £22. Contact the president, Jim Fredericks, at **jim@peach.web.com** for current rates and costs.

Some online payment processors have built very elaborate online facilities that attract many thousands of visitors every day. A pioneer in this has been SoftLock Services with its Downtown Anywhere Web site, which is a good choice if you want to complement your online activities with conventional toll-free order line and credit card processing facilities in the US. Downtown Anywhere has a forum which it calls The Marketplace for Ideas and you can check out this and its other facilities on the Web at **http://www.awa.com**.

There is little doubt that processing credit card and other forms of electronic cash and credit in cyberspace will become an acceptably secure routine for the international business community. But the most challenging online billing problem remains – how to protect and remunerate writers, artists, publishers, researchers and others who release their intellectual property into cyberspace. Once out there, the very qualities that make the medium so effective also make it very easy to replicate original work. The difficulties of policing copyright and other rights in cyberspace are enormous, and often beyond the resources of even substantial companies, let alone individual entrepreneurs and other originators of creative materials.

Canada is now the location for the most ambitious trial anywhere of a possible solution. The Intercom Ontario Consortium is running the world's first system capable of providing accountability for content on the information highways, including cable television and other services. Code-named IVY, and jointly developed by Disus, SOCAN, and the CulTech Collaborative Research Centre, it is testing a technology for both protecting intellectual property and also distributing royalty payments. The protecting of IPRs (Intellectual Property Rights) is only one part of the equation – the other is to have an effective way of making properties readily available and collecting revenues from those wanting the rights to use them.

The test of the IVY system is part of a much wider social experiment of potential significance to Britain. Intercom Ontario's interactive community research trial is unique in the way that it is researching how ordinary people, institutions, and businesses will use and pay for cyberspace services. The organisers are creating a fully "wired" microcosm of Canadian society within which they will test the efficiency of supplying and collecting money for services involving IPRs of different kinds.

"Without fair compensation there will be no valuable content on the infoway," says Paul Hoffert, Executive Director of the Intercom Ontario Consortium. "Through IVY we have transformed theoretical discussions to a working system for use not only in our trial, but by others."

IVY combines software with a complete online enrolment and management system for delivering works and enabling trusted organisations to monitor usage and collect payments. The aim is to extend into cyberspace the procedures that protect the rights in intellectual properties that are distributed in physical forms, such as books, CDs, or video tapes. Using IVY, Intercom Ontario can determine use patterns on broadband networks, track the content traffic, and ensure that content providers are fairly compensated. The research benefits will include valuable data about how users interact with applications, what they choose to access, how long they use it, and what, if anything, they'd be willing to pay for it.

Figure 7.2 Using a touch-screen display

"Content providers wanting to take advantage of the infoway now, can either self-publish and expose their work to an anarchic system from which they may receive very little business and no payment, or they can sell all rights to an international media giant who will handle all distribution, and take complete control," says Tom Jurenka, President of Disus.

"Allowing any and all creators to register with copyright collectives using IVY provides a third distribution option: one that provides access to a greater audience, ensures copyright protection, and provides users with an option of becoming registered creators."

The system works like this. A consumer requests content from the retailer who has been authorised to deliver it over the network by a distributor. As the distributor provides the content, IVY sends notice of the transaction to the copyright collective. The content is decrypted and sent to the consumer from the appropriate media server on the network. IVY authenticates the request, checks the distribution contract and ensures that all terms are fulfilled. At the end of each billing period, IVY calculates invoices for distributors, and payments for content owners.

Only authorised users can access registered content, but IVY has enough flexibility to adapt to alternative distribution chains, including direct owner to customer transactions.

The technology has been implemented first at Intercom Ontario's beta site at Calumet College, York University, and as the network expands embraces a residential community, and a number of content centres and businesses in and around Toronto.

More than 60 organisations in both the public and private sector are collaborating in this cyberspace trial in Ontario, and the experiences in the residential community of Newmarket could provide valuable pointers for similar operations among comparable communities in Britain, Europe and other territories. The resulting data could be very important for town and country planning purposes.

One of the key players is SOCAN , the copyright and performing rights society that licences, collects and distributes licence fees as royalties to Canadian composers, lyricists, song writers and their publishers, and affiliated foreign performing rights societies. British writers and composers may soon see royalty revenues flowing to them from this unique project which could foretell how creative people will earn much of their income in future.

There is political significance as the development of information superhighways in Europe generates some hot political potatoes, including the way that some governments are dragging their feet or putting restrictions in the way of private enterprise's desire to drive forward as quickly as possible. In contrast, the Canadian, Ontario and municipal governments are all backing these trials, and the proportion of corporate and other private sector involvement is increasing in a truly collaborative venture unlike anything envisaged in Europe. The estimated cost is some CA$111 million over four years.

Right through to the end of the decade consumers, businesses, schools, universities, libraries, government departments, and cultural institutions will be joined together through a network supporting interactive applications that could change the way people play, work, and live. The results need to be watched by business interests everywhere because we will see the first details emerging of users' real world needs for bandwidth, peak loads, hardware and software.

8. Your cyberspace business plan

Don't forget the human values

Preparing a conventional business plan when launching an enterprise into cyberspace is rather like filing a flight plan when you don't know what kind of aircraft you will be using, how much fuel it carries, and which way the wind is blowing. In both situations you risk getting hopelessly lost, even crashing. However, as neither your bank manager nor your corporate financial controller, if you have one, will respond well to excuses about not drawing up a business or marketing plan, we should try to make what can be a painful process as pleasurable as possible.

When seeking funds or budgetary approval it won't increase your chances of success to emphasise the vagaries of this new, rapidly evolving and unstable business environment. But in your plan's preamble do sound a word of caution about the difficulties in quantifying just how rich are the media-hyped gold strikes to be found in them thar hills to which the information highways lead.

You may well find yourself dealing with an absolute Luddite when your business plan comes to be evaluated. It is astounding how ignorant of the new technology are many loan officers, bank managers, advisors at government sponsored small business development facilities, and others who wield power over would-be entrepreneurs. This is a very serious inhibiting factor for British entrepreneurs seeking to start enterprises online. It is very difficult to get across the credibility of opening a New York office and an international marketing programme from your spare bedroom with £500 start-up capital and monthly operating costs of under £100!

Despite the fluidity of the cyberspace business environment and the consequent difficulty in forecasting what is going to happen, drawing up at least a skeleton business or marketing plan is essential, if only for your own edification. It will give you a framework within which to plan and monitor your

INTERNATIONAL TRADE NETWORK

If you are seeking to establish an international business through cyberspace, a subscription to the International Trade Network provides contacts for shipping agents and other essential services, as well as opportunities to advertise what you are offering. The annual cost is about £13, and you can get details by email to **majordomo @world.std.com**, with the message **info intltrade**.

NEWSPAPERS LEAP INTO CYBERSPACE

"The world's newspapers are leaping into cyberspace. From *Aftonbladet* in Sweden to *L'Unione Sarda* in Italy to the *Weekly Mail* in South Africa to the *Los Angeles Times* or *Hartford Courant* in the US, newspapers are hurtling along the infobahn at such speed that it is hard keeping track of them," said the *Financial Times* in April 1995.

You can try to keep up by accessing the international database of online newspapers at **http://marketplace.com/e-papers.list.www/** on the Web. Online journalism resources recommended by the *FT* include Newslink (**http://www.newslink.org/newslink**) and John Makulowich's journalism list and links to other sites through **http://www.clark.net/pub/journalism/verbwork.html.**

Steve Outing, who runs the database of online newspapers, predicts between 1,000 and 2,000 newspapers will be operating such services in 1997.

progress, but don't regard anything in it as inflexible. Use a spreadsheet that does not impose a rigid structure to record how and when you will deploy your resources. Make your estimates of costs on the basis that in many categories prices will continue to fall steadily. Project management software can also be a useful tool in both the planning and monitoring procedures.

Be prepared to accelerate your timing at any stage. Once you get involved and start monitoring lists and newsgroups in your areas of interest, you will find that the pace is such that you may need to move faster than you probably anticipated to maintain any competitive advantage you may have – or to catch up with competitors who have overtaken you.

In contrast, delay as long as is sensible your final decisions in buying hardware, software and online services. The tendency is for them all to get cheaper as they get better. Of course, don't delay past the point of common sense; there is a tendency to keep holding out another week for a new upgrade or a better price, but this can result in diminishing returns. You probably already have one or more PCs or Macs capable of handling much of your preliminary work, but once you have got to the point of identifying what software and hardware you will need to be fully operational with the new venture, go for it as soon as practically possible. Buy the latest versions at the best prices you can get at that time. The payoff in increased proficiency and productivity could be the best investment you make.

Before you sit down to put your plan together, talk over your concepts in as much detail as you can with people whose opinions – and confidentiality – you trust. If you are already online, you may be able to do this very quickly and to good effect by using email. While writing this chapter I was asked by one of the users of my *Writers Electronic Publishing Kit* for comments on a project he was considering launching. You may find the following edited version of my email exchange with Dan Gardner helpful.

Every day brings me a variety of enquiries from people in all walks of life who see wonderful new opportunities for their pet projects in the new business world of cyberspace. Very few are worthless, but many are personal dreams that will succeed only if you remove two obsessions from the equation, and I feared at first that Dan Gardner might be afflicted with both and I would have to start advising this physician to heal himself!

The first – and most frequent – is the conviction that, because a particular idea turns on the originator, then there are bound to be lots of other people who can be reached in cyberspace and who will be prepared to throw money at it. Thousands of business or publishing projects flounder because the passion of the originator is not shared by a viable market that can be reached cost-efficiently and is prepared to pay enough to make the project profitable. It can be very difficult to convince people with a passion for a book or a product that their idea is only worth pursuing if they do not expect it to make them rich overnight.

There are entrepreneurial rewards beyond money which should be factored into every business plan, if only for your own personal consideration or to share with family members and colleagues who will be affected by the project. Thousands of businesses fail for reasons that do not figure in the cold statistics that measure such readily quantifiable factors as lack of capital, inappropriate location, market shift, etc. Often, as I know from personal experience, a business fails because other family members do not buy into the concept and provide the support and motivation that can make all the difference between success and disaster.

Such human factors tend to be overlooked in our preoccupation with trying to get the figures right. We have created a society in which money has become the yardstick of merit in so many things. We tend – and publishers and bankers are among the worst examples of this – to try to put a cash value on everything in order to be able to quantify its worth. But a book that you have dreamed about publishing for years, or a business or invention that you want to bring to market to enhance the quality of your life or hand on to your children, may not require a large cash advance from a major publisher or loan approval from a bank manager to verify its merit.

The payoffs may be in the ability to move from an urban to a rural area, with lower income-earning potential more than compensated for by lower living costs and the enhanced quality of the environment. Bank managers tend not to like business plans that show that the principal will be earning less than at present, even if there are strong personal motivations to launch the enterprise.

It is particularly difficult to put monetary cost and revenue projections to a creative work or a carefully assembled database – two prime categories for entrepreneurial ventures in cyberspace which have values in addition to earning

"The development of the online newspaper industry in the immediate future depends fundamentally on whether news providers can work out how to charge for their services and achieve economic viability," commented the FT.

Outing believes newspapers should provide an "electronic town hall" for their subscribers, because "any newspaper, big or small, can succeed if it can position itself to be the No 1 online information provider in its community."

He expects publishers will not turn their online services into profitable ventures by receiving subscriber fees, but by selling advertising or sponsorships; receiving commissions from online transactions between readers and advertisers; and charging for premium services, e.g. access to archives and personalised electronic clippings services.

Delphi provides several online news services, including Reuters and – useful for entertainment industry people – Daily Variety. The keyword is News.

One Program may Launch a Business into Cyberspace

There are myriad new business opportunities hiding in cyberspace among the tens of thousands of software programs that can empower entrepreneurs. You can establish a business just on the basis of one specialist program that gives you the power to provide services or create products that will be in demand. For example, there is a remarkable program called MetalMan that enables sheet metal designs to be created very rapidly. It could be the basis for consultancy and design prototyping services, even to clients who have a CAD design capability already.

MetalMan works in Windows to simulate sheet metal fabrication. You use it to make parts as if you were painfully developing prototypes in the workshop using punch and drill presses and other machine tools.

power in the benefits they can bring readers and the personal satisfaction and possible career enhancement for the originators that may be impossible to quantify in conventional monetary terms. There are many rewards beyond money for entrepreneurs seeking real quality in their lives and careers and you should include these – as well as any necessary sacrifices – in your business plan.

A book of merit that appeals only to a small niche market can now not be denied publication; cyberspace offers practical publishing opportunities impossible in the print medium, just don't expect it to be a best-seller! You can leverage a book in electronic form into the many opportunities to advance a career or promote a service, or just for personal satisfaction of a kind that you cannot buy at any price.

An example of this is one of those dogged seekers after the truth of the authorship of the works attributed to Shakespeare. There are thousands of them around the world, particularly in the United States, but collectively they hardly make up a viable market that can be reached easily for the many books that have been written to advance the cause of Bacon, the Earl of Oxford, Ben Jonson, and other seemingly better qualified candidates than the glovemaker's son from Stratford.

In addition to the 4,000 or so books and papers already published on Shakespeare authorship, there are thousands more manuscripts that their authors dream of getting into print. Many are well researched and written – fascinating insights into the first Age of Enlightenment. The fact that they cannot get past acquisition editors and peer reviewers into print causes great frustration and bitterness among their authors, some of whom have invested their savings in vanity presses or self-publishing to try to get their messages out. I know of none of these that have been profitable ventures. One of the best, a superb research effort into Francis Bacon by retired lawyer Penn Leary, has not made a profit after two print editions – hardback and paperback – and an electronic version on floppy disk.

But Penn regards pursuing that interest into print and electronic publishing as one of the best investments he has ever made. He has completed a major intellectual task and become a player in one of the most competitive commercial environments, publishing. His work has given him an abiding interest and has been seen through to tangible, permanent forms that are a testimony to his intellectual abilities, and determination. I was privileged to present a summary of his work to a meeting in Beverley Hills marking the tenth anniversary of the Shakespeare Authorship Roundtable, and to participate in the electronic publication of his book. We still have not shown a profit on it after more than two years, but it represents a credit in our balance sheets of life experiences.

Another Shakespeare authorship investigator who further illustrates the point is Ethel Griffing, a retired teacher and librarian who accepted that her efforts to publish in print would never succeed because of the harsh realities of commercial print publishing. Now, approaching eighty, she has learned how to use a computer for the first time and is venturing out into cyberspace with electronic publishing ventures about Thomas Heywood being the likely author of many Shakespearean works, new evidence about the execution of a Welsh participant in the Babington plot against Queen Elizabeth I, and some fascinating stuff exploring the historical background to the current revival of interest in angels. I have observed the remarkable changes in her that these activities have stimulated, enhancing her life as she coped with the physical realities of old age and the loss of her husband. The fact that electronic publishing in cyberspace is readily available to Ethel gives a sense of purpose and permanence to what otherwise might be considered just a hobby.

Ethel celebrated her 78th birthday by buying a new computer and high speed modem. She is one of the now tens of thousands of senior citizens who are becoming cyberspace entrepreneurs. Some will make good money, but most who try to publish, use their expertise to gain consultancy work, or launch small business ventures may generate little monetary profit. Nevertheless, they can greatly enhance their later years by stimulating their minds through such ventures in cyberspace.

Senior citizens with these kinds of entrepreneurial missions are less vulnerable to the bad legal advice that others among my correspondents are getting. A vital issue for many would-be cyberspace entrepreneurs is "how do I protect my intellectual property?". They may, if they can afford it, build expensive legal services into their budgets and business plans.

My answer to these thorny intellectual property rights issues is " expect to protect your copyrightable works with great difficulty at best, in most cases not at all. Before you pay a lawyer to tell you this, consider carefully if it really matters".

You select the metal you want to use – aluminium or mild steel, for example – design the part and then go through the actual manufacturing process on screen. It will work in three dimensions and also create flat design views to plot drill holes and fold and cut marks. When the virtual prototype is satisfactory, the program creates mechanical specifications, estimates of manufacturing costs and times, and can be customised to match the actual machine shop in which the real life fabrication will be done.

Any entrepreneur who knows metalwork could use this program to create an international consultancy through cyberspace, as well as provide a face-to-face service to local clients. The pricing in Europe is under $1,000, and the best way to find out more is to email Metalman president David Baltz at **72302.1027@ Compuserve.com**.

NEED FOR BLIND FACILITIES

Online services are very variable in the facilities they provide for blind people, yet they represent an important niche market which we have a social responsibility to serve. The commercial pressures to introduce user-friendly graphical interfaces risk leaving the blind denied access to many cyberspace benefits as the text-based interfaces of old are replaced.

It remains to be seen to what extent the main commercial providers will keep the commitments they have made not to abandon their blind users. As they are already over-stretched trying to grab their shares of such a rapidly expanding market, there will probably be a continuing need for specialist services to help blind users continue to use their speech and Braille output systems.

The British Computer Society operates an online service of information to help disabled people. Details by email from **k.davis@dircon.co.uk**.

I've just heard from a woman who has devoted many years to researching what could be turned into a very unusual and interesting ebook or database of information. As part of her planning, she consulted her lawyer about marketing this online and was advised not to do so because of the difficulty of protecting her copyright. So she has abandoned the project, and almost certainly will not be able to pursue it as a viable conventional print publishing or business activity.

How sad. She is very disappointed and will always regret that decision because she never brought to a conclusion those years of research and a developing passion for a subject for which the Internet probably offers the only cost-effective way of reaching her small and fragmented potential market. Her work – like most of the cases that come to me – is not going to be pirated to any degree, if at all. Even if there was a lot of illicit copying, it would be less damaging to her than not going ahead because a lawyer warned her of the difficulty of getting copyright protection.

We deal with copyright and other forms of intellectual property protection elsewhere. Just let me emphasise here that piracy is the most over-blown issue in publishing and other business ventures in cyberspace. There is so much original work going on that your chances of being illicitly copied are comparatively small. Even if you are, you may well be able to turn this to your advantage – even encourage it. Cyberspace pirates may prove valuable additions to your sales force!

The third barrier against which I see many cyberspace ventures falling is the excessive research and complexity that form a carry-over legacy millstone from the traditional ways in which large corporations do business. These traditions in management and business planning techniques are still being perpetuated by academics and former corporate managers teaching in business schools.

A big company involved in a traditional business must pay great attention to detail and research long and intensively because just a small mistake or misjudgement can have enormous consequences. Take the minivan as an example. Several European motor manufacturers are facing heavy losses because they misjudged the potential of this market sector, while in the US Chrysler's stock fell after it announced the biggest recall in history to modify the door locks on some four million of its minivans. Small mistakes can cost millions in that kind of traditional business because of the high costs inherent with marketing and supporting large volumes of conventional physical products.

That is not the case with cyberspace, where the up-front costs can be tiny and the risks all down the line from mistakes or misjudgements can be very little. That's why cyberspace is such an ideal environment for the one-person or small business venture that has little capital, but can move quickly to market without the inertia and inhibitions existing in large corporations.

The biggest mistake – and I see it so often – is to apply big business practices to small entrepreneurial adventures. This happened to a business in San Francisco for which I was a consultant. Run by former executives with large organisations, they managed to secure a substantial investment which proved their undoing. So much time and cost were devoted to researching the planned products and establishing a corporate infrastructure that the investor got cold feet, cut off the money flow, and the whole venture collapsed after wasting about £300,000. That wastage included setting up a computer network, when all the key people involved worked in adjoining offices and could just as easily, at least at the beginning, either exchange their digitised information by a simple modem link through their telephone lines, passed floppy disks one to another, or actually walked a few steps to talk to each other!

For the time and money spent on research, we could have created and test-marketed products and services that would have generated an early revenue flow without any significant risk of damaging our longer-term prospects. Pensioner Ethel Griffing achieved more working alone at her old computer than we did with all our resources – and she didn't spend £300,000 in the process.

Recently, I've been dealing with someone who wants to launch over the Internet a range of products and services linked to helping people with addiction problems. Much of his effort is going into preparing the pitch and meeting the people he is wooing to put up the significant amounts of initial capital that he feels are required. Now, presumably to impress them, he wants me to do a lot of research into the software alternatives and rank the core products by the varying degrees of interactivity that can be achieved online.

I try to be kind, but the best advice to him would be to stop worrying about details and get on with actually doing something with his basically good idea.

ECONOMIC FACTS AND FIGURES

If you need to track commercial and economic trends, there are many sources for national, regional and global information. Three of the best are accessible by *Gopher* – **cwis.usc.edu**, **zeus.nijenrode.nl**, and **una.hh.lib.umich.edu**.

News and discussions about many individual industries can be tracked down on the Web through **http://www.clarinet.com/index.html**.

KEEP UP TO DATE WITH THE COMPETITION

To find out what your competitors are doing on the Web, go to the Commercial Sites Listing at **http://www. directory/ com/** and What's New on the Web at **http://www. ncsa.uic.edu/SDG/Software/Mosaic/Docs/whats-new.html**. These will lead you to new developments in creating Web pages – which are quite easy to reverse engineer to see how they are done – and the opportunities for posting your own cyberspace advertising.

He doesn't need those outside investors, and the choice of software is already obvious. Adding too much interactivity in the search for what the movie business calls "production values" is as redundant as the fins on a 1970's Cadillac. The more bells and whistles he grafts on to his core concept, the slower it will run online, the more difficult it will be to use, and the less it will meet the need that exists for it.

He can – with little computing knowledge – create a Web site, market directly to the people in various online special Internet groups that offer him his best sales prospects, and focus on steadily increasing his entrepreneurial venture rather than drawing up budgets and fancy proposals to generate money he thinks he needs to achieve grandiose objectives.

So forget the big business games when venturing into cyberspace. If you budget and plan to set up a structure that, for example, results in the typical £5 it costs a big company to write a letter, then you're probably dooming your cyberspace venture to disaster.

Occasionally, I receive a query which makes me feel good because all the elements seem to be coming together well and the plan reflects the honest realism about doing business in cyberspace – including the human factors – that are key ingredients for success.

That was the case when Dan Gardner emailed me before drawing up his detailed business plan. Dan is a physician specialising in psychiatry, psychoanalysis, and neurobehavioural medicine.

"Bringing together an interest in writing and computers, and inspired by current enthusiasm about cyberspace (including your book), we're embarking on producing and distributing epubs," he emailed me. "Qualified Insights Press, our company, is composed of my wife Dianne, (a professional speaker and trainer), our son Max (a computer aficionado) and our friend and chief consultant Sean Stallings, who knows about graphic design and cyberspace communications."

I replied: that sounds close to a dream team for a family business in cyberspace. There are two experts in specialities in which information-based products should be in strong demand. One is a professional speaker, so products created for online marketing can be adapted also for back-of-the-room sales at seminars and workshops. The online activities can be used also to promote speaking opportunities in a variety of cross-pollination ways to help the business to grow.

The medical qualifications held by you and your wife could be essential when communicating with fellow professionals, and a major asset when broadening the market to the increasing numbers of people seeking information about their medical and related problems.

Having a computer-literate child in the family provides the boy – or girl – power to do much of the online locating of these special interest groups and posting messages to them. Youngsters who enjoy cybersurfing are particularly useful for the time-consuming research necessary to locate Internet sites, BBSs and VANs which offer marketing opportunities and to which links should be made to attract traffic to your virtual store.

Having advice from someone who knows graphic design and cyberspace communications is a big bonus. Sean's programming skills can come in very useful for modifying applications, or creating routines and small self-executing programs that can give a custom look and added functionality to either online operations or to disk-based products. The graphic design capability – rare in programmers, despite what some of them like to believe! – will help to create the attractive screen displays that are becoming increasingly important.

"We're focussing on the areas of healthcare, self-help, psychology, and professional speaking and training – our areas of expertise," Dr. Gardner continued.

Yes, concentrate on what you know best and leverage your knowledge into credible products and services that bring tangible benefits to your target markets. There is a tremendous amount of online activity in the healthcare and self-help fields – cancer, neurological diseases, addiction, co-dependency, and a wide range of psychological and emotional issues are just some examples of forums and support groups whose members value quality information about their problems.

You will not be able to market aggressively through these on-line resources, but if you contribute creatively to their information needs, many will follow through for more information about your products and services, or visit your own online resource regularly. Stimulating their word-of-mouth recommendations is probably the single most important marketing activity that you can undertake.

DIRECT MAIL SUMS

To identify potential savings from using cyberspace in place of conventional direct mail, add up the design, printing, mail list rental, folding, envelope stuffing and postal costs of sending out the shot, and divide by the number in the mailing to get the unit cost. Then add up the production and transmission costs to reach the same targets on line. The unit cost through cyberspace can be under one per cent of the cost for a conventional hard copy direct mailing, particularly if it is international. Of course, the calculations are only valid if your targets are accessible electronically.

The savings get greater the larger and more international the mailing. In effect, you can increase the size of the mailing without increasing the total cost, whereas doing it with paper pushes the cost up in direct proportion to numbers involved, with some compensation for economics of scale in the printing.

PROFITABLE PUBLICATIONS

Most print publications have built up large reference resources on specific topics, much of which can be recycled into digital databases for marketing online as well as off the printed page. This can be tried at minimal cost by assembling related texts and graphics on to a set of floppies using a simple ebook compiling program such as Jeff Napier's Writer's Dream, which can be found online in most good shareware collections. Dream will run on virtually any DOS or Windows system straight off the floppy, so is about as universal and foolproof as you can get, particularly if your readers tend to have older systems. Dream automatically adds straightforward text search facilities, so you can quickly turn a bunch of word processor or desktop published files and scanned images into a viable database. The newer Macs will run your ebook as a DOS program also, or can get at the texts as plain ASCII files.

"To get off the ground, we're in the process of producing four subscription electronic newsletters: a weekly medical humour letter (yet to be titled), *Brain Injury Update*, *NeuroLaw Letter*, and *NeuroPractice* newsletter. (The last three are electronic versions of current print publications.)"

It seems that you are segmenting your market sensibly and targeting closely matched titles to them. Your experience in print publishing should stand you in good stead – and there is now software that will enable you to take the word processed texts for your print newsletters and convert them quickly and easily into the HTML language for publishing over the Internet's World Wide Web, and into *Windows* Help files if you do any distribution in that form. (I recommend *HotMetal Pro* and the new *WebAuthor* for HTML, and *RoboHelp* and *Word for Windows* templates to create *WinHelp* files.)

"We're developing a proprietary newsletter reader which will allow us to email encoded text directly to the subscriber's email address. This newsletter reader software will decode the text and make it accessible only on that particular subscriber's hard drive. This production and distribution method addresses the problems of easy accessibility and theft prevention."

Those are two prime practical issues that you seem to have solved before you start. Newsletter publishers experimented extensively with non-copying paper and other devices to try to prevent illicit copying of their printed editions. Many still avoid cyberspace because of their – often unjustified – fears of piracy. Even if illicit copying is not a major issue, adding that coding feature will help to enhance subscribers' perceptions of the value of the content of your publications. Also, of course, you can offer trial subscriptions and cut off the bad payers with speed and flexibility.

Distributing directly to subscribers by email can be automated into a very efficient process. However, try to make what you email as compact as possible if your target readers include those who have to pay personally for their online services, unlike institutional and corporate users who are not as concerned about online charges.

"In addition, we're producing free promotional epubs which will advertise the print publications of several publishers."

Such co-operative promotions can be very effective, but they can also dilute the individual messages of the participants. Remember that cyberspace is not used best in most situations as a mass marketing medium, but as a way of targeting specific people who, hopefully, have a need to know your information and will really benefit from it. It can be counter-productive to commingle your promotional message with those of others who may not be as finely focused on the target market you need to reach.

Anything that makes a document being distributed online longer than it needs to be to achieve your objectives is counter-productive. We are all getting swamped by massive amounts of text which we have to read from the screen and there is a real risk of online promotional material stimulating the adverse reaction we have to the junk snail mail that bombards us daily. Don't risk becoming an intrusion on the time of your target subscribers.

"We plan to produce the epubs in WinHelp format, believing that DOS is on its way out and that most Macs will soon have *Windows* capabilities." (You can download a sample from America Online's EPUB area, for which European access should be available soon after this book is published. Go to keyword **EPUB > Software Libraries> electronic books> WinHelp file: Gender Quotes.**)

You are correct in predicting that *WinHelp* must emerge as a *de facto* standard for electronic publishing, but there are perhaps nearly a hundred million computers around the world that do not read *WinHelp* files easily, if at all, and that hardware will remain in use for a long time. If you need to reach the widest possible audience – particularly internationally – then you may have to offer DOS and Mac versions also, or ASCII texts that can be used by both systems. In America, one tends to forget just how many DOS only systems are used in other countries where hardware and software are more expensive, so that the life cycle of computing equipment is much longer. Also, there are parts of the world – the Far East, for example – where the Mac penetration is greater than in the US.

Similar considerations apply when distributing in physical media. CD-ROM drives are still only available on a small proportion of computers in use around the world, many of which also cannot accept the 1.4MB high density disks that are becoming the standard in the US.

Consider another approach – providing access to the full text online in HTML documents which can be read in a predictable way using DOS, Mac or Unix

Print labels and a jacket and duplicate disks as required and try out the concept first with advertorial in your own publication to your existing readers. Keep the price at or slightly below what they might expect to pay for a conventional book covering the same ground – under £15 for a three-disk set, or under $10 for a single are good yardsticks. It is the perceived quality of the information, not the number of disks, that leads to buying decisions.

A pig farming magazine, for example, could plunder its archives to create databases on such subjects as farrowing, herd record keeping, weaning wrinkles, heavy hogs, baconers, tricks and tips for successful showing, etc.

RECRUITMENT AND CAREER DEVELOPMENT

If you are looking for new career opportunities, or seeking to recruit staff, there are now many on-line speciality forums, lists and classified advertising areas. All the main VANs now have such facilities, including Compu-Serve's Professional area and America On-line's Talent Bank. On the Web, JobWeb is located at **http://www.risetime.com/risetime/preview.html**

BRUSHING UP BUSINESS

The Internet is proving a great way to generate requests for new product samples. Smithkline Beecham posted a message about its new Aquafresh Whitening toothpaste to the **alt.consumers.free-stuff** newsgroup and pulled in a big response. However, that is a cyberspace location used specifically by people looking for freebies, and making such an overt commercial pitch to other groups would guarantee flaming.

browsers. You can distribute the same documents on disk if there is enough file space to provide also browser software that will simulate an Internet connection on the end user's system.

"We have a rudimentary (soon to be upgraded to professional quality) BBS and plan to distribute the epubs to appropriate BBSs and FTP server sites and WWW home pages. We plan to distribute the enewsletters via a list server from our BBS."

That is a good example of how to integrate a BBS and a mix of online media into an effective distribution and marketing operation. However, it may be that your main target markets for these professional publications will increasingly be using the Web and you might want to concentrate less of your effort on the BBS and more on your own Web site, building graphical and hypertext links to and from it to link with other sites that will help your business to grow.

It might help your marketing to move quickly to secure a distinctive and easily remembered Web address appropriate to your business – just like a memorable telephone number can be an important business asset. The investment you make in developing your Web site now may enhance the assets of your business more than a BBS if you want to sell your business later.

You can build equity value into a Web site and, unlike a BBS, it has mobility if you plan to change your own physical location – or sell the business – later. The Web address – if you pick your service provider well – can stay the same, irrespective of the location where it is being operated. A BBS is tied to the telephone services and needs a new number if the location changes.

You may also investigate a university, hospital, charity, association or corporation that has Internet facilities which would be enhanced by carrying your enewsletters. However, such an association must not compromise subscriber perceptions of your editorial independence.

"Hopefully, we can get enough product to get a forum on America Online. The forum would, of course, contain epub files to be downloaded by interested parties. It would also have several discussion topics moderated by epub authors."

While AOL is the fastest-growing service and has many merits, it is not the biggest, and only acquires a European presence in late 1995. CompuServe, Prodigy, Delphi and other VANs may be more useful in reaching a larger North American audience, and for the international market.

"Against that background, I have some more detailed questions.

1. What is your general impression of our approach?"

> You have the basic elements together for a successful electronic newsletter publishing business, but only your own knowledge of your very specific target markets will enable you to evaluate if they are viable, receptive at this time to electronic publications, and accessible online. If they meet these requirements, then your chances of success are much greater than the print newsletter publishing ventures that have burned so many entrepreneurs.
>
> By marketing and publishing online you avoid most of the costs in direct mail marketing which requires substantial initial capital to launch a printed newsletter. You can save a lot of money – and be far more efficient also – in being able to fulfil subscriptions online. Online fulfilment is particularly important if your content is highly topical and time-sensitive.
>
> If your existing print newsletter subscribers are not eager to switch to online delivery, you may be forced to keep the print editions going. You may decide to offer print and online editions for all your publications if that is what your marketing indicates is important to maximise potential revenues. In that case, you might offer more attractive pricing for the paperless versions.
>
> As a compromise, you might be able to offer most of your subscribers who are not receptive to online fulfilment the option of physical delivery on floppy disk. The unit price of a 3.5 inch floppy bought in quite small quantities is now well under 30p, and they can be run off quickly and economically on any PC using programs such as *DiskDupe* or *DiskDuplicator*. I do most of my disk duplicating while watching television or listening to the radio. So the time involved is not a factor, and unit costs become competitive with printing.

SCAMS UNLIMITED

Scams online are almost unlimited in their variety and ingenuity. But cyberspace consumers are getting together to share experiences and sound warnings. A key sources for this information is the newsgroup **alt.consumers.experiences**.

QUICK CAPTURES

It is necessary to capture screen images quickly and easily for a whole variety of cyberspace business activities. Your favourite draw or paint program may have this facility, but perhaps in a form that is not sufficiently versatile as your needs develop. *Paint Shop Pro* – available widely as shareware – is efficient and easy to use. There are a number of good graphics file format converters available on line also. Look out for those from Alchemy, experts in graphics software.

Medical Economies

Virtual patient records available through cyberspace might be able to reduce NHS costs by over 15 %. Lost, unavailable, out of date, inadequate or innaccurate patient records are a major cost factor for doctors, hospitals, ancillary services and health administration. Just the waste of time and resources moving patient documents around costs millions every year.

Consequently, a lot of attention is being given to ways in which patient records can be removed from the cost and vulnerability of their traditional paper formats and moved online into virtual databases. In addition to reducing costs, the quality of care should improve, with patients less at risk of faulty diagnosis or treatment when their records are but a few keystrokes away at any time, anywhere.

"2. Have I left any important considerations out?"

Not if you have really done your homework on your prospective markets – particularly the numbers of potential subscribers and how much they will be prepared to pay. Of course, we are assuming that the CONTENT of your products provides tangible benefits for readers that they cannot obtain readily elsewhere at lesser or no cost. Without such content, the renewals won't come.

In print newsletter publishing, it is often only at renewal time that a subscription actually becomes profitable. Until then, it should be listed in the books as a liability because the cost of acquiring that subscriber and servicing him or her for the first subscription period often exceed the revenues generated. Electronic marketing and publishing can make a subscriber theoretically profitable from Day 1, but the business as a whole will not be viable unless there is a high renewal rate.

"3. Can you recommend a source for sample contracts (e.g., between publisher and authors)? We hope to help naive-about-the-net, sceptical businesses (including print publishers) dip their toe in the electronic waters by offering to produce and electronically distribute promotional epubs at no upfront cost to them. In return, we'd ask for a percentage of the sales of their print publications. In theory, this no risk, win-win scenario sounds great – but......"

My experience indicates you are at the ones at risk – of being bombarded by would-be electronic publishers who either do not have viable concepts, or lack the determination and staying power to turn ideas into tangible products. A percentage of something that doesn't sell would not cover your time and costs. If you really feel that you can provide a good service, charge a reasonable up-front fee, with perhaps a lesser percentage.

Don't take on any publications which you do not feel comfortable in identifying with, and which you are reasonably confident will be successful. Otherwise you risk diverting the essential effort you will need to put into making your own business a success.

Sample contracts are available online, and from writers' organisations. A simple exchange of letters outlining the agreement might suffice.

"4. How can we track the sales for each business? How practical would it be for us to collect payment, then send orders to the businesses we're promoting for fulfilment? We're concerned about liability if the orders aren't promptly fulfilled by the businesses. If the consumer purchases the products directly from the businesses, how can we reliably know the sales revenues?

"Also, once a customer buys a product through us, the business will send him a catalogue along with his first purchase and take his future orders directly. Any ideas how we can offer a no-risk, no- money- upfront deal and get a percentage of sales?

> There, you've listed some of the main problems facing anyone offering an e-publishing, or other online trading service to others! Let's tackle them in order.
>
> "How can we track the sales for each business? " You could modify almost any good financial software package to do this. *Quicken*, for example, has the necessary power and flexibility.
>
> "How practical would it be for us to collect payment, then send orders to the businesses we're promoting for fulfilment? We're concerned about liability if the orders aren't promptly fulfilled by the businesses."
>
> It is attractive to many start-ups if you offer to process credit card payments for them – and you should make sure that you include provision for this in your percentage split. You can process checks and the various forms of electronic cash and credit payment systems now emerging. Don't get involved in COD arrangements – the hassles and return rates do not make it worthwhile.
>
> You should insist that all suppliers have an email address, then you can automate the passing on of orders to them in a quick and easy process. Hold all the funds you receive for at least six weeks, preferably 2-3 months, to allow time for the payments to be processed, and any fraudulent use of cards, bad cheques, etc. to have surfaced. Allow a sufficient period for any reasonable credits to be made to clients who have genuine reasons to seek a refund.

The big pay-off nationally will be the ease with which patient records can be researched to indicate which are the most cost-effective treatments, and reveal trends in the national state of health. The main concerns centre around privacy.

Such issues are discussed by several cyberspace groups, including *Physicians Online*, which is free to the nearly 20,000 doctors who use it. The funding for this service – you must be a physician to join – is entirely from advertising, and there are considerable entrepreneurial opportunities to set up similar ventures in the various medical disciplines.

Reach the Demand Drivers

When marketing business-to-business cyberspace products and services do not make the mistake that has put many start-ups out of business by concentrating too much on selling high tech concepts to the technical people in companies who you think are the only ones who understand the merits of what you are offering.

Technical managers and staff are often not the main "demand drivers" in companies. The initiative to purchase may well come from administration and operations staff, line managers, finance officers and others who have little technical knowledge but scour computer magazines and roam exhibitions looking for solutions to their problems.

Then deduct your commissions and any other fees before making payment to the outside supplier. Make clear in your order form that you are acting as an agent and that the product will be drop-shipped by the supplier directly, who is responsible also for after-sales support. Don't get caught servicing someone else's product, nor assuming other responsibilities for it.

Of course, customers who buy a product through you may be sent a catalogue by the supplier, along with their first purchases, so that there is the risk of you not being involved in future orders. There is no effective way to protect yourself from this, so your percentage should allow for it and not be geared to the anticipation of handling second and further sales after the initial purchase.

Remember that you get the customer's details also, and may be able to build mailing lists useful to your own business from the responses that your client suppliers generate for their products. What you lose on the swings, you might more than gain on the roundabouts. Anyway, many of your suppliers may prove to be only one product businesses, with minimal repeat orders.

"5. We are in the process of getting other healthcare professionals involved as authors and acquisition editors. I understand the standard author's share for an ebook is 40%. How about for a newsletter distributed weekly or monthly? Since the time and effort is considerably more, would 30% be fair to the author. How about a percent of sales for the acquisition editor, who finds suitable authors and helps them deliver a high quality, edited work for conversion to an epub? Is 10% a reasonable figure?"

All these are "reasonable" figures, depending on individual circumstances, but no set levels have emerged yet. Actual revenues may fall far short of expectations, which risks leaving your acquisitions editors, who do much of the hard work, without adequate remuneration. In many cases, 10% would not prove sufficient for the editor, and a flat fee with no more, or much lower, commission would be appropriate.

Percentage deals should be proportionate to the input in work, costs and risk-taking. Authors who have tried seriously without success to get works accepted by commercial publishers and now want to try electronic publishing without doing the extra work themselves, should be ready to take royalty rates that are closer to the miserable levels existing in print. At the least they will get paid every month, while it is normal in print publishing to wait six months or a year.

Royalties or fees should also reflect the way in which products/ titles are delivered to you, the publisher. Do they need to be scanned from hard copies, converted from word processor and graphics forms, extensively reformatted into HTML or *Windows* Help documents, etc.?

"6. How about a reasonable purchase price for the electronic rights to print publications? I'm negotiating with a publisher for the electronic rights to several books written by my colleagues. Again, what percentage is reasonable?"

> No typical standard rates or percentages exist at present. I'd start by offering to create and market electronic versions at rates very favourable to you because of the publicity you will generate for hard copy sales. Each case will be different, and you should stick out for the best deal for yourselves on titles for which the publishers are not generating significant back list revenues. They may be about to put the books out of print any way. One of the best things about paperless publishing is that books not viable to keep in print, can be made available electronically with minimal costs.

"7. What about liability insurance? Do publishers need this?"

> In theory, as a publisher you assume liability for defamation and for the consequences of advice given in anything you publish. However, liability and libel insurance can be prohibitively expensive. If you are careful in what you accept for your imprint, and publish all the usual disclaimers, the risk can be made acceptable to carry yourself.
>
> But this is an increasingly litigious society, so you need to pay particular attention to even the most unlikely consequences of what you publish. Also bear in mind that your files may be corrupted after they've left you, so keep archives and issue appropriate warnings and disclaimers.

That is why any promotion, including trade shows aimed at techies, needs lively, entertaining and easy to understand aspects. A classic example of this is the way that AT&T added multimedia humour through an interactive kiosk to promote its ISDN services at shows. The cost of around £20,000 is expected to save over £60,000 in the first year just from the savings in personnel and demonstration equipment, with the added impact on the true corporate demand drivers being the main benefit.

SECURITY IS A SERIOUS ISSUE

Security on the Internet is only becoming a major issue with the arrival of the business community, and organisations like the CIA which have secrets they want to keep while exploiting this system set up for the free sharing of information. There are many ways to protect data and reduce the risk of confidential networks being penetrated by hackers, spies, viruses and villains from cyberspace. Effective systems are emerging also to protect the integrity of financial transactions taking place online. Perhaps the biggest risk of all is being so preoccupied with security issues that you do not exploit the entrepreneurial opportunities available. Just as a supermarket budgets for an acceptable proportion of losses, so a cyberspace business venture must take sensible precautions, but accept that some losses will occur.

"8. Any suggestions about "hot" (saleable) epub healthcare topics (e.g., weight loss, nutrition, alternative medicine, etc.)?"

> There are increasing numbers of publications on these topics, with highly variable quality. I would start from leads generated by the market research for your existing titles pointing you to topics in which there is a viable interest and which are not at present adequately covered. New treatments and techniques that promise to solve problems are the most viable topics, while collections of information – databases – are particularly appropriate for electronic publishing. Indeed, if you have a lot of information, market it as a database with easy search facilities rather than a publication. There is a higher perceived value. A *Windows Help* file packed with information can justifiably be promoted as a database rather than an epub.

"9. Do you know of others who are producing and distributing subscription electronic newsletters?"

> They are cropping up all over cyberspace, but the quality is very variable. Many cover information that is available without charge over the Internet, so they are not profitable unless they save people with the capacity to pay a lot of time searching online. You need to zero in on the basic requirements of newsletter publishing: providing information that your target readers really need to know, enhancing that information into knowledge that provides readers with tangible benefits, then charging them as much for it as they are prepared to pay.

"10. Do you know of any toll-free credit card processing services that will take payment, then send us the payment and orders for fulfilment?"

> Yes, I have used SoftLock Services and others are emerging all the time. Don't get locked into any particular system at this time, but leave yourselves flexible to seize the fresh opportunities for electronic trading that are being developed.

Dan Gardner and I continue to exchange messages about his interesting projects and he is pulling advice in from a variety of expert sources that he tracks down online. As a result, his business plan is well founded with realistic objectives and much practical detail so that it goes a long way to becoming almost a manual by which he and his associates can run his business day-by-day.

Bear in mind that traditional advisors may not have the expertise to help you plan a cyberspace enterprise. You may only be able to get the advice that you need for key aspects of your project by going online to find people with appropriate knowledge and experience.

With that background, let's build a typical cyberspace business plan. We'll call it a business plan, although it may in your case be more of a marketing or promotional plan than one covering the building of an entire business. If you are new to this process, or have what the Americans call Business Plan Phobia when they sell £80 an hour consultancy services as professed cures for the disease, you might find it helpful to copy the following steps and paste them on to the covers of ordinary card file folders. Then you have them for ready reference, together with the documentation inside the folder needed to compile each section of your plan.

Step 1 – Broadly define your business mission and your corporate and personal objectives.

> Don't waste time vaguely wondering how you can exploit cyberspace. Decide what it is you need to achieve, and then seek out the best opportunities to use online services to gain those objectives. In many respects, you may well be pioneering with no precedents to guide you. If you have firm goals and approach the new media with imagination, you will find that you can do things with the cyberspace facilities that they were not designed to do, and no one has tried before.

Step 2 – Refine those objectives

> Draw up a detailed list of your goals, probably dividing them up into four main categories:
>
> - saving money
> - increasing efficiency
> - research and development
> - marketing
>
> It may be difficult – or impossible – initially to quantify the savings and benefits you can anticipate in each of these categories by exploiting cyberspace. You may find it difficult to convince colleagues that tangible benefits are obtainable. That's why Step 3 is important.

If security is a serious consideration for you, there are so many variables in circumstances, threats, and defences that it is essential to get professional advice. Conduct a comprehensive risk analysis, and apply and maintain appropriate security measures.

The risk of vandalism to Web sites is very small unless you are a high profile target, and not difficult to repair. The biggest concern is likely to be penetration of a corporate network through an Internet gateway, with the attendant risks of virus infections, data being stolen or corrupted, transmissions being intercepted, and tampering with financial transactions.

There are now both commercial and shareware firewall programs which enable a network to create effective barriers against this kind of intrusion. Your network administrator, or experts with your suppliers, should be able to advise which is the most appropriate for your

Step 3 – Start an email system, if you do not already have one

circumstances. There is an Internet mailing list packed with expertise which you can get by email to **major domo@greatcircle.com** with the words **subscribe firewalls** in the body of the message.

Even the best firewall won't do much to protect your secrets and data from internal attack from your own employees, which in many cases is the biggest risk. Computer security is as much a human resources as technological problem. It is also as important to protect against physical dangers as from electronic intrusion, so an effective disaster protection and recovery plan is essential to cope with familiar hazards such as fire, flood and interruptions to the power supply.

If you or your organisation – and let's use "you" use as an all-embracing collective pronoun from now on – do not have an email system operating yet, then the anticipated savings and improvements that you can list under categories 1 and 2 could more than justify the entire costs of a major cyberspace project. In other words, you might only need to justify an email facility to get a much more ambitious cyberspace project moving. It could be the easiest way over the first hurdle in raising funds or getting management approval.

Email is the single largest online activity, and it is a safe and demonstrably effective way to start moving an organisation into cyberspace.. CompuServe alone handles some 100 million email messages annually just between its members, with another two million messages monthly going outside its network for transmission or reception via the Internet. The transmission cost of each message is trifling, and it is a faster and more convenient way of communicating in most circumstances than either conventional internal or external mail, fax, or even voice telephone. Staff reluctant to accept email soon become dependent on it and will be seduced by the time-saving efficiency to switch as much of their work as possible into email communications.

Typically, many will come to spend 20% of a working day handling email as a key element in completing assigned tasks. Europe is moving rapidly to the situation already existing in the US in which millions of professional and business people have become dependent on email to function. Over five million American professionals take a portable with them on business trips, and around two thirds of these use email both on the road and at their desks. Email has become a tool not associated primarily with nomadic workers, but as an everyday routine for the majority, mobile or deskbound, in the same category as using the telephone or fax machine.

You will need email sooner or later just to communicate with collaborators, clients, customers and other business contacts. IBM alone handles over half-a-million email messages with external contacts every month. So if you want to do business with IBM, you'll need an email address. Much of the research for this book was done by email. I – and millions of others in all walks of life now depend on email to function in our business and professional activities. Britain is being put at a serious competitive disadvantage because we are proving so slow to introduce email in our companies, organisations and professions.

Whether you have it already, or need to introduce it, include email prominently in your business plan as your top priority. You can budget it at as little as £10 per month per user providing you have local telephone call access to your cyberspace gateway, e.g. CompuServe or Delphi. The cost-benefits speak for themselves if you have significant expenditure on telephone calls and faxes – particularly internationally – or use courier services to transport documents. But you don't need to be operating nationally, or even nationally, to get benefits from email. It might well be the easiest, quickest, and cheapest way to enhance communications between colleagues within a small local organisation, and improve liaison with external customers and suppliers.

Email is highly relevant also to R&D. Using email alone can greatly reduce the cost and increase the tempo and accuracy of much research and product development work. When you are preparing to go to market, email again functions as a low cost, high return tool.

If I was trying to get budget approval for a cyberspace marketing communications presence, such as an advertising site on the Web, from a resistant manager or client that had not yet even networked its computers, my most likely line of attack would be to sell them on email and build the advertising or sales promotion project in as a subsidiary bonus.

Step 4 – Find out what the others are up to

Use your email capabilities, and acquire also the abilities to access the Web, and use Internet Relay Chats, *Telnet*, FTP, etc. to carry out some low level industrial espionage. Roam around cyberspace and listen in on the newsgroups, subscribe to the mailing lists, penetrate the Web sites dealing with topics of

INCOMES HIGHER WITH A PC IN THE HOUSE

One reason businesses are so attracted to cyberspace marketing is that there is a close correlation between personal computer ownership and income levels. This has been quantified for the first time by the Census Bureau in the US, which found that households with incomes above $75,000 (about £47,000) are from three to five times more likely to own computers than households with incomes from $25,000 to $30,000. (about £15,000 to £19,000). Where the head of the household has a college education, there is 11 times more likelihood of computer ownership than households headed by people who have not completed high school.

Those are particularly interesting figures for British cyberspace exporters aiming at selling intellectual products into North America.

Codes to send Files as Email

There are many situations in which it is useful to send email containing binary files with special formatting, such as a spreadsheet, or a word processing document containing a particular layout. You do this by using special coding and decoding software for the sender and recipient respectively, with the formatted file moving between them as the standard email ASCII characters.

One of the most popular ways to do this is using the DOS programs *uuencode.com* and *uudecode.com*. There are equivalents for Macintosh and Unix systems also. Suitable software may be available directly from your Internet service provider, or you can download these ASCII encoders from good software libraries.

concern to you. Budget for 10 hours a week of this activity over at least a month, and £40-£100 per month in connection costs. (Bear in mind that much of your writing and reading of email can be done off-line without incurring charges from your service provider and telephone company.)

Check through the mailing lists and other resources in Chapter 10 and the Appendix for pointers to places in cyberspace where you are most likely to find the information that you seek. A particularly useful resource at this stage could be the Net-happenings list, which you can get by emailing the message subscribe net-happenings, followed by your first and surnames, to **majordomo@is.internic.net**.

If you can't spare the time for this basic research, delegate some of the preliminary investigations so that when you go online you have specific destinations identified as needing personal visits. If you don't have staff for this, employ a teenager. He – it almost certainly will be he – may do preliminary research far quicker than a middle aged manager finding it difficult to adjust to cyberspace communications.

If the budget is tight, hook up a cheap dot matrix printer with a pile of low cost continuous feed paper and don't be mean about printing out hard copies of anything of importance that you gather online. Although I'm evangelical about the merits of paperless publishing, it is still easier for most of us to evaluate the kind of information that will be collected if it is categorised and sifted it in hard copy form. However, it pays also to dump all your captured online information and sources into a free-form database, or even word processor files, so that you can search through it quickly to find specific references.

Step 5 – Select your service provider

Now that you have a better idea of what you are going to do, you are in a stronger position to decide who you are going to do it through. Make a list of the facilities that you need as a result of reading this book and the other inputs you have had for your cyberspace project. Remember that you will need your own node or a full service provider to be proactive in such ways as having your own FTP or *Gopher* site, or Web page.

This demands more sophisticated resources in terms of hardware, software and personnel, and significantly greater expense. You may need to hire staff or consultants, identify a provider who will give you comprehensive technical support, lease a dedicated telephone line or get an ISDN connection, etc. etc.

For most projects, it will help to divide your needs into two lists. One will detail the resources you need to reach online primarily to gather information and react with others in a limited way, perhaps only through email. The other list should contain your planned more proactive activities, e.g. marketing products and services. The type of connection, hardware, software and service provider will be significantly more advanced for this than the former type of activity. Then – *before* seriously considering the option of establishing your own independent Internet node, go out shopping and try to find a VAN or a specialist Internet gateway that meets your needs with the best deal.

No printed book should try to make specific recommendations in this area. The deals and the facilities offered are developing so rapidly that even print magazines cannot keep up. My only firm recommendations must be to shop around, and ask as many other users as possible with similar needs about their experiences. Your best single source is probably the newsgroup on Usenet at **alt.internet.access**. Bear in mind that your needs may change, and you should allow for this. A VAN such as CompuServe may provide easy cheap access in the early days, but you may soon need more comprehensive Internet facilities and then either have to change services, or add additional ones.

If you cannot put together a package from service producers that ties in with your needs and objectives, then move towards evaluating the requirements for your own direct independent Internet access or node. If operating independently, consider whether there are appropriate strategic alliances that you can forge to help with this. If in a corporate situation, there may be other departments evaluating cyberspace activities – or already engaged in them – with whom you can join forces.

FED UP WITH HIGH PHONE CHARGES?

The Internet is offering alternatives to high voice telephone charges, particularly for international calls. *Internet Phone* is the first of what promises to become a wide selection of programs that enable computers fitted with modems and sound cards to establish connections for voice communications. The conversation is compressed at each end before transmission and travels between the computers as digital information like an ordinary Net connection. Only one person could speak at a time in early versions, as with most speakerphones, but that's a small hassle compared to the big savings that can be made by exploiting the Net's benefits of calling the other side of the world through a cheap local connection.

SAVE MONEY BY CAREFUL LICENSING

Before finalising a corporate licensing arrangement for software, do a careful audit of past and likely future usage patterns. There are now specific software metering programs that will help with this task. Millions of pounds are being wasted annually by companies paying unnecessary licensing fees. Metering programs can be used to log usage patterns, share licenses between different elements of an organisation, manage access to licensed programs – including forming queues if more users want access at one time than the license permits – and show which programs are not being used cost-efficiently under existing licensing agreements.

Step 6 – Draw up the marketing plan

If you intend to be really proactive in cyberspace, i.e. aggressively seeking exposure or generating orders, you should now draw up a specific marketing plan as a sub-set to your main business plan.

In this, identify the types and numbers of lists, newsgroups, etc. you need to target, and the nature and scale of your own home base – e.g. virtual store or consulting rooms – that you have to establish. It may be practical to differentiate clearly between the resources that you will need for research and those you will need for marketing. A Web site might be entirely devoted to marketing, while facilities for email, FTP, and *Telnet* play essentially research and related functions.

However, bear in mind that the same Intenet resources that you use for research are probably among the best places to generate awareness of your marketing facility. Post discreet, non-commercial messages drawing attention to information or other helpful facilities provided at the Web site and create hypermedia links to that site wherever and whenever you can while doing your research.

Include all the online and off-line media available to you in your marketing plan. You might get useful exposure through the VANs, even if you have an independent Web site not associated directly with any of them. The print media – particularly trade or special interest magazines relating directly to your projects – should be used to get exposure for your new online facilities. In many cases the very fact that you have created a site in cyberspace for news about widgets should merit editorial coverage in trade journals dealing with the widget industry. Consequently, you may be able to budget for a campaign with the emphasis on comparatively low cost below-the-line PR activities, rather than the more expensive creation of display advertising and space buying.

Step 7 – Firm up your hardware and software shopping list

Now you know enough about your needs to finalise acquiring the necessary hardware and software. If you had taken these decisions earlier, you could have wasted a lot of time and money. The service providers, for example, are improving their own software packages which it will be preferable – even essential – to use in preference to what is obtainable elsewhere. The VANs are producing integrated Web publishing packages that could save you a lot of money, and perhaps avoid the need to use expensive technical consultants.

The software choices should be made first – pick the software, irrespective of platform – that you feel will meet your needs best. Then get the hardware that will operate that software now, and cope with expected upgrades over the next 18 months.

Expect to be steered towards *Windows* programming and a 486 Pentium or better PC. The harsh reality, if you are a confirmed Mac enthusiast, is that most software development in this field is now for the *Windows* platform. Monopolies are worrying, but as we make Bill Gates even richer it is comforting that his business acumen and the brilliance of his programmers are helping to establish the standards that make cyberspace viable as a readily accessible place to do business. You need to produce very pervasive business arguments to yourself – as well as your backers – if your cyberspace hardware and software purchases are not *Windows*-based. There is, sadly, not enough momentum behind the Macintosh platform, and Unix is losing its technical edge by not attracting the creative and monetary investment necessary to prevent *Windows* from being the majority medium of choice for most cyberspace ventures.

Plan also for the need to distribute some of your products or promotional materials off-line in physical form on disks or CD-ROMs. *Windows* compatible formats are preferable for those also, particularly Help files which can be made to simulate Web and other Internet activities on the majority of personal computers.

Consider budgeting to produce demos and promotional and other documentation in Help form as part of your business and marketing plans. They can be useful tools – and a great way of distributing publicity material to the media, reducing the need to re-keyboard well-written press releases now that carpal tunnel disease is endemic among journalists.

If you are using technical staff, don't finally commit to purchases until completing Step 8.

INTERNATIONAL CONSULTANTS ONLINE

There are many sources online to get initial advice free on almost any business topic, and to locate expert consultants around the world who you could consider retaining for specific assignments. State your needs through a message in the appropriate Business section of your online service – in the case of CompuServe you can go directly to the Computer Consultants Forum by entering **GO CONSULT**.

HOW MUCH TO LAUNCH A BUSINESS IN CYBER-SPACE?

The cost of establishing the capacity to be a cyberspace business offering products and taking orders can vary from under £100 to over £100,000. At the low end you can do it yourself in a low key way, or create a really significant corporate presence on the Web or the VANs for about £1,500 and up, depending on how much you are prepared to do yourself.

The deals offered vary enormously and there are lots of virtual malls and mail order catalogues from which to choose. Monthly fees range from about £20 to over £2,000, but come down as competition increases. There may be a charge for the space you take up on the provider's disk storage, which should stabilise at around 50p per megabyte.

Step 8 – Identify human resource requirements

You may well need to recruit staff or consultant contractors, or retrain existing staff, in which case you should get their input before finalising hardware and software purchases. However, do not let their dedication to particular systems or programs override the merits of the more dispassionate choices you may have made already.

Personnel may well change as the project progresses, which is one good reason not to pander too much to personal preferences at this stage. Also, you need to be prepared for situations in which backups are required because key personnel are no longer available. If you let a technical person dictate the choice of software tools at the beginning, you may become too dependent on him or her later.

Ease of use as well as sheer technological power are key human resource factors to consider in implementing the decisions reached in Step 8. *Windows* programs are becoming as standardised in their command structures and ease of use as Macintosh programs have always been, but Mac die-hards are reluctant to admit this. There could be particular problems in persuading graphic design people being assigned to Web projects to adjust to *Windows* programs.

Be aware in your planning that there are very few consultants around who combine hands-on business experience, realistic assessments of consumer needs, and online technical know-how. Managing a cyberspace project demands particular people skills to achieve the right mix of talent to get end results that cater for the demographical makeup of the online community as it has existed for the past decade, and which will be in tune with the cyberspace population as it broadens in age, gender, attitudes, and computing prowess. The potential is enormous for creating Edsels destined to rust away, broken down and neglected along the highways of cyberspace.

Step 9 – Budget and plan to give as well as take

Cyberspace in general, and the Internet in particular, only function because so much available there is free. Businesses are geared to charging as much as is possible for the services and products provided with corporate structures and the planning of projects geared towards maximising profit potential as the final objective.

In many situations it is impossible to budget and plan to make profits directly on line in the conventional monetary sense. Be realistic about this in your business plan and be prepared to evaluate in detail how much you will have to give away to the cyberspace community to become a player there, and whether the potential returns need to quantified by other than direct monetary measures such as sales revenues.

The most successful sites with the highest traffic charge the most. CompuServe, the world's largest online subscription service, has been getting a very high rate of renewals for its package deals which allow for displaying details of up to 100 products, including full colour images for 25 of them. That, early in 1995, was costing about £12,500 annually, plus two per cent commission on sales actually made on-line.

Figure 8.1 Portable offices provide cyberspace access

We have touched on these points earlier. Now, if you are committing a firm business plan to paper, you need to be realistic about it to yourself, your management, and to your financial supporters. While most information-related products and services are appropriate to online direct marketing, many other categories are not. In many cases you should plan to go into cyberspace to increase the efficiency of an existing or start-up business and to exploit its power for global marketing communications, always giving generously with soft sell information, entertainment and assistance.

DEMOGRAPHICS CHANGING

Although accurate analysis is impossible, it has been assumed that the average Internet user has the demographic profile of a male aged 18 to 34 years. This is now changing, particularly with the growing popularity of the easier to access multimedia World Wide Web with its growing emphasis on entertainment and commerce, in contrast to the serious academic and scientific research activities, and the young computing enthusiasts which have dominated other areas of the Net.

Probably the best source for well-conceived continuing demographic analysis of the Web is the Michigan Business School online survey at **http://www.umich.edu/~sgupta/hermes.htm**. Initial results from 3,500 Internet users yielded an average age of 31, over 90% male, 70% with college degrees, and an average income of nearly $60,000 (£37,500). 26% of the

There are so many shopping malls opening on the Web, that the easiest way to visit over a score of them is through the Hall of Malls at **http://nsns.com/MouseTracks/HallofMalls.html**. Watch particularly for a repeat in cyberspace of the successful retailing pattern of an anchor store creating a favourable business environment for the smaller boutiques.

My file of case histories contains some impressive statistics and clippings of media reports of products such as cars being "sold" over the Internet. This can be very misleading. Only a very few cars have actually been sold online – or ever will be. But no automotive manufacturers can now ignore the fact that, to be competitive, they must use cyberspace for a variety of marketing communications tasks that motivate buyers to want to visit their local dealerships. You could emulate the motor industry's effective use of the Internet for creative niche marketing, its main role in the marketing mix, but don't expect success just by dumping electronic versions of sales brochures on line.

General Motors, for example, created an online news service about the America's Cup yacht racing with a subsidiary message inviting visitors to request product information. Toyota is engaged in a number of cybermarketing projects to target specifically higher income business professionals interested in luxury cars, and young adults considering their first new car purchases. Toyota moved one its promotions off-line onto CD disks, a quarter-of-a-million of which were given away to business class fliers with an incentive of 1,000 frequent flier miles if they followed through with a visit to a dealership for a test drive.

Several manufacturers are putting virtual test drive demonstrations and interactive games featuring their models onto CD disks, and making these programs available online for free downloading. This illustrates the potential of generating interest by giving away games, a comparatively unexploited aspect of business-to-business marketing. (Europress Software, Britain's top-selling producer of educational software, has a neat program called *Klik & Play* which can be used to create games and entertaining tutorials for a range of target markets. The voice phone contact for further information is +44 (0) 1625 859333).

Ford has been tailoring its online promotions to the demographics of the VANs – using the Prodigy service with its emphasis on home users for family cars, and the more sophisticated CompuServe for technically-orientated messages.

Volvo and Chrysler are among the manufacturers who make a more general pitch on the basis of the fact that many of their prospective buyers are online computer users. Chrysler has pioneered using the online services to test consumer recall of television advertising. You will find many more examples throughout this book of worthwhile activities that that you can build into your plan to demonstrate potential returns from cyberspace that cannot be forecast as direct sales.

Again, look out for collaborative opportunities. Professional sports organisations in North America are starting to use the Internet because the demographics – predominantly educated young men aged between 18 and 34 – so closely match their prime markets. The global scope could be particularly attractive for soccer, for example. The American National Football League and Rupert Murdoch's News Corp. have already used the NFL's Web site to promote their World League tournament in Europe. Individual sports teams are now opening Web sites also, while others would do so if they found corporate sponsors and technology partners.

Step 10 – Keep on testing, listening, and refreshing

Whatever you do in cyberspace, try to build in an element to stimulate feedback – it is, after all, essentially an interactive two-ways communications medium. The responses you get, together with the continual testing of your products, services and online business presence, will enable you to refine your cyberspace projects and keep them fresh.

It is essential to keep on listening to your target publics and responding to their changing needs in these dynamic new

survey used the Web for business research, 59% for education, and 66% for entertainment. The majority chose online magazines and newspapers as their first choice to find product information, but the trend seemed strongly towards commercial Web sites steadily becoming more popular. Indeed, some forecasts indicate that commercial Web sites will eventually become more important sources for product and servicing information for online users than conventional printed direct mail.

ONLINE TUTORIALS

Tutorials as well as lot of up-to-date information about creating a business presence on the Web can be found at **http://www.wired.com /Staff/justin/dox/started.html**. For a tutorial on writing Web documents in HTML, go to **http://www.ncsa.uiuc.edu/General/Internet/WWW/HTMLPrimer.html**.

media. You also, because there is much new happening out there, need to budget and plan for a continual refreshing of your online presence. This is essential to remain competitive and to encourage repeat visits. You need to budget for this continuing research function and the at least occasional technical expertise to reverse engineer particular sites and projects that might teach you important lessons.

Everybody is learning in cyberspace, and it is a process that will never stop.

9. Your shopping list of hardware and software products and programs

Let's go shopping! You can leave your money behind on your first shopping excursion into cyberspace. Most of the essential tools that you will need are either free, or readily available for extended trials without charge.

Companies and individuals have been able to recover the entire first year's cost for online access by the savings achieved from the freeware and shareware programs they have downloaded from VANs and the Internet. If you are not familiar with these terms for software trading, you need to know that there is a distinct difference between the two.

Freeware programs are put out into cyberspace for anyone to use without charge, but still usually with the originators retaining copyright and stipulating that the programs are not to be sold for commercial gain. Commercial programs may also appear as freeware demonstrations – *demoware* – in which important features are either disabled or missing. You may not, for example, be able to save or print work done with them. There is also *giveware* – a program distributed as freeware with a request that users send a donation to the author's favourite charity.

Shareware programs are being marketed in cyberspace with profit as the objective. It is a distinct method of marketing particularly appropriate for cyberspace products. These programs are released with permission for them to be copied and distributed in their entire original forms for evaluation only. After a trial period, usually 30 days, you are asked either to delete the program from your system, or formally register as a user and send the requisite fee to the author.

In some cases you receive an updated version of the program with more features, perhaps also a printed manual. The increasing tendency is for the shareware version to be fully featured and incorporate comprehensive documenta-

Your First Cyberspace Tools

The very first thing that you should do when you have online access is to download two files which are to be found in almost every good collection of shareware or freeware in cyberspace.

The first is called *DIR10.zip*, and the second *WINZIP.zip*. (These file names may vary slightly to identify different editions of the files. Check to see that you have an edition that is up-to-date. The basic information in the reference file is reasonably timeless, but WinZIP keeps improving and you should use version 5.6 or later).

The *Desktop Internet Reference* is contained in the *DIR10.zip* file. It is one of the best hypertext references to the Internet available at any price, and has 18,000 pages with well designed cross-references and hypertext links to provide you with the answers to most of the questions that you may have about the Internet.

tion in the form of a text file manual that you can print out, or as a *Windows* Help file providing context-sensitive instructions linked directly to the particular functions that you wish to use.

There is a gross misconception prevalent in business circles that freeware or shareware are inferior to commercial packaged software that usually costs much more, but comes in a tangible physical form on floppy or CD disks in an impressive box accompanied by a properly printed manual. This is not true. There are superb shareware programs that beat anything available in a box at a fraction of the price. The first example on your cyberspace shopping list should be Nico Mak's *WinZIP*, a unique utility running in *Windows* which enables you to decompress and unpack the other programs that you can obtain online.

WinZip is essential because most shareware programs are distributed as single compressed files, with their elements packed tightly into a single package which prevents individual files from getting lost or damaged. The compressed packages occupy minimal space on the server systems where they are available, and take the shortest time possible to travel from there through cyberspace to the downloading computer.

Compressed files may be self-executing, and identified by the filename extension .EXE. You type the file name and hit ENTER – or click on the name in *Windows File Manager* – and they execute automatically, decompressing and unpacking themselves using programming contained within them. It's similar to the self-contained metamorphosing process independent of external resources that a chrysalis demonstrates when it turns from a caterpillar into a butterfly.

You can create compressed .EXE file packages quite easily for electronic publications of different kinds so that they run as simply as possible for your end users. The *BigText* and *NeoBook* electronic publishing programs, and the Lotus *ScreenCam* computerised movie capture program are examples. However, such files are not very safe or secure. They can get damaged or corrupted quite easily in the rough and tumble of moving around cyberspace, and are particularly vulnerable to computer virus attack. Consequently, the system operators of many bulletin boards and other cyberspace locations will not allow .EXE files to be uploaded to their sites.

So you may wish to limit your use of .EXE files to products or demonstrations that you distribute physically on floppy or CD disks and so can control better. At the least you can write protect a floppy by moving the little flap to the write-protect position, while a CD-ROM is intrinsically secure. However, even with such physical distribution, there are still advantages in compressing and archiving an .EXE file with *WinZip* to compress it even further, perhaps and to protect it.

Most shareware available online is distributed in archived compressed files which usually carry the extension .ZIP. In fact, they may have been compressed by one of several alternative methods, not only by the proprietary *PKZIP* program which became a *de facto* standard. Alternatives include LZH, ARJ and ARC. *WinZip* handles them all with aplomb, and you will find a copy of this useful utility for free evaluation on thousands of bulletin boards and Internet locations, as well as the main VANs.

WinZip added valuable Internet features in 1995, so if you have problems finding version 5.6 or later, go directly to the source – email to **70056.241@compuserve.com** or **info@winzip.com**, visit the WinZip Web home page at **http://www.winzip.com/winzip/** or download directly from **ftp.winzip.com**.

You will find this an essential tool for both unpacking and creating compressed files in a variety of online and business situations. Initially, if you are new to this aspect of computing, *WinZip* greatly simplifies the installation and, if necessary, removal of other programs that you obtain online. You may move on to compress your own files as a way of safely and economically distributing digital products, or just use *WinZip* as a basic email tool to compress data or graphics files that you attach to email messages.

There is a valuable companion program called *WinZip Self-Extractor* which offers a more efficient and safer way of distributing multiple files in one compressed self-extracting package than as the vulnerable self-executing files mentioned earlier. You pay one small registration fee to use this program without any liability for additional royalty payments for the products you create with it. In effect, you get unlimited free, secure and efficient packaging for your cyberspace products.

Remarkably, it is free and must not be sold – a symbol of the philosophy of sharing information in cyberspace that you will need to learn to be a successful entrepreneur there.

The second program is the remarkable WinZIP file compression and decompression utility that makes it so easy to use Windows simple point and click actions to handle files that you send or receive online. You need such a utility to decompress the *Desktop Internet Reference*. WinZIP is the best and a shareware program – you can obtain it without cost online, try it free for a limited time, but are expected to pay a small fee to register and continue using it.

The *Desktop Internet Reference* is based on Peter Scott's Hy*Telnet*, a really comprehensive DOS and UNIX reference to the Internet, and runs under Windows as a Help file. It demonstrates how Help files will become one of the most effective formats for electronic publishing, and will introduce you also to hypertext concepts that you will find on the Internet, particularly the World Wide Web.

When you decompress the file you find electronic versions of the following works also : The Hitchhikers Guide to the Internet, NSF's Internet Resource Guide, Zen and the Art of the Internet, Introduction to the Internet: A Reading List, Putting your home PC on the Internet, the Public Dialup Internet Access List, The Totally Unofficial List of Internet Muds, and High Weirdness on the Internet.

Practical topics covered include *Archie* user commands, how to get individual access to the Internet, and a list of anonymous FTP sites.

"I feel that The Desktop Internet Reference is special because it brings together a large number of useful documents into a single cross-linked, easily accessed form," says the compiler, John Buckman. "I hope it will make the Internet more

I cannot recommend *WinZip* too highly, and it has improved significantly since winning the 1994 Shareware Industry Award for Best Utility. It is a better conceived, developed and technically supported full feature *Windows* product than many I have reviewed in fancy boxes at, literally, ten times the price. Registration is under £20, with another £30 for the *WinZip Self-Extractor* developer's tool.

Sadly, there is so much shareware available that much of the good stuff gets hidden among the clutter and you can't see the cyberspace wood for the trees. Few programs get such wide distribution as *WinZip*, but you will still find a very large selection in the software for downloading sections of the leading VANs and bulletin boards. Two of many university FTP locations holding substantial collections are **archive.umich.edu** and **oak.oakland.educ**.

Mosaic, Netscape, email handlers, TCP and FTP software, and other basic essential online navigational and search tools you will almost certainly get from your VAN or Internet service provider when you join. It pays to keep alert to the updates and additions being introduced all the time, so your web address book should include the What's New List at **http://www.ncsa.uiuc.edu/sdg/software/mosaic/docs/whats-new.html**. Check in regularly also with the founders of the Web, the European Centre for Physics Research in Switzerland, at **http://info.cern.ch/hyptertext/www/linemode/defaults/default.html**. The source for ongoing information about Mosaic is where it was born and continues to be nurtured through successive generations – **http://www.ncsa.uiuc.edu/SDG/Software/Mosaic/Docs/help-about.html**.

A good service for the latest versions of a varied collection of Internet access tools is by FTP to **ftp.cic.indiana.edu**. If you are using *Windows*, move on into the **pub/pc/win3/winsock** directory to pick up a powerful *Windows Gopher* client, the universally popular Trumpet Winsock package for TCP/IP connections(which includes *Telnet* and FTP utilities), and one of the best email handlers, *Eudora*.

Sometimes the access software for a particular provider makes such a quantum leap in speed, ease of use, or special features that you might consider changing services just to get it. However, the VANs are so competitive that, to avoid the hassles of changing your email address, it might be better in most situations to wait until your own service catches up, or moves ahead again.

When shopping for an access provider, there is an international list on the Web at **http://www.netusa.com/net/lsp**. If you do fall out with one and want to move to another, the email forwarding service operated by The Internet Company could be useful. Details from **messenger@internet.com**. For help with problems dealing with email in Europe when away from your usual local connection – or if wanting to use an American VAN without direct access from Europe – contact **info@EU.net**.

Delphi, which has played a leading role in connecting Britain to cyberspace, has a slick email handling program called *Apollo* which can be downloaded free for evaluation. You can save a very high proportion of online charges with such programs, which enable you to work on your email without being connected. Just hooking up to send or receive your email files can be done in seconds.

Delphi is the home of the online version of the *Sunday Times*, and scores of British discussion groups. Access Delphi by modem with your communications software set to Data bits: 8, Stop Bit 1, Parity: none, Flowcontrol: XON/XOFF, and the speed anywhere between 2,400 and 14,400 baud. The UK number is +44 (0) 171 284 2424. For voice help, call +44 (0) 171 757 7080. The deal at the time of writing was that you can sign on immediately and get five free hours, with a subscription of about £10 per month.

If you are facing the challenge of hooking all the users on an existing network into the Internet simultaneously, it might be worth talking to Britain's Performance Technology, who have a hardware and software package called Instant Internet that offers a turnkey solution. But you will have to pay about £2,750 for it. The voice contact number in the UK is +44 (0) 1344 382 020.

You can pick up a lot of freeware and shareware for business applications – as well as useful information for a wide range of business activities – by *Gopher* or FTP access to the University of Vaasa in Finland- **garbo.uwasa.fiport 70**. The Free Software Foundation also has useful programs which you can FTP from **ftp.uu.net**.

Some sites specialise in Macintosh software. Stanford University has a choice at **sumex-aim.standford.edu**, and Rutgers University at **rutgers.edu**. (While at Rutgers you can tap into the CIA's more constructive operations by accessing the CIA World Fact Book, which is packed with information on all the

9. YOUR SHOPPING LIST OF BASIC PRODCUTS AND PROGRAMS

accessible to the average computer user."

The latest version is available by anonymous FTP at various sites world-wide, and can be downloaded from many bulletin boards and online service providers – the Value Added Networks such as CompuServe, for example. The FTP site **ftp.uwp.edu** always carries the latest version in the directory /pub/msdos/dir. You can contact John Buckman by email at **jbuckman@aas.org**.

NETSCAPE FOR NOTHING

One of the most highly praised Web browsers which just keeps on getting better and is being adopted as the standard by some very big cyberspace ventures is Netscape Navigator. There are Windows, Unix and Macintosh versions available by FTP to **ftp.mcom.com**. No charge for evaluation and continuing non-profit or educational use, and there is a full commercial version for about £25. Netscape has also some of the best Web server and monetary transaction software – information by email from **info@netscape.com**.

MILLION-DOLLAR CAVES

Virtual reality experiences over the Internet are predicted to be a major growth area as the technology is refined to make this practical. Already there is a virtual reality equivalent of HTML called VRML – the Virtual Reality Markup Language. Both Windows and Mac versions have been under development and should be available through the Web site at **http://www.eit.com/vrml/**.

Silicon Graphics are among the leaders in the Internet's VR development, and you can see some of what they are up to at **http://www.sgi.com**. Their WebForce authoring and server packages are expensive, but among the most powerful and sophisticated available.

world's nations. You get there by *Telnet* to **info.rutgers.edu**, or by FTP to **nic.funet.fi**, or buy it as a database on CD-ROM. A rich resource for Bank of England, World Bank and government statistics is to be found with a *Telnet* connection to **sun.nsf.ac.uk**.

There are literally thousands of such contacts to be made for free or free trial software and data in cyberspace, and you will find more leads through the mailing lists in the Appendix. However, some things you have to pay for, and here are some cyberspace entrepreneur's toolkit suggestions of good values on- and off-line.

The best hard copy resources to online databases is the annual *Gale Guide to Internet Databases*, which you can at least try out free for 30 days. It is well indexed, non technical, and a well constructed reference to 2,000 databases available over the Net, some free, others charging fees. To get more information email to **72203.1552@compuserve.com**. (Gale also produce excellent directories of other computer-readable databases on portable media such as CD-ROM, and its *PR News Casebook* of 1,000 public relations case studies is the best single source I have ever found for sparking off good promotional ideas.)

Your toolkit will probably at some stage include several CD-ROM telephone and address directories. They are falling dramatically in price and have moved from costing thousands of pounds to well under £100 for some lists of literally millions of contacts which you can sort and use for direct mail or telemarketing purposes. Some of these directories on CDs are still being crippled, e.g. you cannot print out more than a restricted number of listings at any one time, or you cannot sort and capture details to do mail merges properly.

However, that's no longer a problem with some of the best products, of which the remarkable *PhoneDisc USA* is an outstanding example. Here, on one CD-ROM, are some nine million business listings with very efficient searching and mailing capabilities. It is a unique resource in which to find, for example, nearly a quarter of a million law firms if you have a legal product or service to pitch. The production of these massive CD databases is getting so slick that they are exceeding 97% average accuracy, and new scanning processes and regular updates enable them to rival the latest editions of printed telephone directories in topicality.

The set of three CDs from *PhoneDisc* gives the latest access details for 90 million people, businesses and organisations in the US. The business disk could be the single best reason for taking a CD player along when prospecting for clients, suppliers, distributors, agents or customers in the US, or just to quantify the size of the different market sectors and how they can be reached most cost-efficiently.

Your software shopping list should probably have the new manifestations of *Lotus Notes* up near the top for a wide range of networking activities. It can be the single most effective solution to many communications needs. Less well-known is the way that *Lotus ScreenCam* has steadily been getting better; now it could be the key tool in making certain types of products for distribution on disk or online, and for demonstrating anything that you can display as a sequence on the computer, such as a visit to a Web site. I used it to show sceptical auctioneers that it is now practical to conduct auctions in cyberspace, and to demonstrate to British Waterways how connecting the canals system to the Information Superhighways might generate additional foreign tourist business.

ScreenCam works within *Windows* just like a video recorder. You can start and stop recording what is being displayed on screen with mouse clicks that simulate pressing the buttons on a VCR. Add a sound commentary and music if you have a sound card, or there is a neat new captioning feature that would work well to cope with foreign language versions. The completed movie can be saved as a self-executing file, so that it will run on any *Windows* system. *Lotus* dealers are everywhere, but not all of them are familiar with *ScreenCam* and as this book went to press it had not achieved wide international distribution, so you may have to nag to get it.

Another program that exploits *Windows* facilities to create digital movies is Blue Sky's *RoboHELP WinHelp Video Kit*. You can use it to create a video sequence that can stand alone, or be triggered by pressing a button or other graphical hypermedia hotspot in a *Windows* Help file.

The *WinHelp* format can be a powerful medium for all kinds of cyberspace products and business uses. There are a number of Help file authoring programs and templates for word processors now available as shareware from many sites, particularly for use with Microsoft's *Word for Windows*. But *RoboHelp* is on the cutting edge of this publishing medium, which I believe has enormous still unexploited potential for all kinds of electronic publica-

The initial trend in online VR has been non-immersive systems, which do not try to completely immerse the user in the experience by supporting headsets, gloves, or full body suits. An interesting development that makes full touchy-feely VR experiences possible over a network is a VR Cave environment that can be created within a small room. Some companies are spending a million dollars to create their own VR Caves.

The front runners in this technology are at the Electronic Visualisation Laboratory at the University of Illinois in Chicago. You can reach the director, Tom DeFanti, by email to **Tom@uic.edu**.

EMAIL WARNINGS

The volume of email that you will send and receive will almost certainly, if you are a new user of this way of communicating, far exceed your initial estimates. Consequently, find out the details of charges being levied for email services before finalising your choice of online service provider. Some charge no more than their basic per hour fee, others have varying rates that may be linked to the numbers and sizes of messages. It can be an expensive hassle if they do not have a program like Apollo and require you to open email messages while online.

Verify also how efficient the service providers are in their handling of email. Not all are equal. Most will move immediately messages between their own subscribers, but may be quite slow in handling messages that travel over the Internet. Don't assume that your messages will be transmitted instantly – you may even send or receive an email no faster

tions, tutorials, manuals and myriad other uses. It is a complete publishing toolkit and is being developed to work with a number of *Windows*-based word processors, so it is worth checking with Blue Sky to see if they have developed a version that meets your needs. The email address is **73473.3633@compuserve.com**.

Microsoft's own help file compiler is widely available online. The current version as this book went to press was in file **HCP505.ZIP**, available from CompuServe, among other places, by download from **GO WINUSER**. (There is a much improved help compiler for *Windows* 95.)

There are several neat tools that facilitate person-to-person or group communications in cyberspace that do not need massive resources of hardware, software, or communications connections. One of the simplest and most effective of the document conferencing programs is DataBeam's *Farsite* for *Windows*, which needs only a computer running *Windows* and a modem at each end of an ordinary phone line to set up a teleconference in which users at distant locations can interactively see and edit files. The cost is typically about 1/40th of setting up a video conference.

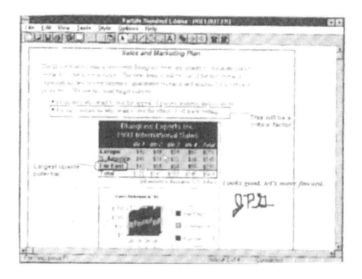

Figure 9.1 Example of a FarSite teleconference

Users share a dynamic electronic whiteboard which appears on the monitor screens at each location, and they can make notes and import text and images on to this virtual board. Scientific researchers use boards as a routine way of comparing notes and talking through problems. *FarSite* and similar programs now make this interactive medium available in an electronic form that can be very useful to the business community in many types of cyberspace projects. It could be worth finding out more from **fs_win@databeam.com**.

There are other programs for teleconferencing, but most are designed to work with LANs and can be difficult to set up.

If you want to establish a business bulletin board, you should probably look first when shopping around at market leader *Wildcat* from Mustang Software; it is the most popular BBS software in the world. Although setting up a board can be comparatively simple, lots of technical issues can arise and the Mustang people have dealt with most of them before. They have a good reputation for international hand-holding, and in addition to their technical support services on CompuServe and other VANs, they have MSI SupportNet echo conferences around the world.

One of *Wildcat*'s enthusiastic users is the Information Clearinghouse, which uses its board to support and demonstrate a unique program called *MarketNet*. It is an expensive bundle for creating very complex catalogues online in various ways. *MarketNet* is almost limitless in the number of products, ordering procedures and simultaneous users with which it can cope, and you can license the source code to tweak it in many directions. Out of the box, it is probably the world's most powerful online order desk and catalogue which can be run from a single PC, yet handle thousands of items. There are some big multinational users, and lots of small entrepreneurial businesses also. To find out more, email to **76300.400@compuserve.com**, or dial up the American BBS at +(1) 310 763 0275 for an online demonstration.

Almost inevitably, you, or people working with you, will need to get up to speed quickly in at least basic knowledge of how cyberspace in general, and the Internet in particular, function. The cyberspace boom has sparked a mini-industry of live seminars, workshops and courses, many of which are overpriced and not very good. Consider adding one or more of the computerised tutorials to the shopping list as a cost-effective and flexible solution. You can download all the information necessary to become a proficient net surfer from the Net itself, but that's not the same as having a properly constructed tutorial that steps you through the different procedures.

than a first class letter if your service provider is inefficient, or adopts a policy of waiting to send external messages or faxes until the cheap telecommunications charges come into effect at night.

Services vary also in the size of messages they allow to pass to or from external networks, and may not permit files to be attached.

Some are not very good at letting you know quickly if your message encountered transmission problems, so you can never be absolutely sure than an important message arrived at its destination.

Do not assume that email is confidential or secure. If secrecy is important to you, then it is necessary to set up effective encryption procedures.

There is a bargain available for this – only about £15 – that does its teaching by creating DOS simulations of actually being online and sending or receiving email, using *Gopher*, conducting searches, downloading files, etc. This cyberspace tutorial is updated regularly – and you learn in the program how to get those updates from the *Gopher* site at California State University. Including such training materials in your cyberspace business plan could solve many problems before they arise. You could even build a business around this program by using it as the basis for workshops for cyberspace neophytes. Training materials tend to be very expensive, but this one represents outstanding value for less than the cost of most computer books. Email to **bridge@crl.com** for more information.

If you want more wide ranging information about cyberspace training materials, the University of Newcastle is operating the Trainmat *Gopher* site to provide a resource for trainers. Email to **margaret.isaacs@ncl.ac.uk** for details.

As the Net is so practical for international business, you may need to acquire foreign language capabilities. Despite the warning by former French telecommunications chief Gerard Thery that European culture and ten different languages are at risk because of the English dominance of the information superhighways, the diversity of language does extend into cyberspace. I forecast the development of a special type of international business communications which takes advantage of the tremendous improvements in software that semi-automatically translates from one language into another.

A text originated in English can be sent to, say, a Frenchman or Japanese for whom English is a second language, with the original English and the French or Japanese translation displayed side by side. The translation may not be grammatically or idiomatically as good as a skilled human translator could make it, but certainly adequate for readers to scan more quickly in their native tongues than they could in English. Where the meaning is unclear, or a specific section needs to be checked, then original language text is right alongside for easy reference.

Among the best programs I have found for these and other translation tasks come from Globalink. They are very bilingual, whereas some other programs tend to be good at going one way or the other between two languages, and their *Power Translator Pro* can top 20,000 words an hour in full-sentence, bi-directional translation. The import and export capabilities are excellent also, making it much easier to do translations in conjunction with your favourite word processor. There is even a speech and pronunciation capability if you have a sound card.

There are translation programs in this series between English and Spanish, French, German and Russian for DOS, *Windows*, *OS/2* and Macintosh systems. Here is another example of not needing to spend very much – about £100 – to get powerful facilities. Globalink also operates a translation service over the Internet so that you can email a file in one language and get it back in another. To get full details, email to **info@glink.com** requesting information.

Pictures can help to communicate across language barriers – in fact, in any kind of communications. The Web is rich in graphics, but they are difficult or impossible to incorporate into the other text-dominated areas of the Net. Consequently, you may want to download some of the ASCII clip art being collected by the Texas Tech University Department of Computer Science at the *Gopher* site **cs4sun.cs.ttu.edu**. The email address is **gripe@cs4sun.cs.ttu.edu**. This is a good source for finding ASCII art – pictures drawn using the standard character set – that you might modify to include in your signature file as the graphic on your electronic calling card.

Almost any good paint or drawing program will suffice to handle the graphical images you may want to process for cyberspace businesses, until you get into advanced areas such as 3-D, virtual reality and animation. However, the general rule is still to keep images small and simple to make your Web site run quickly and efficiently, so you may well find that the draw and paint accessories that come with *Windows* or your Macintosh are all that you need.

A useful addition to these for technical artwork and diagrams might be Shapeware's *Visio*, with its enormous range of templates. This program also simplifies drawing complex flow and organisation charts for such tasks as planning the structure of a complex Web site and planning links to and from it. *Visio* is widely available internationally, and you can get information about it on CompuServe from **GO VISIO**.

GET YOURSELF A WEB CRAWLER

The Internet Voyager newsletter likened finding specific information on the Internet to "trying to find the bathroom in a house with 250,000 unmarked doors". To help find what you need in a resource growing by some 2,000 new destinations every month, you can recruit a software robot roaming tirelessly through cyberspace. One of the best is Lycos, to be found on the Web at **http:/ /fuzine.mt.cs.cmu.edu./ mlm/lycos-all.html**. A good place to start a search – and pick up an automated search robot – is the Yahoo site at **http:// akebono.stanford.edu/ yahoo**. The WebCrawler searching software can be found at **http://web crawler.cs.washington.edu /webcrawler/web query.html**.

Hardware

The hardware on your shopping list will not come free, but it need not require significant outlay. Most 386 or better PCs or Macintosh System 7s can do a great deal of powerful cybersurfing with only the addition of the appropriate software and a modem with a data transfer rate of 14,400 or better. If you have such a system, you can be in business for an additional £100 or so, plus your actual online costs.

However, your capabilities increase significantly with a 486 or Pentium running *Windows*, particularly *Windows 95* with its greatly improved telecommunications capabilities and processing speeds. Make sure you have the largest hard drive you can afford – or add a second one.

A scanner could be your most useful peripheral after the printer, and this is another area in which it is easy to be tempted by false economies. Scanner technology has improved greatly in recent years and it does not pay to chose less than a TWAIN compliant sheet or flatbed colour scanner coupled with really efficient OCR (optical character recognition) software. A hand scanner may suffice if you do not anticipate having much need to scan, or will do your image and text capturing in situations such as reference libraries where you can only use a hand scanner with a portable computer. In that case, select a portable scanner designed to run directly from the computer's parallel port, then you can transfer it easily between systems.

If you do have to buy new hardware, there are many places online to shop around for good deals. Marketplaces are developing in cyberspace for used equipment also, but it is very much a "let the buyer beware" situation.

The newsgroups, mailing lists or other resources that you use online to keep in touch with your areas of interest could be the best sources at any given time for access provider and hardware and software recommendations tailored to your needs.

10. Dare to be different

Every cyberspace entrepreneur is a publisher

Whatever the products or services that you are considering marketing in cyberspace, to do business in this new environment you will need to be a publisher there, a disseminator of information in virtual formats. So it could be helpful if we look more closely at publishing in the new media and how it compares to traditional practices in print.

Almost every business involves publishing to some degree. Big corporations, such as the motor manufacturers, can have publishing operations that are larger than some of the best known names in book publishing. So it is in this area that businesses may have most to gain from the creative use of cyberspace. Indeed, manufacturers and other business enterprises are in many respects ahead of the publishers in daring to be different in the new media.

This book tries to strike a balance in covering both the practical "how to" details of conducting business in cyberspace, and the cultural, social and other less tangible aspects of this new environment. The former are the easiest to research, communicate in an objective way, and to understand. The latter are much more difficult to analyse, but are far more important . You can automate many of the practical tasks of cyberspace business and let the machines play the roles for which they are so well suited. What you cannot avoid – if you are to stand any chance of success – is devoting a large part of your entrepreneurial effort to finding ways to be creatively different from how you publish and otherwise communicate in the physical business world.

This is not being taught to any significant degree yet in business schools, but the lessons are being learned the hard way by the pioneers of cyberspace. One that I admire greatly for the depth and range of her thinking is Laura Fillmore, founder and president of the Online Bookstore. Laura has launched two of my previous books online, and I hope that she will take this one under her

CYBERGATEWAYS ARE OPENING

Entrepreneurs are opening all manner of gateways through which special interest groups will pass to enter cyberspace. It's rather like having the prime selling position near the entrance of a department store or supermarket, or being by the check-out. An example is the start-up NetNoir to launch a series of online services to act as "cyber gateways between the traditional online world and Afrocentric culture".

The project is global, including Afro-Caribbean, Afro-Latin, Afro-European, continental African and African-American cultures. Interactive distance learning, online shopping, advertising, travel, health, music and sports are among the activities.

wing also. We have not made many sales together, but that is because we were both several years into the paperless publishing business before we began fully to learn the lesson of the need to dare to be very different in these new media.

"The longer we publish on the Internet, the clearer it becomes that the language we've imported from the tangible 'real' world ceases to apply in cyberspace," says Laura. (The OBS has been focusing on two main areas – distributed publishing, which is full-text online publishing using the Internet itself as the medium, and its BookFinder service enabling readers to order any in-print book in any of 269 languages. BookFinder networks bookstores together, and they do the fulfilment.)

"We are faced with conundrums at every turn. Does the term 'publishing' make sense when suddenly everyone is empowered to publish? What is Internet publishing after all, but the making public of words and thoughts, whether in the form of a software manual, .GIF files of marketing information from a family florist shop, a multimedia multi-million-dollar multinational phone company's Web site, or a schoolgirl's love poem?

"If, in its Internet incarnation, 'publishing' no longer exists in its traditional sense, then, by extrapolation, what is an author, an editor, and even a business? If one puts up a Web page on a server, listing URLs for a given subject area, such as Mayan ruins, is one a publisher, an author, a link editor, an indexer, or an online jeweller selling culture URLs?"

Laura emphasises that it is a false analogy to view cyberspace as a new way of bottling old wine. While the wine analogy seems apposite at first, in fact it illustrates the fundamental truth that we cannot use old words to describe new thought processes and activities in cyberspace.

She and other cyberspace pioneers with practical experience of the market have had to come to terms with the incontrovertible fact that there has been a great reluctance actually to spend money online. The exceptions that prove the rule are when the invitation to spend is an integral part of the whole complex interactive process. That is why we need to dare to be different in how we position cyberspace products, and also where we expect to generate revenue from our goods and services. Laura illustrates the point from her viewpoint as a publishing professional moving from the print to electronic media.

Figure 10.1 The Online Bookstore

D.I.Y. DISCS

If you have particular expertise in a subject that lends itself to hobbies and DIY projects requiring detailed instructions, you may have all that is required to launch a cyberspace business. Using any of the now enormous selection of drawing and presentation or electronic publishing programs, you can create a product promotable online and which can be marketed as a downloadable file or supplied physically on a floppy disk.

Look for examples of such projects in shareware libraries and software outlets. One of the most-praised titles is *The Greatest Paper Airplanes*, which adds value by means of clever 3-D animations and the ability to print out designs complete with fold lines. Many DIY projects lend themselves to files of plans, construction details and materials lists that the users can print out.

Most projects like this should not be sold through computer or book stores, but through outlets catering to the specific target markets – DIY topics in ironmongers stores, paper aeroplanes in model shops, for example.

What Modem?

The modem is the essential link between the computer and the telephone line that leads to cyberspace. They come in a bewildering variety, and much of the advertising for them is deceptive.

Modem standards are set by the International Telecommunications Union-Telecommunications Sector, and it is important to get a modem that meets recent versions of those standards. Get the best that you can afford. In 1995 and 1996, that would be V.34 bis modulation delivering 28.8Kbps transfer rate, V.42 bis compression, V.42 error control, with CCITT Group 3 fax.

The V.32 bis modulation delivering 14.4Kbps will still suffice for many uses, and such modems are significantly cheaper than those to the V.34 standard. This speed may well be all that your online service provider or the bulletin boards you use will permit. It is

Figure 10.2 The Online Bookstore's German interface

also more than fast enough for typical email and for downloading small to medium-sized files. However, V.34 is the standard of the future, and could quickly pay for itself if you download large files, or are establishing a corporate system.

Don't get a 9,600 bps modem unless funds are tight and the cost of time online is not a significant factor. Beware misleading packaging and advertising which do not indicate the true speed of DATA, as distinct from FAX, transfer rates. Most dedicated fax machines already installed do not run faster than 9,600 bps, so that is sufficient if you are primarily interested in sending faxes.

Figure 10.3 The Online Bookstore's search service

"Readers and publishers have become accustomed to thinking about publishing as a process resulting in a concrete object, a book, which is distributed to and paid for by readers," the OBS president says. " Our business models have been refined with the introduction of word processing, computerised typesetting and production technologies, but, until very recently and the advent of Internet publishing, our end product was still a physical product, a book, and recently, a CD or a disk. So the basic business models for selling ideas, information, and entertainment enjoyed a concrete basis.

"Now we must subtract the physical incarnation of the product from the equation. This does not eliminate the actual substance of what is for sale. However, the exponentially increasing use of global computer networks as a publishing medium requires us to examine the fundamentals of the publishing process, and asks us to recognise that process for what it is: an ongoing and evolving method for transferring ideas, information, and entertainment among people around the world. Shifting from the paper and disk-based media to the evanescent networked media offers significant opportunities to expand and redefine what it is publishers are doing and, ultimately, what they are selling in the world-wide market."

However, to make that adjustment as an essential preliminary to operating a successful cyberspace business, one must learn how the medium itself, as well as the products appropriate to it, are so very different from our established commercial realities.

"We will not succeed in furthering the evolution of the publishing process on the Net by simply using it as a global distribution medium for digitised versions of books, or as a 'front end' for selling CDs or other physically contained disk-based publications. We must make the distinction between publishing a concrete physical object such as a book or a CD, and beaming ideas, information, and entertainment."

She describes the very different process of publishing online as "pubnetting", with these very distinctive attributes:

- it's immediate
- it's global
- it's interactive
- it's kinetic
- it's multimedia.

HARD FACTS ON SPEED

The hard disk is still – because of its mechanical functions – the component that dictates the speed at which many computer tasks are carried out. Nevertheless, hard drives illustrate the remarkable rate at which the technology as a whole is developing. In the past five or six years, hard disks have become fifty times more reliable, and you can buy ten times the storage capacity for about a twentieth of the price. A better hard disk can be the single most important reason to upgrade a system, although for sheer performance increasing the RAM is still the most cost-efficient upgrade option.

128

"Anything that can be digitised can be transmitted over the networks: texts, pictures, videos, sounds – even people, via email links to them. But the transactions involved are completely different from traditional publishing's economy of scarcity, in which one is selling finite objects. If I am a print publisher someone buys, steals or borrows one of my book products, then I am poorer because I am without it.

" Pubnetting operates in an economy of abundance. If someone makes a million copies of the files off my machine or my server, I still have the original files and am none the poorer for the transaction. The currency becomes the 'attention' of the reader, and the challenge before us in the evolution from publishing to pubnetting is to construct a commercially viable business model for pubnetting, What matters – and what is for sale – in the tactile environment is fundamentally other than what is for sale in the instantaneously accessible online environment, where the issue is not *distributing* a tangible thing, a copy of a book or a disk which the buyer then owns or possesses, but rather *accessing* ideas and information.

"How does a pubnetter sell access to ideas and information, to whom, and for how much? That becomes the issue."

You can *give* things away very effectively in cyberspace, as Capstone Software demonstrated in 1995 with their successful give-away online of thousands of CD copies of their new *Zorro* action adventure game, downloadable demos, and associated merchandise. It was a commercial success because they dared to be different and instead of building protective barriers round their product, as so many software publishers still tend to do, they opened up in this new, free environment to give potential buyers ready access to it.

(Capstone also used traditional business practices effectively by building into the online promotion a response element so that they captured names and addresses. You don't always need to do *everything* differently!)

The Online Bookstore has survived and progressed by steadily giving more and more away to enhance the access facilities it offers. Laura sees this as the inevitable route towards generating sales of conventional hard copy books, as well as stimulating reader participation in the new form of publishing which she describes as "distributive". In this, the content of the book and its structure online evolve by the dynamic interaction with it of readers and events.

If your cyberspace projects involve video, you certainly need massive hard disk capacity. A 30-second advertisement gobbles up 15MB, and while optical CDs have enormous capacity, they are inherently slower and so have limited potential. Silicon chip cartridges due to appear for the new generation of Ninetendo game players in late 1995 are said to be two million times faster than CD-ROMs, but have a fraction of the capacity of a CD, or a of a modern hard disk.

Most authors and publishers find it difficult to relate to this concept, which involves considerable loss of control and acceptance that a book published through the medium of cyberspace is not an end product in itself. Consequently, there is a tendency for authors and publishers dipping their toes into these unfamiliar – and perceived to be potentially toxic – waters to go in only a short distance, pushing their conventional book products before them. The bookstores springing up throughout cyberspace are making some progress in attracting buyers for the printed books on their virtual shelves, but only if they add online features that are not available from their competitors in the malls and high streets, or by direct mail.

The OBS, for example, has sophisticated online title search facilities that beat going through card indices, the tightly packed pages of *Books in Print*, or the microfilm readers of the typical library or bookstore. The interesting BookZone project on the Web quickly built up to 7,000 visitors a month by providing a café-like social chat and message area right from the beginning, and putting much of its start-up effort into building over 1,000 "Literary Leaps", hypertext links to other book-related locations on the Net.

Both BookZone president Mary Westheimer and Laura Fillmore regard the creation of hypertext links as essential.

"Just having a site on the Internet is not enough," emphasises Mary. "You must draw people to it. They may go away, but they will come back again because we are providing this service to help them to pursue their interest in books."

The BookZone focuses on helping small presses and author-publishers to market their conventional books online. It is essentially a service facility for publishers which works by being a friendly environment for readers, their buyers. The orders can be placed online, but the transactions are essentially directly between publisher and reader with no commissions being charged.

The Online Bookstore is conducting some fascinating experiments in "distributive" publishing online which could provide guidance for you for a variety of cyberspace enterprises. For example, links that are more varied and commercial than the BookZone's "Literary Leaps" were used for the online digital version of Nelson Mandela's autobiography.

"For the Mandela book we used several different types of external linking which indicate how in the future they may be used for licensing agreements which generate revenues and add value for the readers," Laura told me. "Some links were uni-directional, simply pointing the reader outside the Mandela book to another site on the Net. For example, from the passage describing how he was forced to wear the same suit for five years, there was a hypertext link to an African clothing store on the Net. In such a case, we might lose our reader to the clothing store, but we could have an agreement stipulating a modest payment from the store every time one of our readers clicks on the clothing page. This is a kind of no-risk advertising established on a pay-as-you-go basis.

"Another link might be reciprocal. We point, for example, to the *SUNsite* educational server and it simultaneously points back to OBS. Through reciprocal links, we offer our readers a semi-closed loop on which to travel: they may decide to visit the *SUNsite* server and simply return to the Mandela book, or go further and explore educational resources on the *SUNsite* server. On the Internet, where attention spans can be short, it is important to offer the readers the capability to customise their own link sets for a particular title.

Figure 10.4 Nelson Mandela's book at the OBS

DISK STANDARD

3.5-inch High Density floppy disks are now established as the international standard for distributing digital products. Although there are millions of computers still in business use which have 5.25" floppy drives, many software publishers no long supply their products in this format, e.g. IBM for its OS/2 Warp.

This standardisation makes it simpler to distribute cyberspace products on floppies, but for some markets you may consider configuring them so that they can be supplied on the 5.25"size also, or at least able to be copied to the physically bigger but smaller in capacity disks. Even if an end user has two floppy drives – one for each size – some programs will not load unless the system is configured to make the 3.5" drive as A, and so the original disks must be copied to the other format just to install the product.

Later versions of the shareware utilities PKZIP and WinZip will compress and archive over multiple floppies.

The Mandela book provided its online readers with internal links to other sections of the text, like any hypertext document, or, for that matter, a conventional book with its index, contents list and footnotes. But, and this is important, the ability to add external links creatively and in an interactive way added extra value not possible in either a printed book, or a digitised publication confined to a physical medium such as a CD disk.

Readers could extend *The Long Walk to Freedom* beyond the boundaries of the book as it was written and so become much more involved in all the issues it raised. They could link to factual information about South Africa, the history of slavery and racial issues, the speeches of Martin Luther King, and much more. You can make similar links in a CD publication, but they are fixed when the disk is mastered. In cyberspace, the links are infinitely variable as the reader, as well as the publisher, choose to make them.

"An external link set is a unique addition to a book, one which can only be made via a computer network," Laura emphasises. "It accommodates the nuances of meaning inherent in a text as they are perceived by the reader, not the author or publisher. The reader can customise this 'living' publication on the Net, making it uniquely suited for his or her own intellectual needs and interests."

She takes this concept even further to explore alternative ways of generating revenue from online publishing without being dependent on actual sales of the book itself. You use – and pay for – the book as if you were buying a ticket on a tour bus. The book, particularly if it is a high profile one like Mandela's autobiography, is the vehicle to attract prospects from a niche market which by its very nature it defines. The distributed book then transports these passengers with their well-defined interests and needs on a cyberspace excursion specifically tailored to them.

"If one were taking a tour of black history on the Internet, one might have the Mandela project as a 'bus' offering customised tours for people with differing backgrounds: young urban blacks, senior citizens, or sixth-grade suburban schoolchildren in France," explains Laura. "Such an approach, using the value-added external links and the readers' attention to which they appeal as the two poles of commerce in the online publishing environment, constitutes a working hierarchy which should preserve relatively free access to thought and ideas.

"The plain ASCII files could be freely available to any who wanted them. What would be of value, and what readers would pay for, would be the customised contextual referencing surrounding the text files – that is the value added. Such a hierarchy preserves the free public library component of paper publishing with the free availability of ASCII, while capitalising on the unique properties of the Net by making possible a kinetic core of content, linked into distributive online context with a protean set of links, customised for individual users."

I suggest, if you want to publish a book in cyberspace, that you seek out the very exceptional Web sites run by people of vision such as Laura Fillmore's Online Bookstore, and the BookZone operation founded by Mary Westheimer and Laurence Palestrant. They are vastly different from the electronic vanity presses and passive, uninspiring virtual book vendors springing up everywhere.

"One of our main motivations was to offer authors and small presses a viable alternative to the electronic carpetbaggers," Mary told me. The two enterprises are very different in nature, and so really don't compete directly with each other. The OBS is located on the Web at **http://www.online-bookstore.com**, or by *Gopher* client to **gopher marketplace.com**, or email to **obs@marketplace.com**. The cost of having a book listed there varies, and there are consultancy services to expand your concept into any direction that your vision and the expert staff can take it. Some big names in publishing are using the OBS, and an entire catalogue can be posted there.

The BookZone also has some big names like Doubleday among its 100 publisher clients, but it is developing more into the cyberspace equivalent of the friendly independent small book store with a free coffee urn where you go to meet like people and dig out the kinds of books that somehow you never find anywhere else.

Its low costs are particularly attractive for small presses and author-publishers. For under £100 a year you can have a detailed description of your book cross-referenced to at least three listings, extracts of up to 3,000 words called "Peeks between the Covers" and other features including a full colour graphic of your front cover. BookZone is located on the Web at **http://ttx.com/bookzone**, and the email address is **bookzone@ttx.com**.

WEBBED POP MUSIC

Music is already big business on the Net, with the number of bands active on line heading towards 1,000. Some have set up sophisticated home pages and make available digitised demo tracks. More informal discussion groups are run by fans, or at least seem to be that way, although there is some subtle promotional PR going on in the background. Publicity and books for live concerts are a tailor-made Internet activity being extended into actual live concerts over the Net. Details of who is making what music in cyberspace from **http://american.recordings.com/wwwofmusic/index.html**.

T-Shirts Sell Well

T-shirts have proved to be effective online merchandise because they can be shipped internationally so easily, and designed specifically for the special interest groups that automatically categorise themselves into attractive niche markets. However, those who have tried it say you must be very discreet in posting to your target newsgroups information that you have a T-shirt of particular interest to them. Apologise upfront to anyone who might be offended and tempted to flame you for your commercial activities. You could temper potentially hostile reaction by linking shirts to a genuine charitable fund-raising objective, or to generate publicity for the target group's objectives.

If publishing is the core of your cyberspace entrepreneurial objectives, then testing your project through either of these locations could be a very good way to start. However, don't expect either of them to make great sales for you unless you are prepared also to put some effort into the marketing. They may, by this time, have created thousands of literary leaps to hypertext link to groups of potential book buyers in cyberspace, but if your book is on, say, nuclear physics, you need also to make the effort to go out and locate the nuclear physicists who are online and woo your specific target audience to seek out your title on the shelves of the virtual book stores.

If you achieve that, you have a much better chance online of converting motivated browsers into buyers because you can use the power of the Web to project your book to them in colourful multimedia, with an extract sufficiently long to show, hopefully, that it is worth purchasing the rest.

Once you embark on that marketing exercise, you may be tempted to go further and explore these fascinating concepts of dynamic, evolving vehicles of knowledge – the tour buses of the Internet.

11. Producing and packaging disk products

Sooner rather than later every cyberspace entrepreneur needs to duplicate and package disks. There are many occasions when it is necessary or preferable to distribute material physically on a floppy rather than to send it winging in virtual form through cyberspace.

The familiar floppy is particularly useful as a way to distribute demos to contacts and as give-aways at trade shows and other functions. You can package a floppy or CD very economically to give it physical substance and add a printed sales message or instructions. A plain disk on its own tends not be seen to have much value nor significance. Appearance and substance are important for retail point of sale situations, and when offering back-of-the-room products at workshops or seminars, or as promotional items at shows and exhibitions.

The CD-ROM is the high profile physical form for cyberspace projects, mainly those requiring very large files of data or multimedia features. It is, at present, the easiest and fastest way to lose money in electronic publishing, so if you can get your product to fit on to a floppy or two this is a much safer and more universal medium to use.

CD-ROMs are getting all the media hype and being pushed by several large companies because it is the one format in which the economies of scale, the marketing and distribution power, and the capital resources of big corporations can make an impact. You should know that informed industry estimates all conclude that the great majority of CD-ROM publishers have remained unprofitable well through the first half of the decade, and by 1995 perhaps only 4% actually make any money. They are, with a few exceptions, not the high profile ones that you have read about, but the specialists with essential information for niche markets that can command hundreds or thousands of pounds for a database on a disk.

Many CD-titles have been developed and never even got to market effectively. The cost of development typically ranges from about £25,000 to over

PROMOTIONAL AND PERSONALISED MERCHANDISE

Online ventures are creating a significant demand for promotional and personalised merchandising, everything from T-shirts to pens, mugs – even underwear. If you have the resources to create appropriate products,you might tap into this market with an online offer to accept email orders accompanied by a graphics file of the logo or other visual image. This is the kind of opportunity that could well be exploited by a small silk screen printing shop, or a craft worker.

Internet Faxes

For many years there will be a need to use the Internet to communicate with individuals and organisations without email address, but with fax machines. An experimental service for this offering somewhat restricted coverage to addresses in Britain, Japan, the USA and Hong Kong had recently started as this book went to press. For information email a HELP message to **tpc-faq@town.hall.org**.

Look out also for better fax , voice mail and email facilities being introduced all the time in the major groupware programs, notably Lotus Notes and cc:Mail, and Novell's GroupWise.

£500,000, and you need major marketing budgets to move large numbers of units to take advantage of volume duplicating that can bring unit costs down to under £1.

You can bring production costs way down if you do most or all of the work in-house. It is possible for a single talented person to complete a compex multimedia production or build a large database on CD-ROM without very expensive hardware or software – a system costing under £2,000 would do it. The actual disk mastering can be contracted out economically, and the new consumer Photo-CD facilities being promoted by Kodak bring this stage to very affordable levels for certain types of production. The duplication costs are coming down also, with in-house equipment to do this becoming well within the reach of individuals and small businesses.

Sponsored CDs can be viable propositions, as are also those that meet clearly defined market needs. The problem is to reduce costs and achieve profitable sales for titles aimed at general consumer markets that have not yet reached anywhere near maturity, and may never do so.

The CD market is glutted, and unless you have something uniquely appropriate to this medium, the risks are too high for even the most adventurous entrepreneurs. This is not a very popular message in the mid-1990s when so many experts expect CD-ROMs to repeat in the personal computing market the remarkable successes of CD audio disks for the music industry. The reality is that these are completely different consumer markets and radically different digital products.

If you still want to get into CD products, prepare your budgets and sales forecasts as conservatively as possible and don't even bother to start unless you can identify and target your markets precisely. Although global CD sales were around 54 million units in 1994, only a tiny proportion of the estimated nearly 15,000 titles available by late 1995 are proving profitable. Most of them are either languishing in storage, being discounted heavily at a loss to their developers, or packaged into very low price bundles given away to promote hardware.

Leading CD-ROM publishers have been shedding staff – Compton's New Media, one of the biggest, laid off 30% of its US workforce early in 1995. A big shake-out is expected among the weaker CD-ROM developers – there may be as many as 2,000 of them.

Even when development costs are minimal, it is proving very difficult to turn a profit except in very specific niche markets. As duplication costs tumble, you might score with what the multimedia enthusiasts deride as "shovelware" titles, in which a lot of content from print or digital databases is shovelled into the CD format without much concern given to the need to add value with interactive multimedia or powerful searching features. If the content is really valuable to the target markets and the search facilities are at least reasonable, then shovelware can be viable.

I am sounding those warnings because CD-ROMs are the most capital intensive medium of electronic publishing. You can get to a potentially larger – and faster growing – market for much less cost and risk online through cyberspace. Nevertheless, the CD-ROM market seems set for continued growth in the UK over the next few years, and if you have the courage and the right product there are opportunities to get a viable slice of it. There will be perhaps half a million drives installed in Britain by the end of 1995, a market penetration behind only the US and Germany. Global sales of drives in 1994 were about 4.4 million, a million more than in 1993, and as prices drop they are becoming a near standard element in both home and business systems.

However, that doesn't mean that PC users are going to make the quantity of impulse CD purchases necessary to support the flood of titles. The pattern seems to be settling into a steady demand for the hot games, educational and reference CD titles, and the rest only moving in small, unprofitable numbers. In the short term at least, most of the CDs on the typical desk at home or at work will contain applications software, as this is an ideal substitute for the packages of floppies that have become necessary for the distribution of bloated word processors, spreadsheets and graphical programs.

CD sales may be helped in Britain because of the national preference to buy to own permanently, rather than rent to use temporarily, and the absence of free local telephone calls to facilitate the alternative PC usage of connecting to the Internet. Our telephone usage is very low compared to the US, and there is an inbuilt reluctance to spend a lot of time online, in contrast to the US where telephones are used without anywhere near as much concern for time and cost, particularly as local calls are usually free.

It is dangerous to make any assumptions that British CD-ROM drive owners will purchase to feed their machines in the same way as they have moved from audio cassettes to CD music disks. The market demographics and motivations are so completely different.

When CD-ROMs are part of the media mix for your cyberspace venture, you must budget for significantly large production runs, which puts you back into the physical handicaps and cost structures of conventional print publishing. Expect also to pay for a high proportion of returns, generous technical support, and other hassles with customers.

As much as 40% of some widely distributed CD-ROM products in the US have been returned by end users, and the average return rate through retailers is believed to be over 20%. Apart from clunky programming, most problems stem from incompatibilities with the users' systems, together with lack of end-user knowledge in fixing what may be very simple adjustments.

The situation is aggravated for manufacturers who make their electronic products too sophisticated for the systems still used by many of their customers. Experts emphasise the need to test on a wide variety of system configurations, and make realistic minimum system requirements prominent in advertising and packaging. It is usually better to lose a sale, than have to cope with one which generates complaints, as has been pointed out earlier.

VIRTUAL BOOTHS

Virtual shopping booths or kiosks could offer hot entrepreneurial opportunities over the next few years. About the size of a small telephone booth, they are being installed in places where people have time to kill, or need to make purchases for delivery elsewhere, particularly gifts. Consequently, cybershopping booths began to appear during 1995 in airports – particularly the airline clubs – and in hotels. The booths may be followed by similar facilities which give metered access to free roaming over the Internet.

There are better prospects for digital video on CD, which could become a major medium for cyberspace entrepreneurs. The files are large and take a long time to download online, despite significant improvements in compression methods and the wider use of faster modems and connections. So a video product could be promoted to its target markets with extracts available online, and the full program sold as a CD or a standard video tape.

(To see what is happening in the field of digital movies, look out online for files identified by .mpeg or .mpg extensions. You can find them at many FTP and *Gopher* sites. Sources include **ftp://havefun.standford.edu/pu/mpeg** and on the Web at **http://www.wit.com**. There are *Windows* and DOS viewers available at **ftp://ftp.netcom/pub/cf/cfogg/mpeg1/vmpeg12a.zip** and a free Macintosh viewer called Sparkle at **ftp://ftp.ncsa.uiuc.edu/Mac/Mosaic/Helpers**. For general information about online movies, try the Web address of **http://www.eit.com/techinfo/mpeg/mpeg.html**.)

Now for the good news!

Virtual businesses that exist largely in cyberspace without the need for physical premises can produce excellent and successful products to sell on floppy disks. The raw materials – the disks – are getting cheaper all the time and unless you get into really big runs you do not need any special hardware. All that is necessary to add to your entrepreneur's toolkit is a program such as *DiskDuplicator*, which effectively turns virtually any PC able to run *Windows* into a dedicated disk duplicating machine.

It is essential to have a program like this to create electronic products and demonstrations distributed on floppy disks. There are many such utilities available as shareware from the online sources listed throughout this book, but few approach *DiskDuplicator* in their capabilities.

It is an example of cyberspace entrepreneurship. The program was created by five software engineers who only have occasional meetings, and those mainly for social get togethers. Virtually all their work in developing *DiskDuplicator* and steadily further improving it has been done online. The leader of the project, Ajay Sharma, told me that their premises were effectively the computer under his desk.

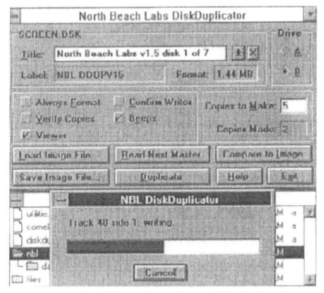

Figure 11.1 North Beach Labs Disk Duplicator

HOROSCOPES ONLINE

Astrological forecasting – long a staple of syndication services in print publishing – are proving a viable business in cyberspace. Some services charge a fee for personalised readings, but there are also many sites that offer free information and downloadable software. A good resource on the Web is at **http://cyborganic.com/ ~justin/astral**, and there is also a very active mailing list which can be joined by emailing to **michael.bulmer@ maths.utas.edu.au.**

Digital City

Europe's first Digital City was set up in 1994 with a £30,000 grant from Amsterdam city council and government subsidies. It was soon attracting 3,000 visitors daily. Such ventures can start with the creation of an electronic equivalent to the town hall, then grow with both social and commercial activities that reflect the real community. In addition to filling local needs, digital cities can play valuable roles to attract tourism and investment internationally.

The original Digital City serves as one of the most interesting models of a community going online and you can get there on the Web at **http://dds.nl**, or by calling direct to Amsterdam 6225222.

"We have found that we actually work more efficiently by communicating online than we do when interacting physically with colleagues in the different companies for which we work," he said.

You can get more information and a shareware version of the program on the Web at **http://www.hia.com/hia/nbl**. Or, if you have only a text-based dial-up connection, FTP to **ftp.aimnet.com** and go to the directory **/pub/users/hia**.

How to package disks and e-books for under 5p each!

Here is a ten-step, low-cost solution to a major problem for the authors and distributors of shareware, electronic books, and other projects on floppy disks. I have looked at scores of different packaging options while researching my ebooks – and found that the best solution is also one of the simplest.

You can create high impact, practical packaging for a disk for under 5p, using standard size paper or light board. The layout is easy to complete using a word processing, drawing, or desktop publishing program. Attractive copies can be made – with the impact of colour – even on basic copiers.

The resulting packages look great on display in stores or at seminars and other point-of-sale situations. They provide also lightweight protection for disks that can be mailed in an ordinary business size envelope.

Perhaps this format could become the standard that all of us involved in electronic publishing need for our disk-based products. Standardised packaging has contributed much to the success of audio cassettes and CD disks. We are handicapped by not having the consistency that enables our disks to be displayed effectively in retail outlets, or to be shipped economically and safely.

Another attraction of basic, honest packaging is that anything more elaborate than the following simple procedure could negate the environmental "green" attributes of publishing online or on floppies.

Here are the simple steps to create great packaging for 3.5 inch disks using A4 or US standard letter-size paper or card. (You need to vary the dimensions, or go to A3 or something in between A4 and A3, or to the US legal size paper or card to package 5.25 inch floppies or CD-ROMs.) I will go into some detail because you can use this method whether you are an independent entrepreneur on a tight budget, or in a large enterprise needing quickly to make up just a few samples or a small run without incurring conventional print and packaging costsand delays.

Step 1

Set your word processor, desktop publishing, or draw program page set-up to landscape (horizontal) standard letter size.

Step 2

Set your margins to 0.5 inches, which is about the tightest that many laser printers will print to the edge of the paper.

Step 3

Use your layout guides, column settings, or frames (depending on the formatting options that you have) to divide the page horizontally into three sections. In many word processors, you can do this just by selecting a three-column format. The first section is at the right edge of the paper and will form your front cover. The second section – in the middle – is your back cover, while the third section on the left will create the inside pocket to hold the disk.

Together they comprise the outside of your packaging, plus the inside flap that forms a wallet. You can experiment to vary the width of these sections, preferably by cutting down the width of the left hand column that forms the flap, and so create larger front and back covers. This may give more impact at point-of-sale when your disk package is displayed, but could pose mailing problems if it will then not fit into a standard envelope.

Take a sheet of paper and fold it along the divisions between the sections, to form a dummy so that you can see how your packaging assembles to guide you through the layout. The narrow Section 1 on the left tucks inside Section 3 and will be glued at the top and bottom to form a pocket. Section 3 on the right is the equivalent to a book cover, or the front of a box. This is where you will put your title, visuals, price, and other information to achieve impact and motivate potential buyers to pick up the package and examine it more closely, as they would when browsing book stores and being attracted by an effective front cover or jacket.

SCOTCH ON CD-ROM

CD-ROM publishing linked to cyberspace promotional activities is a growing trend, although linking ad rates to megabytes of disk space occupied is not a viable pricing structure unless backed up by adequate circulation to the appropriate demographic target markets. The best titles can charge high rates – Dewar's paid about £24,000 for its pioneering 15 megabytes on the April 1995 premier edition of the Launch CD-ROM magazine.

"A CD-ROM magazine is the perfect vehicle for Dewar's," said brand manager Denise Luft, in the *Wall Street Journal*. "It talks to young, hip people who like to experiment."

Export Accents

The reputation of the British for being different underpins many of our export successes, particularly in the entertainment business. Now it is being promulgated in cyberspace through the newsgroup **alt.fan. british-accent**, which the hip American magazine *Wired* described as "absolutely fabulous".

Flattening Gender Differences

"Technology doesn't get enough credit for being the feminists' friend. Technology has killed hierarchy. When you get into companies that have email systems, you don't have to be the loudest man or the biggest braggart. It flattens gender differences." Harriet Rubin, executive editor of Currency/Doubleday, quoted in *Inc. Technology*.

Section 2 is your equivalent to a book back cover, or the back of a product box. Here is where you put the supplementary information to convert a browser into a buyer. A summary of your ebook or software, favourable reviews or comments by users or experts, and the system requirements to run the disk all belong here.

Section 1 – the tuck-in flap to form the pocket for the disk contains the first text that buyers see when they open the package. It is right next to the disk – they can't miss what's there when they remove the disk – and so is a good place to put simple instructions on how to run the disk and install the program or ebook that it contains. Practical help, rather than hard-selling copy, is appropriate for this section.

Step 5

Create the texts and visuals for each of these three sections that form the outside of your packaging. Centre your content in each section. If you have made Section 1 narrower to give you more space for your back and front covers, the install instructions that go here look effective as a left- or right-aligned narrow column of short paragraphs.

Section 2 – the back cover – can be visually enhanced by enclosing all or sections of the text in a panel or box.

Section 3 – the front cover – should have strong visual elements if you need point-of-sale appeal. You can go to 48 points, or even larger type, to make the title come across clearly. This is the place for your International Standard Book Number (ISBN), if you have one, and the retail price.

Step 6

If you plan to print or copy with a second spot colour, cut and paste into the same position on a duplicate layout the elements of your design that you want in that second colour. They might be a visual, the title, a flash across one corner, or other features that you wish to highlight in colour. Some graphics programs allow you to create your entire illustration first, and then separate out different colours. Or you may be able to work in two colours on different layers which you can print separately.

If you only want to print or copy in one colour, you can still enhance your packaging by using coloured paper or card stock. I have made extensive use of green paper to put across my theme of environmentally correct Green Paperless Books. I found a great green with an appropriate earthy kind of texture among the packages and pads of construction paper and card sold for children's projects. These tend not to be of standard metric or US sizes, so you will need either to trim them or vary your layout dimensions. They don't usually load well from the copier's paper tray, so you need to hand feed them, and some copiers may not like them and print unevenly or jam. However, most machines will produce good results.

There is a good selection available of other coloured and pre-printed papers and cards. You can get really great results using metallic coated card, if your copier will take them. You need to hand feed card through a machine that has a reasonably straight paper path and be sure that the leading edge of the card is not likely to cause damage to the drum as it passes through.

If I have only a few card covers to run, I use an almost exhausted replaceable drum and toner cartridge unit in a personal copier. When these disposable units first start indicating that they are close to empty, you still have quite a lot of copies left and can revive them by shaking the replacement unit vigorously from side to get remnants of toner powder down into the bottom hopper. If a card does damage the drum, then you've not lost anything.

Some copiers will not heat and fix toner adequately on very glossy card – particularly metallic cards. The image may become rub-proof if left exposed for some time – but this may take days. You can spray the surface with a clear varnish or fixative available from an arts supply store, which gives a more professional glossy finish. Experimentation pays off.

I add impact sometimes by using coloured labels that I have printed commercially at instant print shops or through mail order offers. They are very reasonably priced and particularly applicable to adding a logo and address details to your disk packaging.

Step 7

You can also use the inside of your packaging effectively. To do this, repeat the set-up formatting instructions in Steps 1-3, but change the dimensions.

CROOKS ONLINE

A phenomenon of the increasing prison population in some countries is the growth of an alternative press of magazines, newsletters and newspapers produced inside prisons. Some of these may find their way online during the next few years as access to the Internet becomes acceptable – perhaps essential – for prisoners doing educational courses. They will also find sources for free expert legal advice online!

The Urge to be First

Oxford University Press was an early entrant to publishing over the Internet for very practical reasons – it immediately cut the lead time from acceptance of a paper for its *Nucleic Acids Research* from 12 weeks to only three. Such speed helps publishers to attract the most important research papers because the first scientist into print has been regarded as implicit acknowledgement of making a discovery first.

That is changing. The ease and speed of publishing online is causing a re-evaluation of the peer review and other traditional processes involved in sifting and assessing scientific research papers. Opportunities for fraud and misleading or ill-founded research being published have increased greatly. For the first time, researchers who have papers rejected now have viable alternatives to get the exposure, acclaim or to further

Section 1 on the back – which is the reverse side of the front's Section 3 (your front cover) – extends in from the left edge of the paper. It appears when your customer opens up the packaging. This is a good place to put additional information, such as more comprehensive installation instructions which will be logically opposite the disk when it is removed from the wallet. Or you can use this space to sell other programs, ebooks, products or services that you offer.

Section 2 of the reverse will be completely hidden, or only a narrow strip if you have made the flap narrower to give more width to the front and back covers. The rest of the page – the reverse side of the front of your packaging – will be obscured by the flap that contains the disk.

If you do have a narrow column showing in this centre section, it will be partly obscured when the disk is in the package, but you can still use it effectively. I include here additional help information, such as a telephone number to call if the user has problems, or needs a different disk format. I also highlight here any particular features of the disk, such as the ability to adjust the display colours for different monitors or for a laptop screen.

Step 8

Now fold your packaging. If you use card stock, you may need to score the folds first using a ruler and the back of a knife or scissors blade to achieve a clean fold.

Step 9

Glue the disk flap at the top and bottom, using a good quality paper glue. I find that quality glue sticks work well, or you might try a hot or low melt glue gun, or the rubber cement that layout artists use.

Step 10

Create a paper or card insert to go into the flap along with the disk if you need to convey more printed information. A stiff card will help to protect the disk, and could be an attractive ready reference. You can also put your business card, or a pre-printed response registration or order card, into the wallet, along with other promotional materials.

If you want to keep the packaging closed, as when on display in a store to reduce the risk of disks being stolen or mishandled, a small self-adhesive label can be used as a seal. Attach it to the centre of the right edge of the front cover, and fold it over to the back cover. You can make the labels a design feature and print them out on your laser or ink jet printer, or make a master to run through a copier. Printing something like "Guaranteed Virus Free & Sealed for Your Protection" can be a positive sales tool.

You may need to instruct buyers to slit the label carefully, or use labels with low-tack glue of the kind that enables Post-It notes to be removed without damaging a paper surface. You can get low-tack glue in tubes and sticks now, so that you could print your label closure on plain or coloured paper, then cut up and glue on by hand. This can get tedious if the quantities are large, but is economical and practical for small numbers.

This form of packaging can work very well for collections of shareware, for racking displays, or for stand displays at the point-of-sale, such as in a cardboard container positioned near the check-out register. You can buy small display boxes at good stationery supply stores. In some of these display situations, you may need to have particular sales or title information at the top of the front cover, so that it is readily accessible as potential buyers flip through a stack.

You do not need the whole height of the paper to create a wallet for a 3.5" inch disk. Attractive packaging for disks can be made by trimming the paper or card. Obviously, you need to modify your page set-up and layout guides to fit a non-standard paper size.

You can juggle with the dimensions to get your disk package into whatever standard or non-standard size envelope you may be using. If you are going over the first class letter weight limit anyway, a catalogue envelope in a tough manila paper works well and adds further protection for your disk.

I mail disks all over the world all the time and very rarely do they get damaged, although if there are other papers in the envelope I put the disk package in the centre of these as a precaution. Sometimes I add plastic bubble pack or a sheet of card, but usually it is not necessary – those hard shell floppies are pretty tough.

You may want to put your disk package into a standard-size plastic bag for protection, and for hanging displays. The re-sealable bags for food work well,

scientific, financial, personal, and academic objectives. An individual, team, department, or college can easily set up and promote to prominence their own Web site or bulletin board – giving them publishing power that can abused as well as used beneficially.

SHOPPING AS ENTERTAINMENT

The trend in retailing to make shopping an entertainment experience is proving essential for successful online virtual stores. While home shopping television channels are increasing the entertainment content of their programming, so cyberspace stores are incorporating virtual elements of the kind of entertainment experience that have been at the root of "showbiz shopping" in the US. Tourists actually queue up to enter some of the top studio stores there, which include over 300 outlets for Disney and nearly 150 for Warner Bros.

MUDDY CHATS

Investigate MUDs – Multi-User Dialogue Dimension Dungeons – and IRCs – Internet Relay Chats – for distributive publishing projects, and as ways of holding real-time online meetings. Both are text-based facilities for enabling people to interact. MUDs are all over the Net, mainly as games, but they can be adapted to more businesslike sessions. A variation called MOOs – MUD Object Orientated – provides more facilities. IRCs can be set up to be reasonably confidential and secure from eavesdropping, making them practical for various business uses. Your service provider may have facilities to help set up MUDs and IRCs.

and you can increase the display impact, protection and perceived value of your disk package if you create also a card of promotional material to slip as a tight fit into the bag. The card helps to keep the bag flat as well as being a sales aid, and is essential if your packaging will be displayed hanging from a hook.

Another way of sealing the package is to use the clear plastic wrapping for foodstuffs that stretches and clings to itself. You can get most of the wrinkles out for a more professional appearance by blowing hot air over it from a hair dryer.

The costs of this type of packaging are so low that you might consider following this procedure for each disk to add perceived value to multiple-disk products. Adopt a common design theme, but vary the text for each of the disks in the package.

If you provide a manual or other documentation in spiral or ring bound form you can fold, punch and bind-in these wallets. Just arrange the layout to clear where the holes for the binding spiral will be punched.

Printing the disk labels is not a problem, as most leading word processors have templates for the standard sizes of adhesive labels. Just make sure that the labels you use are compatible with your printer or copier, and that their adhesive will withstand the heat for hours within a disk drive. Customers get very upset with suppliers of disks with labels that become detached and snarl up expensive drives!

12. New business models for the information age

The core activity in cyberspace, as we have seen, is publishing. Just as, in the past, communities have been founded and flourished on mining, agriculture, textiles, military bases, automotive manufacturing, iron and steel foundries, and other core industrial and commercial activities, so the cyberspace community is being nurtured by the core activity of processing information into publishable form.

The entrepreneurial challenge in cyberspace is that information is not a commodity in the same sense as the raw materials that go into most consumer and industrial products. Nor is the medium definable and controllable in ways that have made other forms of publishing viable business propositions in the past.

During the last five centuries, publishers have achieved considerable success by developing business models of various publishing processes by which information can be acquired, processed, packaged and marketed as printed products in ways that work well for cornflakes and cars. But those models are not proving valid in the new publishing media appearing in the information revolution era. Publishing's new product categories have more similarities with the broadcasting media than they do with print products that market knowledge between the covers of a book, or on the pages of a newspaper, professional journal or magazine.

Broadcast, cable and satellite radio and television services provide better prospective models for business in cyberspace than does print publishing, but there are fundamental differences that every entrepreneur venturing into these new media must understand.

Radio and television – particularly television – are passive one-way media. They have achieved effective total saturation of the populations in developed nations – and much of the Third World also – because they are such accessible and undemanding mass media. Viewers can passively receive without signifi-

FLY THROUGH CYBER-SPACE

Flying is a very popular activity in cyberspace, creating a substantial niche market still wide open to entrepreneurial ventures. Flight simulation programs are available from all the larger shareware libraries, and there is a thriving business in creating add-in modules for scenery and different airports around the world. Most of the interest is in the market leader, the Microsoft Flight Simulator, but virtual pilots are always seeking out new thrills and experiences.

Keep in touch online with what is happening in this field by emailing a subscription request to **flight-sim-request@grove.iup.edu**.

cant intellectual effort, or being called on to respond. This has resulted in fundamental changes in our cultural, social and consumer habits. Now several generations have ceased to regard newspapers as their prime source for topical information, and there is a crisis in some nations – the United States in particular – in literacy levels. Radio – still potentially the most powerful of all the information media – is now in decline in this respect as even public broadcasting services feel it necessary to compete with entertainment services to capture larger mass audience shares.

Radio and television services generate revenue for their products and services mainly by sponsorship, usually from commercial organisations paying for advertising space around programming that attracts audiences with the size and demographics that the advertisers seek to reach. Government sponsorship through licence fees or grants is a diminishing factor which may be eliminated altogether in some territories, including the United States.

An important part of the mix is made up of cable television channels that provide programming perceived to be of a premium nature and which viewers purchase by subscription. Although smaller, these are still large markets which are expensive to reach and not very tightly defined. Cyberspace, in contrast, is the very opposite of a mass market. Even as it doubles in size annually, according to some estimates, it remains predominantly a complex web of clearly defined niche markets. It is almost as different from broadcasting as it is from print publishing.

However, broadcasters are expanding their revenue sources by adding physical products, notably video and audio tapes, printed books, newsletters and licensed merchandise. These radio and television activities do provide many valid models for cyberspace publishing, particularly sponsored publishing and the development of product lines that are marketed through online exposure – the "second sale" concept. The first "sale" does not generate profit, nor even revenue, but stimulates the consumer's interest – it "sells" the concept or imagery necessary to achieve the second, real, sale for which money passes from buyer to seller.

In contrast, print publishing generates primarily physical products as its main source of revenue. Sponsorship – routine in broadcasting and now spreading in cyberspace – is alien to book, newspaper and magazine publishing. These print media share with online publishing the features that television lacks –

displaying words and pictures in a form that demands at least some degree of interactivity. But the fundamental difference is that print publishing is geared to the first – and often only – sale of a physical object. Only in magazine publishing is there any significant up front giving away of information or products to generate revenue from a sustained relationship with the consumer. Anyway, subscriptions are essentially advance payments for a physical product sub-divided into instalments.

Most of the book publishing industry, already in a critical state, is dabbling in cyberspace publishing by carrying over into the new media these business models which have worked for it in the past and which are essentially geared to the first sale of physical products. The industry is stuck in this business rut because it has been a manufacturing industry in the past, profitability hinging on the efficiency with which the raw materials of ink and paper could be turned into physical products, books, for marketing in ways that work for other consumer products.

As a result of this reality, the need to manufacture and market with increasing efficiency to remain competitive has resulted in imprints which offered much diversity of information and entertainment in the past being merged and often lost for ever in large publishing houses which re-engineer their staffing and corporate cultures to maximise the profitability potential of their production processes. Resources – particularly marketing resources – must be concentrated on the titles/product lines that have the greatest volume sales potential. The resulting rationalisation process extends right through to the shelves of the major book selling chains and, inevitably, also into the small book stores, libraries, and book reviewing activities. The cultural impact of this has been enormous – on writers and artists as well as readers.

The momentum given to the comparatively small number of high volume selling books creates a push-pull effect in which consumer demand is further distorted to feed the publishing production process.

There are many parallels in other product categories – automobiles and food and beverages are prime examples where actual rather than perceived choice has become eroded. For example, it is almost impossible to buy custard powder in an American supermarket because consumer demand has been manipulated to alternative desserts which have higher profit margins because of the standardised ways in which they can be processed and packaged. The

TELEWORKERS REPRESENT HUGE MARKET

Although telecommuting is still in its infancy in Europe, the way in which it will grow here and in places like New Zealand, Australia and South Africa has already been demonstrated in the US. There exists now a very large market across the Atlantic for products and services that will benefit the nearly seven million American telecommuters, who are heavy users of on-line services. The largest survey of self-employed people anywhere, conducted in the US in 1994 by the Computer Intelligence InfoCorp, revealed that the professional self-employed person with a computer generates 42 % more household income than one without.

The Telecottage Association is a prime source in Britain for information about telecommuting, and its pioneering telecottage shared computer resource centres have spread from rural into urban areas. More information from **10203 696986**, **ISDN:0203 692731**, and **100114.2366@compuserve.com**.

shelves are stacked with what seems to be a large choice, but in reality the basic packaging and contents are standardised, with the differences being achieved at minimal cost through labelling and artificial flavouring. The auto industry's badge engineering to achieve pricing flexibility and appeal to different market segments is a more complex, but basically similar ploy.

The larger companies in the print publishing industry have been following such models in their early responses to the challenge from the new digital electronic media. That is why they have been failing in their efforts to mould these new paperless media to support their traditional ways of doing business and generating profits. The enthusiasm by print publishers for CD-ROM publications as the medium of the future rather than online services is because they offer the best prospect of being able to preserve traditional commercial publishing practices of the past.

Intellectual property is acquired on the most favourable terms possible, processed and packaged in ways in which the economies of scale available to large organisations can best be exploited, and then marketed aggressively as physical products to maximise sales and profit potential. This traditional business model is not working. The CD titles produced by major print publishers have largely not made back their initial costs and there have been drastic cutbacks in budgets and staff deployed on these projects. The minority of CD titles that have been financially successful are distorting the real picture. They are predominantly games, reference or teaching materials ideally suited to the CD-ROM medium's strengths of vast capacity to store data and programming that will enhance data by providing easy reference, interactivity and multimedia capabilities.

CDs will continue to have inherent advantages in these respects for many years but, like parchment before paper, they may prove to represent an intermediate technology with a far more limited long-term future than publishing through the online medium of cyberspace. There will always be a place for products which are clearly superior, but many attempts by print publishers to repackage their intellectual properties in CD form are neither appropriate for the new media, nor well-executed to give added value as electronic publications, or both.

Again, the exceptions prove the rule, such as Dorling-Kindersley's superior CD titles and the best of the CD-ROM interactive encyclopaedia and infor-

FREE-NETS HELP COMMUNITIES TO GROW

Forming a local consortium of private, business and public sector interests to create a local Free-Net is a proven successful way to bring the social and economic benefits of access to cyberspace to communities. A Free-Net is, in effect, a self-funding network of computer users connected by public telephone lines in a particular locality. The usual aim is to foster economic development in the area, from which everyone benefits.

There will be nearly 100 community non-profit networks in the United States by the end of 1995. The process often starts with a public meeting leading to the formation of a steering com-

mation-rich databases. There is nearly always a profit awaiting superior – or problem-solving – products in any field.

Things are likely to get worse before they get better for print publishers dabbling in CD-ROM because the production technology and pricing structures for CD publishing are changing in ways that the large publishers cannot control to protect their trading positions. The technology is developing so that individuals and small enterprises can create and manufacture CD titles at much lower cost. Although similar forces, notably desktop publishing, have helped small presses to exploit market niches left unserved by the major publishers, the beneficial effects remained constrained because of the physical cost and complexity inherent in manufacturing print products which demand volume runs. Desktop publishing is really only equivalent to the research and development phases of producing, say, a motor car. It does not eliminate the usually far more expensive process of replicating the prototype consistently in large numbers which can be sold at unit prices sufficiently high to amortise all the overheads and expenses incurred in bringing the product to market, and to show a profit also.

In the new media of cyberspace – and there are many different types of media emerging there, not just one new way of doing things – the manufacturing processes involved with publishing print are largely eliminated. Most of the traditional product acquisition and marketing models vanish also, along with the basic concept of building businesses around products which are sold as units priced according to the conventional yardsticks of cost of development + cost of production + cost of sales (including distribution and resellers' margins) + profit = selling price.

Distribution and marketing, which at present comprise the major costs for a printed book, are drastically reduced online. Over 90% savings in these costs are easily achieved. Consequently, authors and illustrators, who are the most important elements in the book publishing process, typically receive much less than ten per cent of the revenues their works generate in print, but should increase that proportion dramatically in online ventures to at least 50%, probably over 80% in some cases. The proportion of revenues allocated to editors, designers and other creative talents should increase also.

These are but the more obvious examples of elements which must be factored very differently into the new business models necessary for cyberspace pub-

mittee to operate a registered non-profit charity. Hardware donations and sponsorship can be sought from local businesses, and schemes work best which try to bring into the network project the most diverse range of business, social, and community activities in the area being served. In the US, public terminals are often created in shelters for the homeless, libraries, schools and other youth facilities.

UNUSUAL WEB SITES

There is much entrepreneurial inspiration to be found at one of the most interesting listings of unusual places on the Web. Compiled by Mark J. Cox of the University of Bradford's Department of Industrial Technology, it is to be found at **http:/ /www.eia.brad.ac.uk/ mark/fave-inter.html/**.

SUBTLE CARE SALESMEN

Car salesmen have had to learn to be subtle when selling their products in cyberspace. The pioneering DealerNet, in which Microsoft is a partner, is an information rich database on current car models through which browsers can look for the right combination of specification, image and price. Having made their choice, buyers can email to have it delivered to their homes or offices for a test drive. All the frustration of haggling with a salesman over price and options can be sorted out by email without any need for a face-to-face meeting.

DealerNet was accessed nearly 160,000 times in its first week and is heading towards about three million accesses every month. The 250 car dealers participating during its first year – mainly in Northern California – paid nearly £9,000 each to get a prominent icon. Many regard it as being as cost-efficient as their radio or print advertising.

lishing. It is an environment geared to eliminate many of the motivations and activities that have fuelled conventional print publishing, and much of broadcasting also. One of the most significant changes is that the information product will generally have much less value if it is available only in a fixed form, like a book or CD, rather than being dynamic and evolving, as the new information technologies make possible.

The methods emerging as being most appropriate for doing business online are alien to many corporate cultures now adapting to cyberspace. The arrival of commerce is having a big impact also on the culture of cyberspace. There is a period of adjustment in which the two contrasting cultures will coalesce into a business environment comprising elements of each. But it promises always to be substantially different from the traditional ways of producing and trading in physical products.

New models are emerging for entrepreneurial opportunities in which individual and organisational enterprises alike are able to blend monetary, cultural, social, political, charitable, corporate and other worthwhile goals. Business projects in cyberspace benefit in this web-like rather than hierarchical environment by giving greater weighting to the cultural and social aspects of what companies do than has been the case in the physical world.

Another intriguing development is that, being an interactive medium, the marketing there needs to be far more creative than is the norm in print and broadcasting. Cyberspace will not, for example, prove receptive to the direct transfer of the hard-sell techniques that have been successful on television's shopping channels and in sponsored infommercials. Europeans have already proved resistant to these "in-your-face" approaches, which have not been anywhere near as successful here as in North America.

Large organisations are inherently slow to adapt and initiate. In many respects they are not a natural fit with the entrepreneurial opportunities opening in cyberspace. Success there is built on creativity, fast response, and the ability to be a participant in an ever-changing international experiment in both the technical and human relations aspects of a completely different medium. Large investments and teams of people, or other expensive resources are not needed. Individuals can achieve significant results very quickly, like the young couple Van and Bonnie Glass who started the Cybercafe from their small apartment and within a few weeks were attracting over 1,000 people to it every day, along with a mounting interest from a number of large businesses interested in renting space or sponsoring projects. (Details from **cybercafe@bid.com**, or visit them on the Web at **http://www.bid.com/bid/cybercafe**.)

Some big companies which have invested quite heavily in cyberspace have failed to find the right formula in an environment of sharing and openness that is alien to them, while independents on shoestrings are building successful presences on the Web. Consequently, with this form of publishing so accessible, expect great changes in the way that enterprises start. Many companies will find that they get better returns from sponsoring Internet activities rather than concentrating on developing their own sites. As publishing is the Net's core activity, so those sponsorship funds will flow to paperless publishing projects and overcome many of the financial problems resulting from the difficulties in making online sales for ebooks.

Such sponsorship will not come just from big companies or the industrialised nations. The cost structures of Net publishing can be so low that small businesses everywhere can participate. Some will tell their own stories – an irresistible opportunity for many entrepreneurs who have devoted their lives to building successful enterprises and who have great corporate and personal stories to tell.

The desire to tell your own story is a basic human trait, partly a seeking after a form of immortality. The telling of stories, already a part of business culture, now takes on new and exciting forms that can vastly increase the pool of disseminated knowledge and experience of business successes and failures.

Organisations of all kinds will sponsor or do their own cyberspace publishing to increase awareness of their activities and as an increasingly important fundraising and opinion-forming activity. Communities seeking to attract employers, investment, tourism or trade now have powerful media to deploy towards these objectives, with a small town in a remote place able to compete for attention with the large cities on the main trading routes.

A particularly strong influence is that geographic barriers fall away online, overcoming many problems for developing nations and remote communites. We see here opportunities for new ways of tackling specific economic and social problems affecting communities suffering because they have been lo-

WIRELESS ACCESS

Facilities to access the Internet from anywhere are expanding all the time, with wireless connections developing rapidly to exploit the expanding market among portable computer users, expected to exceed ten million world-wide by the end of the decade.

You do not need to be a major manufacturer or online service provider to get in on the act. There are lots of opportunities for creative packaging of readily available hardware and software products, and telecommunications services. Australian computer products distributor Sourceware has done this around a Motorola Personal Messenger PM100D modem which retails for under £500 in Australia. Plugged into a PC, it establishes a connection to Telecom's Mobile Data network.

cated on the back roads of the world's industrial and commercial highways. They range from crofts and villages in the Highlands to former mining communities in Wales, to declining urban centres abandoned by shipping and other manufacturing industries.

India has been attracting a lot of attention from the software industry because of its low cost and comparatively high levels of English literacy and programming skills. But other, less obvious places, have great new opportunities to tackle some of their economic and social problems through their new high speed, low cost cyberspace trading links with the world.

Take New Zealand and South Africa as examples. Such agricultural activites as sheep farming in both countries have suffered badly from their geographical isolation and the changing international food and clothing preferences and trading patterns. There was little that could be done to counter this before, but now cyberspace offers new opportunities in which such countries can draw on their strengths in surprising ways.

New Zealand is producing children with average reading and learning skills that are way above those in North America and much of Europe. In this new era in which knowledge/information is becoming the single most important commodity for international trade, New Zealand has unexploited resources to market education-related products to remote industrialised countries where over the next decade much learning will move online. Education is a cyberspace growth industry and there is the talent in New Zealand to teach the world a wide range of subjects, from pre-school to degree levels. Additional talent could be attracted there because of the quality of the environment and the reduced sense of cultural isolation resulting from the global networking of minds and cultures.

(The first degree courses from academically creditible institutions conducted entirely online are expected to be launched in cyberspace during 1995. Student fees could be affordable by almost anyone, and the savings on text books alone will bring higher education within the reach of millions more people around the world).

South Africa is a particularly interesting case. The most fascinating real-life experiments in social engineering are going on there, and information about the successes and failures could be of benefit to the whole world. As South Africa tries to rebuild its economy after decades of damage caused by its

CHINA IN CYBERSPACE

The China Education and Research Network (CERNET) and other state networks give Chinese in 700 cities Internet access via local dial-up calls. Hundreds of millions of pounds are being spent on telecommunications and it is becoming a business necessity to have an Internet address. CERNET will link all China's 1,090 universities by the year 2000 , and the leading 100 of them were coming online during 1995. The Chinese leaders feel that they have no choice but to make this massive investment if they are to be internationally competitive. The political situation in China will be transformed by the availability of uncontrollable information dissemination.

economic isolation, the political changes have not alleviated the geographical distancing and expensive telecommunications that further isolate the country from many of its major potential markets. These problems are aggravated by the large distances between communities away from the three major urban centres.

Like China, which is making a big play to become a major cyberspace force, South Africa has many products that can be promoted – even marketed – effectively online. Furthermore, South Africa has English as the major language, high literacy levels, competitive wage rates and technological sophistication. It can be a better place to go for data capture services than China, and the remarkable degree of independence in research, development and manufacturing capabilities achieved as a direct result of sanctions has generated many assets that beg to be exploited internationally.

Cyberspace greatly levels the international playing field for South African entrepreneurs – and the benefits can spread right down from the office towers of the big cities into the townships and remote villages. For example, when this book is finished I have to evaluate a cyberspace project to market beads from Africa to industrial countries, where they are becoming one of the hottest categories of collecting and crafts hobbies. That's an information age reverse flow twist on the earliest medium for international commerce!

Trading beads in cyberspace can be both viable commercially as well as a socially worthwhile project. Bead workers and collectors have several groups online, and *PhoneDisc*'s new CD-ROM with some nine million American business addresses provides very low cost access to hundreds of speciality bead shops, as well as to stores serving craft workers. Combining the two electronic media with conventional "snail mail" can open the overseas market directly to rural South Africans living in remote towns and villages who can supply collector beads for the premium side of the market, as well as add value through their traditional craft skills to more ordinary beads assembled into jewellery and clothing.

We can eliminate many of the costs of distribution through middlemen to ensure that the hundreds of small bead shops and tens of thousands of collectors and craft workers in the USA who need beads get attractive prices and a wider range of inventory. The African suppliers get new sources of income. We can even create a facility – *a Cyberspace Bead Exchange* – to handle both

and on to the Internet service provider, OzEmail, which also provides such online services as fax, MCI and CompuServe mail, file transfer and LAN access.

Networks can be set up so that a remote user with only the radio link can operate as if hard-wired to the network. There is no need to log on for email. The system sends a new message as a quick burst of data, and the notebook beeps like a pager to say there is a new message to read. Telecom's Mobile Data Network is a digital packet data network similar to a cellular phone network, and is compatible with other digital data networks throughout Europe and Asia.

TRANSFER THOSE OLD FILES

Transferring files created years ago on now obsolete systems so that they can be used in cyberspace projects is nowhere near as difficult as it may seem. File conversion software is now much smarter than it used to be, and newer Macs can read and write DOS and Windows compatible disks. If transferring text files without needing to preserve the original formatting, then a common solution is to try a text only transfer. CPM to DOS file converter software is available online, and there are also user groups for old and new operating systems and specific hardware where expert advice is available for the asking.

If saving to disk is not a practical way of making a file physically portable, and the file cannot be sent through cyber-

routine transactions as well as special online auctions of the more valuable collector items.

One of the inspirations for this is President Mandela. When his biography went online, the Web's hypertext facilities were used to generate international exposure for South Africa by linking to information about tourism and commercial activities, as well as to disseminate culturally important information about such topics as race relations.

The important South African wine industry can participate in the wine marketing experiments taking place in cyberspace. There is a unique type of tea in South Africa called Rooibos, and a distinctively tasting chicory blend, both of which can be introduced to large potential markets online through the virtual cafes and natural foods groups springing up in cyberspace. Coffee roasters already devote considerable effort to reaching the thousands of people every day who visit cyberspace cafes; they have created a marketing communications route open to South Africa at minimal cost.

Some of the best brains in business and science are to be found in South Africa, where intellectual and commercial entrepreneurism have flourished in many areas despite – and sometimes because of – the isolation from the rest of the world. They have much knowledge to market or share freely now that their country is liberated from the confines of print communications as well as political and economic barriers.

Figure 12.2 MCI Network Communications

Dr Mark Gillman at the South African Brain Research Institute has over 15,000 case histories to share of the successful techniques he has developed for treating addictions, the world's number one health problem. This could be a far more important development in health care than Dr Chris Barnard's pioneering heart transplant operations in South Africa. Now, thanks to cyberspace, the world can hear about solutions to alcohol and nicotine addictions in detail through a communications medium able to combat the enormous opinion forming advertising and PR capabilities of drug companies and the powerful tobacco lobby which have inhibited the free flow of such information in the past.

Businesses that are socially responsible can achieve much in cyberspace to advance their commercial interests as well as the more philanthropic contributions they make to their communities. In remote South Africa there are excellent examples of this, with executives, line managers and factory floor supervisors having practical knowledge that needs to be communicated to every business school.

An outstanding example of this is Toyota SA, an entirely South African owned and operated company that has been consistently one of the most successful automotive industry enterprises in the world. Against tremendous odds, it has achieved consistently higher penetration figures across more market sectors in a fiercely competitive business environment than probably any other car and truck manufacturer anywhere else in the world. It was as much Toyota's success as political pressures that drove Ford, General Motors, Renault and other manufacturers out of the South African market in the 1980s. Renault France found to its embarrassment that at one time Toyota SA was training unskilled Zulu tribesmen to assemble Renaults to a higher quality standard than was being achieved in the French factories.

Although you may not have heard of them before, Brand Pretorious, Bert Wessels, Colin Adcock and their colleagues in the past and present Toyota SA management team can contribute enormously to the international dissemination of business knowledge through cyberspace. They have more hands-on practical experience in a wider range of real-life management situations than you learn about at vast expense in a week of typical business seminars. Already there is quality information about management issues circulating through scores of online business discussion groups, and as South African entrepre-

space by modem from one system to another, consider a direct serial to serial port connection. Almost any communications program will work on the newer receiving machine, including the standard Windows Terminal and its much more capable reincarnation in Windows '95. If the sending system cannot run a suitable communications program, try printing the file to the serial port to get it to move across.

You need to assemble the appropriate hardware to get the two serial ports to communicate with each other including a null-modem cable or a null-modem adapter with a standard cable, and any necessary gender changers and 9-pin to 25-pin converters.

157

How Much to Launch a Business in Cyberspace?

The cost of establishing the capacity to be a cyberspace business offering products and taking orders can vary from under £100 to over £100,000. At the low end you can do it yourself in a low key way, or create a really significant corporate presence on the Web or the VANs for about £1,500 and up, depending on how much you are prepared to do yourself.

The deals offered vary enormously and there are lots of virtual malls and mail order catalogues from which to choose. Monthly fees ranged from about £20 to over £2,000, but come down as competition increases. There may be a charge for the space you take up on the provider's disk storage, which should stabilise at around 50p per megabyte.

neurs come on line they will be able to contribute much, as well as learn also about markets and techniques from which they have been insulated for so long.

If we probe further into the business structure in remote South Africa, we find other cyberspace opportunities that can inspire entrepreneurs elsewhere. I wondered, in evaluating the international bead exchange concept, about the very real practical problems of bringing cyberspace access to hundreds of South African communities where personal computers are not yet commonplace. The economic and social benefits of the political changes are proving slow to reach beyond the main urban centres and, as the need for the telecottage movement in Britain has demonstrated, the spread of personal computers and modem connections to individuals and small businesses is in most countries way behind the penetration in the US.

Then I remembered that perhaps the biggest single achievement of Toyota SA has been its building of a network of some 300 independent dealers spread right across the nation. They include some of the first successful black businessmen, helped by Brand Pretorious and Bert Wessels to launch enterprises despite the obstacles created by the then government's apartheid policies.

The Toyota dealers are among the most efficient businesses in their communities, usually the most advanced in their adoption of new technology and the raising of local skills levels. Consequently, they are ideally placed to act as catalysts to bring their communities into this new information age, providing Internet gateways for bead makers, authors, artists, musicians, tourist facilities and other local enterprises. Here is an existing physical network that can provide the core resources to build a strong cybernetwork stretching from towns to cities to a national web that seamlessly stitches South Africa into the global Word Wide Web.

In such ways we have opportunities to create completely new business models for cyberspace. That South African automotive dealer network could demonstrate to the whole world that it is a model of an existing resource that can exploit Internet opportunities for economic development more effectively than the creation from scratch of the telecottages and small business initiatives which have had mixed success in Britain.

The social, as well as economic, implications are far-reaching. If you are a frustrated would-be entrepreneur living in Klerksdorp – or in thousands of other small communities in many countries – it has always seemed necessary in the past to head for the big cities or to other lands to try at least to develop your dreams. The resulting drift of skills and talented young people from such communities has been because of their frustrations at being unable to pursue their studies and careers close to home. Now the Internet brings many big city benefits and opportunities through the telephone line into homes, offices and classrooms everywhere.

As radio links to the Internet in Australia and elsewhere demonstrate, and with the introduction of new Internet voice communications, the need for telephone lines and the cost of international calls become much less inhibiting. Mains electricity is no longer a requirement either, as any personal computer can be run from batteries and inverters that can be charged by cheap solar panels, a particularly attractive proposition in sunny South Africa.

The large scale, expensive experiments like the $100-million Intercom Ontario project may grab the headlines, but entrepreneurship in cyberspace is being developed largely brick by brick by individuals and small ventures in the most unlikely places.

The most successful sites with the highest traffic charge the most. CompuServe, the world's largest online subscription service, has been getting a very high rate of renewals for its package deals which allow for displaying details of up to 100 products, including full colour images for 25 of them. That, early in 1995, was costing about £12,500 annually, plus two per cent commission on sales actually made online.

NODES FOR NOMADS

As nomadic working and telecommuting become more prevalent, so the need increases to be a major player in cyberspace wherever you may be. A first step may be the need to remain a fully functioning member of the corporate LAN. You can do this without remote-control software to dial up and operate your desktop system over the telephone. Now there is an increasing selection of remote node programs that permit you to take your network node wherever you.

Apple PowerBook portable computers have the Apple ARA program installed to permit easy access to a host network, but there are no set standards for the DOS/Windows world. The best approach is to confer with your network administrator and software supplier. IBM's LAN Distance, for example, is a good solution if the host system runs under OS/2 and the remote node has either Windows or OS/2.

"As a result of the Information Age, economies are moving away from dependency on centralised manufacturing to distributed information creation, processing, and dissemination," says Michael Strangelove, in his book *How to Advertise on the Internet* (for reviews go to **http://www.phoenix.ca/sie/**). He emphasises the often misunderstood difference between the commercial interests building the information superhighways to provide the physical telecommunications facilities used for accessing the Internet, and the unregulated free individual and entrepreneurial forces of the Net community that generate the content.

"In the old economy, information was paper-based, centralised, and isolated. In this new economy, information is digital-based, wired (networked) and decentralised (distributed) ... the emerging economic paradigm of the wired, digital Information Age removes the central means of production from the elite and places it squarely in the hands of the intellect worker. In the information age, the primary means of production is no longer the "factory" but the independent, creative mind and a $1,000 computer (an information storage and processing system) ...

"Unlike the information superhighway, the Internet democratises access to global markets. It levels the playing field of international markets. In the emerging wired, digital information paradigm, the means of distribution to thirty million Internet consumers today, and half a billion at the dawn of the third millennium, is accessible to all at an insignificant cost through the Net.

"The Net would have no significance in the old economic paradigm because it would be ineffective for distributing products and services. But in the emerging information economy it reverses temporal, spatial, production, and distribution dynamics of elitist and monopolistic systems. At the turn of the third millennium, Capitalism will have lost its main social controlling force ...

"This is the beginning of a mass exodus from the corporate world as entrepreneurs engage the power of cyberspace."

(For ordering information on *How to Advertise on the Internet*, email to **Mstrange @fonorola.net**, or go by to *Gopher* to **fonorola.net**. Michael Strangelove's interesting views and practical information about business in cyberspace are contained also in a selection of helpful free documents available on request from the same address. Stipulate the file names for the documents you require:

The Essential Internet: The Birth of Virtual Culture and Global Community (From *Online Access*, by Michael Strangelove) – File **ESSENTIAL**.

Index of the *Internet Business Journal* – File **INDEX**.

Advertising on the Internet FAQ – File **AD-FAQ**.

Directory of Internet Trainers and Consultants – File **TRAINERS**.

The *Directory of Internet Marketing and Advertising Agencies* – File **MARKET**.

The Geography of Cyberspace – File **GEO**.

The latest Windows versions of Traveling Software's renowned *LapLink* is probably the cheapest, easiest and most practical solution for mobile networking if you do not need full node capabilities. The UK contact voice number is +44 (0) 175 381 8282, with a technical support bulletin board at +44 (0) 175 379 0308. It is particularly good at transferring files quickly, and has some effective security features. Connections can be made between systems by modem, cable, or a Novell network, and it can link to multiple computers at the same time.

If you seek a Web gateway to information about portable computing, radio phones, and other aspects of nomadic working, go to Mobile Office at **http:// www.mobileoffice.com**.

Using the Internet for Marketing: A Publisher's Secrets – File **PUBLISHER**. This is an essay that appeared in the European cyberspace magazine *WAVE*, September 1994.

VIP – *Gopher* to **gopher.fonorola.net** for the official *Internet Business Journal Gopher* archive.

Appendix I – Electronic mailing lists

Many Internet connections permit only electronic mail exchanges, but that still allows you to use the Net as a powerful research tool. Email also can be a vehicle for some discreet marketing promotions online, but you must disseminate quality information, not stray even close to the electronic equivalent of junk mail.

If you have a Net email facility, then you can participate in the cyberspace phenomenon of mailing lists. There may by now be over 5,000 of these on almost every conceivable topic. Most are free, and you can use them to participate in group discussions, or to be a more passive recipient of the information they distribute directly to the electronic mail box of every subscriber. There is also the possibility of creating your own email discussion group quickly and easily for a whole variety of objectives.

The following is but a small selection of the lists available, most coming from the venerable BITNET section of the Internet, of which the European EARN is a part. BITNET is not getting a lot of media attention amidst all the hype for the World Wide Web, but it is a unique resource where a cyberspace entrepreneur can track down expertise on almost every subject under the sun – from defrocked priests to nuclear physics!

This listing contains sources that can provide additional infomation on the main topics covered in this book, contacts and data on a wide range of business topics, groups that can enhance such cyberspace business skills as technical writing and multimedia creation, places with the potential to generate input and find buyers, and some surprising activities to illustrate the enormous variety of academic, scientific and business activites on line.

To find more listings, you can download the latest List-of-Lists by FTP to **ftp.nisc.sri.com**, or by email to **LISTSERV@BITNIC.cren.net**. Also get the interim updates contained in *New-List*, by emailing to **listserv @ndsuvm1.bitnet**.

You subscribe to a list by sending an email message to its administrative address (which may well include the word *"request"* in it). If your access provider software permits, leave the subject heading blank, and for the message type *subscribe yourfirstname yoursecondname.*

You should receive a response very quickly because it is probably automated. The first message will give you any further instructions for that particular list. Those instructions will tell you also how to end your subscription. Usually you send a message saying: *unsubscribe yourfirst name yoursecondname.* Many problems can be resolved by sending a message containing *help,* which should generate a response about access procedures.

Do take a few moments to scan the following addresses – they may spark ideas for entrepeneurial ventures, or new ways to seek solutions to a variety of business research and development problems. Just a glance should show you that it is wise not to assume that there is not at least one special interest group online that you can use beneficially for even the most way-out business concept.

Remember that lists come and go – some stay around for years, others only for a few weeks. A list can be started for a specific topic, to tie in with a conference – or actually to conduct one online. Here are some of the most versatile and information-rich communities in cyberspace.

A

AAASEST	AAASEST@GWUVM.BITNET
	Perspectives on Ethical Issues in Science and Technology
AAASHRAN	AAASHRAN@GWUVM.BITNET
	AAAS Human Rights Action Network
AACSB	AACSB@UMSLVMA.BITNET
	Business School Accredidation
ACCIBD	ACCIBD@UKCC.BITNET
	ACCI – American Council on Consumer Interests
ACCRI-L	ACCRI-L@UABDPO.BITNET
	Anesthesia and Critical Care Resources on the Internet
ACCT-L	ACCT-L@ECUVM1.BITNET

Accounting Research Listserver

ACHNEWS   ACHNEWS@UCSBVM.UCSB.EDU
Newsletter of the Association for Computers and the Humanities

ADDICT-L   ADDICT-L@KENTVM.BITNET
Academic & Scholarly discussion of addiction related topics.

ADVTHE-L   ADVTHE-L@UGA.BITNET
Adventure Therapy Discussion

AE   AE@SJSUVM1.BITNET
Alternative Energy Discussion List

AGING   AGING@SUVM.BITNET
Economics and demography of aging.

AGNEWS   AGNEWS@VM.CC.PURDUE.EDU
News Service Agriculture News releases

AIBI-L   AIBI-L@UOTTAWA.BITNET
The Computerised Analysis of Biblical Texts Discussion Group

AIRCRAFT   AIRCRAFT@IUBVM.BITNET
The Aircraft Discussion List

AIRLINE   AIRLINE@CUNYVM.BITNET
The Airline List

AIRNEWS   AIRNEWS@MCGILL1.BITNET
AIRNEWS user list

ALCOHOL   ALCOHOL@LMUACAD.BITNET
Alcohol & Drug Studies

ALGAE-L   ALGAE-L@IRLEARN.BITNET
ALGAE-L : digest information on botany

ALLMUSIC   ALLMUSIC@LISTSERV.AMERICAN.EDU
Discussions on all forms of Music

ALMS-NN   ALMS-NN@UA1VM.UA.EDU
AL-MS Neural Network Discussion List

ALPINE-L   ALPINE-L@HEARN.BITNET
Cultivation and Botany of Dwarf and Alpine Plants (Rock Gardens)

ALSBNEWS   ALSBNEWS@MIAMIU.BITNET
Academy of Legal Studies in Business (ALSB) News

LSBTALK   ALSBTALK@MIAMIU.BITNET

Academy of Legal Studies in Business (ALSB) Talk

ALXFOCUS   ALXFOCUS@RUTVM1.BITNET
Alexander Library Electronic Focus Group

AMALGAM   AMALGAM@DEARN.BITNET
Mercury Poisoning from Dental Amalgam

AMCA-L   AMCA-L@MCGILL1.BITNET
Alumni and Friends of Croatian Universities

AMEND1-L   AMEND1-L@UAFSYSB.BITNET
Free Speech Discussion

AMINT-L   AMINT-L@PSUVM.BITNET
Academy of Management International

AMNESTY   AMNESTY@SUVM.BITNET
Amnesty International communicates with members

AMODLMKT   AMODLMKT@UMSLVMA.BITNET
Applied Modeling Issues in Marketing

AMPUTEE   AMPUTEE@SJUVM.BITNET
List for Amputees

ANCANACH   ANCANACH@UABDPO.BITNET
Clan Henderson Society of US & Canada

ANCIEN-L   ANCIEN-L@ULKYVM.BITNET
History of the Ancient Mediterranean

ANGLICAN   ANGLICAN@LISTSERV.AMERICAN.EDU
Anglican Mailing List

ANIME-L   ANIME-L@VTVM1.BITNET
Japanese animation news.

ANMGT-L   ANMGT-L@UNLVM.BITNET
Animal Management Discussion Forum

ANONYM-L   ANONYM-L@UCSFVM.BITNET
(Use only to send anonymous mail)

AQUARIUM   AQUARIUM@EMUVM1.BITNET
Fish and Aquaria

AQUIFER   AQUIFER@IBACSATA.BITNET
Pollution and groundwater recharge

ARCANA   ARCANA@BROWNVM.BITNET

166

Discussion and Study of the Occult

ARCITRON   ARCITRON@KENTVM.BITNET
                Architronic: The Electronic Journal of Architecture

ARTCLIPS   ARTCLIPS@SJUVM.BITNET
                Access Art-Clips Distribution List

ARTLIST   ARTLIST@LISTSERV.ARIZONA.EDU
                Discuss Issues Relevant to Contemporary Art

ART193   ART193@GWUVM.BITNET
                Fine Arts Computing Group

ASAT-STC   ASAT-STC@UNLVM.BITNET
                AG-SAT Satellite Telecommunications Coordinators

AUSTLIT   AUSTLIT@NDSUVM1.BITNET
                Austrian Literature

AUTOS-L   AUTOS-L@TRITU.BITNET
                The List For Classic And Sports Cars

AZARC-L   AZARC-L@KSUVM.BITNET
                Association of Zoos and Aquariums Research Coordinators

AZSRACAD   AZSRACAD@LISTSERV.ARIZONA.EDU
                Staying Active After Retirment

B

BALLROOM-M   BALLRM-M@MITVMA.BITNET
             Moderated Discussion List for Ballroom and Swing Dancing

BALT-L   BALT-L@UBVM.BITNET (Peered)
             Baltic Republics Discussion List

BATECH-L   BATECH-L@PSUVM.BITNET
             Technologies in Business Education

BBS-L   BBS-L@SAUPM00.BITNET
             Forum about the creation, usage and maintainance of BBSs

BEE-L   BEE-L@ALBNYVM1.BITNET
             Discussion of Bee Biology

BEER-L   BEER-L@UA1VM.UA.EDU
             Homebrew Digest Redistribution List

BEGIN-PHOTO   BEGIN-PHOTO@LISTSERV.ARIZONA.EDU
Beginning Photograpers

BEHAV-AN   BEHAV-AN@NDSUVM1.BITNET
Behaviour Analysis

BETS-L   BETS-L@UICVM.BITNET
Business Ethics Teaching Society

BILLING   BILLING@HEARN.BITNET
Chargeback of computer resources

BIOREP-L   BIOREP-L@HEARN.BITNET
Biotechnology Research in the European Union

BLIND-L   BLIND-L@UAFSYSB.BITNET
Computer Use by and for the Blind

BLKADR-L   BLKADR-L@PSUVM.BITNET
Blackadder List

BOOKTALK   BOOKTALK@NERVM.BITNET
Childrens literature and classroom use

BRAIN   BRAIN@UTORONTO.BITNET
BRAIN – Brain and Behaviour Discussion List

BRDCST-L   BRDCST-L@UNLVM.BITNET
Broadcasting Discussion List

BREAST-CANCER   BREAST-CANCER@MORGAN.UCS.MUN.CA
Breast Cancer Discussion List

BSCS-L   BSCS-L@EMUVM1.BITNET
Business School Computing Support

BSN-D   BSN-D@KENTVM.BITNET
Business Sources on the Net – Distribution List

BTECH94   BTECH94@UMSLVMA.BITNET
Business Technology

BUDDHIST   BUDDHIST@JPNTUVM0.BITNET
Forum on Indian and Buddhist Studies

BULLY-L   BULLY-L@HEARN.BITNET
Bullying and Victimisation in Schools

BUSETH-L   BUSETH-L@UBVM.BITNET
Business Ethics Computer Network

BUSFAC-L	BUSFAC-L@CMUVM.BITNET
	International Business Faculty Discussion
BUSLIB-L	BUSLIB-L@IDBSU.BITNET
	BUSLIB-L – Business Libraries Discussion List

C

C+HEALTH	C+HEALTH@IUBVM.BITNET
	The Health Effects of Computer Use
C-ALERTL	C-ALERT@JPNYITP.BITNET
	Alert by Elsevier Science Publishers
CADAM-L	CADAM-L@SUVM.BITNET
	Computer Aided Design and Manufacturing Interest Group
CADLIST	CADLIST@SUVM.BITNET
	CAD General Discussion Group
CAEDS-L	CAEDS-L@SUVM.BITNET
	Computer Aided Engineering Design (CAEDS) Interest Group
CAPSL	CAPSL@BLEKUL11.BITNET
	Discussion list on accessibility of digital documents
CARECON	CARECON@YORKVM1.BITNET
	Caribbean Economy
CATIA-L	CATIA-L@SUVM.BITNET
	Computer Aided Three Dimensional Interactive Applications
CBEHIGH	CBEHIGH@BLEKUL11.BITNET
	Computer Based Education in higher education
CBW-L	CBW-L@UMINN1.BITNET
	Conference on Basic Writing
CDROMLAN	CDROMLAN@IDBSU.BITNET
	CD-ROM products in LAN environments
CENASIA	CENASIA@MCGILL1.BITNET
	Former Soviet Republic – Central Asia Political Discussion
CENTAM-L	CENTAM-L@UBVM.BITNET
	Central America Discussion List
CEPES-L	CEPES-L@HEARN.BITNET
	European Centre for Higher Education

CERES-L CERES-L@WVNVM.BITNET
Collaborative Environments for Conserving Earth Resources

CERRO-L CERRO-L@AEARN.BITNET
Central European Regional Research Organization

CESSDA-L CESSDA-L@HEARN.BITNET
Council of European Social Science Data Archives (CESSDA)

CFS-WIRE CFS-WIRE@SJUVM.BITNET
Chronic Fatigue Syndrome NEWSWIRE

CHAETHIC CHAETHIC@HEARN.BITNET
Policies, Ethics and electronic synchronous communication

CHAUCER CHAUCER@UICVM.BITNET
Chaucer Discussion Group

CHEMCOM CHEMCOM@UBVM.BITNET
Chemistry in the Community Discussion List

CHEMCONF CHEMCONF@UMDD.BITNET
Conferences on Chemistry Research and Education

CHEME-L CHEME-L@ULKYVM.BITNET
Chemical Engineering List

CHILDLIT CHILDLIT@RUTVM1.BITNET
Children's Literature: Criticism and Theory

CHILDMUS CHILDMUS@RICEVM1.RICE.EDU
CHILDMUS – A Forum for Children's Museum Professionals

CHINA-NN CHINA-NN@ASUACAD.BITNET (Peered)
China News Digest (Global News)

CHINANET CHINANET@TAMVM1.TAMU.EDU
CHINANET: Networking In China

CHMINF-L CHMINF-L@IUBVM.BITNET
Chemical information sources discussion

CIMTLK-L CIMTLK-L@QUCDN.BITNET
Metallurgy Club

CINEMA-L CINEMA-L@LISTSERV.AMERICAN.EDU
Discussions on all forms of Cinema

CIVIL-L CIVIL-L@UNBVM1.BITNET
Civil Engineering Reasearch & Education

CLASSM-L   CLASSM-L@BROWNVM.BITNET
              Classical Music List

CLAYART   CLAYART@UKCC.BITNET
              Ceramic Arts Discussion List

CLINALRT   CLINALRT@UMAB.BITNET
              Clinical Alerts from the US National Institutes of Health

CMC   CMC@RPITSVM.BITNET
              Computer Mediated Communication

CMDNET-L   CMDNET-L@KSUVM.BITNET
              Conflict Management Division List

COGS   COGS@UICVM.BITNET
              Computing on a Grand Scale List

COMANDO   COMANDO@NDSUVM1.BITNET
              Mandolin Playing and Enjoyment

COMCRI-L   COMCRI-L@PLTUMK11.BITNET
              Computer related crime

COMDEV   COMDEV@RPITSVM.BITNET
              Communications & international development

COMICW-L   COMICW-L@UNLVM.BITNET
              Comic Writers Workshop

COMLAW-L   COMLAW-L@UALTAVM.BITNET
              Computers and Legal Education

COMM-L   COMM-L@SAKAAU03.BITNET
              Communications/Modems/BBSs Discussion List

COMSOC-L   COMSOC-L@LISTSERV.AMERICAN.EDU
              Computers and Society ARPA Digest

CONSIM-L   CONSIM-L@LISTSERV.UNI-C.DK
              Conflict simulation games

CONSLINK   CONSLINK@SIVM.BITNET
              CONSLINK – The Conservation Network

CONSSCI   CONSSCI@UKCC.BITNET
              Family and Consumer Economists, Consumer Educators

CPSR   CPSR@GWUVM.BITNET
              Computer Professionals for Social Responsibility

CRYPTO-L   CRYPTO-L@JPNTUVM0.BITNET
               Forum on Cryptology and Related Mathematics

CTCIV   CTCIV@TEMPLEVM.BITNET
               Court Technology Conference IV

CYBERIA   CYBERIA@EMUVM1.BITNET
               Medieval Electronic Journal Discussion

D

DAIRY-L   DAIRY-L@UMDD.BITNET
               Dairy Discussion List.

DE-CONF   DE-CONF@MORGAN.UCS.MUN.CA
               Committee on Computer Conferencing in Distance Education

DE-L   DE-L@PDOMAIN.UWINDSOR.CA
               Forum for Instructors of Distance Education

DEAF-MAGAZINE DEAF-MAG@LISTSERV.CLARK.NET
               Deaf Magazine

DERR-L   DERR-L@CMUVM.BITNET
               Distance Education Research Roundtable

DEVEL-L   DEVEL-L@LISTSERV.AMERICAN.EDU
               Technology Transfer in International Development

DGTLCLAS   DGTLCLAS@MCGILL1.BITNET
               Digital and Multi-Media for instructional purposes

DIABETES   DIABETES@IRLEARN.BITNET
               International Research Project on Diabetes

DIALIN   DIALIN@INDYCMS.BITNET
               For questions with the new dialups

DICKNS-L   DICKNS-L@UCSBVM.UCSB.EDU
               Charles Dickens Forum

DISARM-D   DISARM-D@ALBNYVM1.BITNET
               Disarmament Discussion Monthly Digest

DITTO-LIST   DITTO-L@AWIIMC12.BITNET
               Data Interfile Transfer, Testing and Operations Utility

DOROTHYL   DOROTHYL@KENTVM.BITNET
               Mystery Literature E-conference

DPMAST-L   DPMAST-L@CMSUVMB.BITNET
Data Processing Management Association

DR-ED   DR-ED@MSU.EDU
Medical Education Research and Development

DRP-L   DRP-L@MARIST.BITNET
Disaster Recovery Plan for Computing Services

DRUGABUS   DRUGABUS@UMAB.BITNET
Drug Abuse Education Information and Research

E

E-POETRY   E-POETRY@UBVM.BITNET
Electronic Poetry Distribution List

E_INVEST   E_INVEST@TEMPLEVM.BITNET
Electronic Journal of Investing

EARLI-AE   EARLI-AE@HEARN.BITNET
European Association for Research on Learning and Instruction

ECDM   ECDM@PDOMAIN.UWINDSOR.CA
Environmentally Conscious Design & Manufacturing List

ECONOMY   ECONOMY@UOTTAWA.BITNET
Economic Problems in Less Developed Countries

EDESIGN   EDESIGN@UOTTAWA.BITNET
Electronic Design and Development

EDP513   EDP513@LISTSERV.ARIZONA.EDU
Research in Educational Technologies

EDRES-DB   EDRES-DB@UNBVM1.BITNET
Educational Resources on the Internet – Database

EDRES-L   EDRES-L@UNBVM1.BITNET
Educational Resources on the Internet

EDUTEL   EDUTEL@RPITSVM.BITNET
Education and information technologies

EEC-L   EEC-L@LISTSERV.AMERICAN.EDU
European Training and Technology List

EEHED-L   EEHED-L@YALEVM.BITNET
Eastern European Higher Education List (EEHED-L)

EJVC-L   EJVC-L@KENTVM.BITNET
Electronic Journal on Virtual Culture

ELAG-L   ELAG-L@HEARN.BITNET
Library Automation in Europe

ELETQM-L   ELETQM-L@BRUFU.BITNET
Open Discussion Forum for the Electrochemistry Community

ELPKG-L   ELPKG-L@BINGVMB.BITNET
Electronics Packaging Forum

EM_TRANS   EM_TRANS@UICVM.BITNET
Emerging Methods in Transportation

EMAILMA   EMAILMAN@VTVM1.BITNET
Learning about accessing electronic information

EMLTEACH   EMLTEACH@INDYCMS.BITNET
Email in Teaching Discussion Group

EMUSIC-L   EMUSIC-L@LISTSERV.AMERICAN.EDU
Electronic Music Discussion List

ENGL8156   ENGL8156@GWUVM.BITNET
Creative Writing Sections 15 and 16

ENVINF-L   ENVINF-L@HEARN.BITNET
List for Environmental Information

EOAA-L   EOAA-L@WVNVM.BITNET
Equal Opportunity/Affirmative Action

ERECS-L   ERECS-L@ALBNYVM1.BITNET
Management & Preservation of Electronic Records

ERUDITIO   ERUDITIO@ASUACAD.BITNET
Knowledge through electronic communications

ET-PERTH   ET-PERTH@SEARN.BITNET
Technology Transfer in Remote Communities

ETHNET-L   ETHNET-L@YSUB.BITNET
Irish and British Ethnographic Research List

EURACT   EURACT@BLEKUL11.BITNET
European academy of teachers in general practice

EURACTCL   EURACTCL@BLEKUL11.BITNET
Council of the European academy of teachers in general practice

EURO-LEX   EURO-LEX@DEARN.BITNET
European Legal Information Exchange List

EV   EV@SJSUVM1.BITNET
Electric Vehicle Discussion List

EWM   EWM@ICNUCEVM.BITNET
European Women in Mathematics

EXLIBRIS   EXLIBRIS@RUTVM1.BITNET
Rare Books and Special Collections Forum

EXOTIC-L   EXOTIC-L@PLEARN.BITNET
Discussion group for exotic pet bird owners.

EXT-MEAT   EXT-MEAT@UMINN1.BITNET
Meat Specialists Extension Group Discussion

F

FAO-INFO   FAO-INFO@IRMFAO01.BITNET
The Food and Agriculture Organization INFO List.

FAOLIST   FAOLIST@IRMFAO01.BITNET
Food and Agriculture Organization Open Discussion List

FARM-MGT   FARM-MGT@NDSUVM1.BITNET
Farm Management

FATHER-L   FATHER-L@UMINN1.BITNET
Importance of Fathers in Childrens Lives

FEEGI   FEEGI@RICEVM1.RICE.EDU
Forum on European Expansion and Global Interaction

FELINE-L   FELINE-L@PSUVM.BITNET
Discussion forum for Cat fanciers

FICTION   FICTION@PSUVM.BITNET
Fiction Writers Workshop

FILM-L   FILM-L@ITESMVF1.BITNET
Film making and reviews list.

FINE-ART   FINE-ART@RUTVM1.BITNET (Peered)
Fine-Art Forum

FINVOL-L   FINVOL-L@VTVM1.BITNET
VCES Satellite Training for Financial Volunteers

FIPEFS-L   FIPEFS-L@UICVM.BITNET
Fiscal Issues, Policy and Education Finance

FLTEACH ·   FLTEACH@UBVM.BITNET
Foreign Language Teaching Forum

FLYFISH   FLYFISH@UKCC.BITNET
Fly Fishing Digest

FOOD-NET   FOOD-NET@UMINN1.BITNET
Exchange of Information about Food Safety & Nutrition

FOODWINE   FOODWINE@CMUVM.BITNET
Discussion List for Food and Wine

FORENSIC   FORENSIC@UABDPO.BITNET
Forensics List

FOREST   FOREST@FIPORT.BITNET
Forest research and studies

G

GAP   GAP@SUVM.BITNET
Prevention, and AIDS awareness group

GARDENS   GARDENS@UKCC.BITNET
Gardens & Gardening

GAY-LIBN   GAY-LIBN@USCVM.BITNET
The Gay/Lesbian/Bisexual Librarians Network

GC-L   GC-L@URIACC.BITNET
GC-L, Global Classroom: International Students Email Debate

GCI-L   GCI-L@DEARN.BITNET
Chinese student group in Germany

GEN-DE-L   GEN-DE-L@RZ.UNI-KARLSRUHE.DE
German Genealogy

GEN-NED   GEN-NED@HEARN.BITNET
Human Genetics Nederland

GENDER   GENDER@RPITSVM.BITNET
Study of communication and gender

GEODESIC   GEODESIC@UBVM.BITNET
List for the discussion of Buckminster Fuller's works

GEOED-L   GEOED-L@UWF.BITNET
Geology and Earth Science Education Discussion Forum

GEOGABLE   GEOGABLE@UKCC.BITNET
Issues relating to geography and disabilities

GERINET   GERINET@UBVM.BITNET
Geriatric Health Care Discussion Group

GINLIST   GINLIST@MSU.EDU
Global Interact Network

GISBUS-L   GISBUS-L@ECUVM1.BITNET
Geographic Information Systems for Business and Management

GLB-HLT   GLB-HLT@UICVM.BITNET
Global Forum on Medical Education and Practice

GLOBALMC   GLOBALMC@TAMVM1.TAMU.EDU
Global Marketing Consortium Discussion List

GLOBMKT   GLOBMKT@UKCC.BITNET
Applied Global Marketing

GLOMOD-L   GLOMOD-L@UHCCVM.BITNET
The Global Modeling Forum

GLOSAS   GLOSAS@MCGILL1.BITNET
Global Systems Analysis and Simulation Assoc.

GOETHE   GOETHE@LISTSERV.DARTMOUTH.EDU
Information concerning the Goethe-Institut Munich

GOLF-L   GOLF-L@UBVM.BITNET
The Golf Discussion List

GUNDOG-L   GUNDOG-L@TAMVM1.TAMU.EDU
Gun Dog discussion list

GUTNBERG   GUTNBERG@UIUCVMD.BITNET
Project Gutenberg Email List

H

H-ASIA   H-ASIA@MSU.EDU
H-Net list for Asian History and Culture

H-FRANCE   H-FRANCE@UICVM.BITNET
H-Net History of France List

H-LABOR H-LABOR@MSU.EDU
H-Net Labor History discussion list

H-MMEDIA H-MMEDIA@MSU.EDU
Multimedia and New Technologies in Humanities

H-NZ-OZ H-NZ-OZ@MSU.EDU
H-Net New Zealand & Australia Discussion list

H-RURAL H-RURAL@MSU.EDU
H-Net list for discussion of Rural & Agricultural issues

H-SAE H-SAE@MSU.EDU
H-Net List for the Society for Anthropology of Europe

H-WAR H-WAR@KSUVM.BITNET
H-Net Military History Discussion List

H-WOMEN H-WOMEN@MSU.EDU
H-NET List for Women's History

H-WORLD H-WORLD@MSU.EDU
H-NET List for World History

HACKERS HACKERS@PLEARN.BITNET
Hackers discusion list

HAM-L HAM-L@TREARN.BITNET
HAM Radio Discussion List

HARMA-PS HARMA-PS@IRLEARN.BITNET
HARMA-PS For Agricultural Statisticians from the EU Periphery

HEALTH-L HEALTH-L@IRLEARN.BITNET
International Discussion on Health Research

HEP2-L HEP2-L@LISTSERV.AMERICAN.EDU
Marketing with Technology (MarTech)

HERB HERB@TREARN.BITNET
Medicinal and Aromatic Plants discussion list

HIWAYMEN HIWAYMEN@INDYCMS.BITNET
Discussion of the Highwaymen's music

HLT-NET HLT-NET@HEARN.BITNET
Initiatives in innovation in health professions

HMEDRSCH HMEDRSCH@ETSUADMN.BITNET
Home Education Research Discussion List

HMG-MOLGEN   HMG-MOLG@HEARN.BITNET
              Human Molecular Genetics

HOMEFIX   HOMEFIX@TREARN.BITNET
              Home Appliance/Improvement Discussion List

HOMESAT   HOMESAT@NDSUVM1.BITNET
              HOMESAT – Home Satellite Technology

HONDA-L   HONDA-L@BROWNVM.BITNET
              Honda Digest

HORROR   HORROR@IUBVM.BITNET
              Horror in Film and Literature

HORSEMAN   HORSEMAN@UCBCMSA.BITNET
              Natural Horsemanship Discussion Group

HOTEL-L   HOTEL-L@MIZZOU1.BITNET
              Hotel and Restaurant Educators Discussion

HOUNDS-L   HOUNDS-L@KENTVM.BITNET
              Discussion of Sherlock Holmes Literature

HPSCHD-L   HPSCHD-L@ALBNYVM1.BITNET
              Harpsichords and Related Topics

HR-INFO   HR-INFO@HARVARDA.BITNET
              Human Resources Information Discussion List

HRACING   HRACING@ULKYVM.BITNET
              Horse Racing discussion

HUMEVO-L   HUMEVO-L@PSUORVM.BITNET
              Human Evolutionary Research Discussion List

HUMOR   HUMOR@UGA.BITNET
              UGA Humor List

HYDROGEN   HYDROGEN@URIACC.BITNET
              Hydrogen as an alternative fuel

HYPERCRD   HYPERCRD@MSU.EDU
              Mac Hypercard Discussion List

H2O-VW   H2O-VW@SJSUVM1.BITNET
              Water-Cooled Volkswagen Discussion List

I

IAAE-L IAAE-L@BRLNCC.BITNET
International Association of Agricultural Economists Forum

IAC-L IAC-L@IRLEARN.BITNET
Irish Academic Computing

IAP IAP@IRISHVMA.BITNET
Small Internet Access Providers

IAPADV IAPADV@IUBVM.BITNET
International Arctic Project Adventure

I-IBMPC I-IBMPC@UIUCVMD.BITNET
IBM PC discussions

IBM-MAIN IBM-MAIN@UA1VM.UA.EDU
IBM Mainframe Discussion List

IBSCG IBSCG@MIAMIU.BITNET
International Business School Computer User's Group

ICADD ICADD@ASUACAD.BITNET
International Committee for Accessible Document Design

ICEE94-L ICEE94-L@UGA.BITNET
International Conference on Environmental Ethics

ICEN-L ICEN-L@IUBVM.BITNET
ICEN-L International Career and Employment Network

ICIS-L ICIS-L@UGA.BITNET
International Conference on Information Systems

IDFORUM IDFORUM@YORKVM1.BITNET
Industrial Design Forum

IJGT-ABSTRACTS IJGT-L@TAUNIVM.BITNET
International Journal of Game Theory Abstracts

IMAMEDIA IMAMEDIA@UMDD.BITNET
Compatability of Multimedia Applications

IMO-L IMO-L@NOBIVM.BITNET
International Management Operations.

INDIA INDIA@CUNYVM.BITNET
The India List

INFORM-L INFORM-L@VMTECSLP.BITNET
Cultural Informatica en Mexico y America Latina

INFOSYS   INFOSYS@LISTSERV.AMERICAN.EDU
Newsletter for Information Systems

INHEALTH   INHEALTH@RPITSVM.BITNET
International Health Communication

INNS-L   INNS-L@UMDD.BITNET
International Neural Network Society

INSEA-L   INSEA-L@UNBVM1.BITNET
International Society for Education Through Art

INTCAR-L   INTCAR-L@LISTSERV.AMERICAN.EDU
Internationally-Oriented Computer-Assisted Reporting List

INTDEV-L   INTDEV-L@URIACC.BITNET
International Development and Global Education

INTER-ED   INTER-ED@UMINN1.BITNET
Forum for International Education

INTER-EU   INTER-EU@HEARN.BITNET
Discussion list for International Educators in Europe

INTERCUL   INTERCUL@RPITSVM.BITNET
Study of intercultural communication

INTERPER   INTERPER@RPITSVM.BITNET
Interpersonal/small group communication

IOOB-L   IOOB-L@UGA.BITNET
Industrial Psychology

IP-NSP-ITA   IP-NSP@ICNUCEVM.BITNET
List of the Internet Network Service Providers in Italy

IRE-L   IRE-L@MIZZOU1.BITNET
Discussion of Investigative Reporting Techniques

IRELAND   IRELAND@RUTVM1.BITNET
Discussion about news about Ireland

IRISHLAW   IRISHLAW@IRLEARN.BITNET
Irish and N. Irish Law

ISACA-L   ISACA-L@MITVMA.BITNET
Information Systems Audit and Control Association List

ISCPES   ISCPES@SJSUVM1.BITNET
International Society for Comparative Physical Education & Sport

ISLMECON	ISLMECON@SAIRTI00.BITNET	
	ISLAMIC ECONOMICS DISCUSSION LIST.	
ISM_LSERV	ISM_LSERV@MTC5.MID.TEC.SC.US	
	Tech Information Systems Managers' List Server	
ISSC	ISSC@CUVMC.BITNET	
	Information Systems Security Committee	
IT-TEAM	IT-TEAM@CFRVM.BITNET	
	I.T. Management/Facilitative Leadership Forum	
ITCOLLAB	ITCOLLAB@HARVARDA.BITNET	
	Collaborative Study on Academic Information Technology	
ITD-JNL	ITD-JNL@SJUVM.BITNET	
	Information and Technology for the Disabled	
ITEC1-L	ITEC1-L@ECUVM1.BITNET	
	Industrial Technologist information and issues	

J

JAPAN	JAPAN@PUCC.BITNET
	Japanese Business and Economics Network
JAZZ-L	JAZZ-L@BROWNVM.BITNET
	Jazz Lovers' List
JEI-L	JEI-L@UMDD.BITNET
	Technology in Education Mailing List members
JOB-TECH	JOB-TECH@UICVM.BITNET
	Technology and Employment Conference
JOBPLACE	JOBPLACE@UKCC.BITNET
	Self Directed Job Search Techniques and Placement

K

KAWALIST	KAWALIST@JPNIMRTU.BITNET
	Forum on Materials Design by Computer

L

LABOR-L	LABOR-L@YORKVM1.BITNET
	Forum on Labour in the Global Economy

LAMC-L   LAMC-L@IUBVM.BITNET
            Academic Discussion of Latin American Music

LANET-L   LANET-L@LATECH.BITNET
            La Net Discussion Group

LANMAN-L   LANMAN-L@NIHLIST.BITNET
            MS *Windows* NT Adv Server and LAN Man Discussion List

LARCH-L   LARCH-L@SUVM.BITNET
            Landscape Architecture Electronic Forum

LASMED-L   LASMED-L@TAUNIVM.BITNET
            Laser Medicine

LDRSHP   LDRSHP@IUBVM.BITNET
            Discussion list about all aspects of leadership.

LEADERS1   LEADERS1@TAMVM1.TAMU.EDU
            Leadership Techniques, Practice, & Practitioners

LIBADMIN   LIBADMIN@UMAB.BITNET
            Library Administration and Management

LITHOARC   LITHOARC@UNBVM1.BITNET
            Desktop Publishing, Printing and Binding Archive

LITHOBID   LITHOBID@UNBVM1.BITNET
            Desktop Publishing, Printing and Binding Tenders

M

MAC-L   MAC-L@YALEVM.BITNET
            Macintosh News and Information

MACHRDWR   MACHRDWR@LISTSERV.DARTMOUTH.EDU
            Macintosh hardware and related perpherials

MACMULTI   MACMULTI@FCCJ.BITNET
            Macintosh Multimedia Discussion List

MACNET-L   MACNET-L@YALEVM.BITNET
            Macintosh Networking Issues

MAPS-L   MAPS-L@UGA.BITNET
            Maps and Air Photo Systems Forum

MARKET-L   MARKET-L@NERVM.BITNET
            For the Discussion of Marketing

MASSCOMM   MASSCOMM@RPITSVM.BITNET
Mass communications and new technologies

MAT-DSGN   MAT-DSGN@JPNTUVM0.BITNET
Forum on Materials Design by Computer

MEANING   MEANING@ASUACAD.BITNET
The meaning of life and other weighty contemplations

MEATQUAL   MEATQUAL@ICNUCEVM.BITNET
MEATQUAL – Residues in meat: First teleconference

MEDIAWEB   MEDIAWEB@TEMPLEVM.BITNET
Film/Video Web sites discussion

MEDIEV-L   MEDIEV-L@UKANVM.BITNET
Medieval History

MEDNETS   MEDNETS@NDSUVM1.BITNET
MEDNETS Medical Telecommunications Networks

MEDSCI-L   MEDSCI-L@BROWNVM.BITNET
Medieval Science Discussion List

MENOPAUS   MENOPAUS@PSUHMC.BITNET
Menopause Discussion List

MICAT-L   MICAT-L@FREESIDE.NRM.SE
Musical Instrument Conservation and Technology

MODBRITS   MODBRITS@KENTVM.BITNET
Modern British and Irish Literature: 1895-1955

MORRIS   MORRIS@SUVM.BITNET
Morris Dancing Discussion List

MSLIST-L   MSLIST-L@TECHNION.BITNET
Multiple Sclerosis Discussion/Support

MSMAIL-L   MSMAIL-L@YALEVM.BITNET
Microsoft Mail Discussion List

MUCID-L   MUCID-L@BRUFU.BITNET
Music and Cultural Industry Discussion List

MUD-L   MUD-L@TREARN.BITNET
Multi-User Dungeons and Other
Simulated Real-Time Environments

MUFC   MUFC@IUBVM.BITNET
Manchester United Football Club (soccer)

N

NABS-L   NABS-L@UCSBVM.UCSB.EDU
               National Alliance of Blind Students' Symposium

NETSCAPE   NETSCAPE@IRLEARN.BITNET
               Discussion of Netscape

NEWINT-L   NEWINT-L@HARVARDA.BITNET
               New Approaches to International Law Discussion List

NEWTON   NEWTON-L@OCLC.ORG
               Newton Support Discussion Forum

NEXT-L   NEXT-L@BROWNVM.BITNET
               NeXT Computer List

NORDBALT   NORDBALT@SEARN.BITNET
               Networking between Nordic and Baltic countries

NOTES-L   NOTES-L@OSUVM1.BITNET
               Lotus Notes Interest Group

NOVELS-L   NOVELS-L@PSUVM.BITNET
               Novel Writers Workshop

NPC-L   NPC-L@UBVM.BITNET
               USA National Press Club List

NURSENET   NURSENET@UTORONTO.BITNET
               NURSENET – A Global Forum for Nursing Issues

NYSLUX-L   NYSLUX-L@UBVM.BITNET
               NY Consortium for Model European Community Simulation

O

OCD-L   OCD-L@MARIST.BITNET
               Obsessive Compulsive Disorder List

ODP-L   ODP-L@TAMVM1.TAMU.EDU
               Ocean Drilling Program Open Discussion List

ONE-L   ONE-L@CLVM.BITNET
               Organization and the Natural Environment

ONLINE-L   ONLINE-L@LISTSERV.CLARK.NET
               In, Around and Online

ONO-NET	ONO-NET@UMINN1.BITNET
	Resource for those interested in the works of Yoko Ono
OSCE	OSCE@BLEKUL11.BITNET
	Organization for Security and Cooperation in Europe (OSCE)
OS2USERS	OS2USERS@MCGILL1.BITNET
	OS/2 Users Discussion List
OTRU-NET	OTRU-NET@UTORONTO.BITNET
	OTRU-NET – Tobacco Research Network

P

PACKRND	PACKRND@NDSUVM1.BITNET
	Packaging Research and Development
PACS-L	PACS-L@UHUPVM1.UH.EDU
	Public-Access Computer Systems Forum
PARKINSN	PARKINSN@UTORONTO.BITNET
	Parkinson's Disease – Information Exchange Network
PCBUILD	PCBUILD@TSCVM.BITNET
	Building PCs
PCSERV-L	PCSERV-L@UALTAVM.BITNET
	Public domain software servers
PCSUPT-L	PCSUPT-L@YALEVM.BITNET
	Forum for the discussion of PC user support issues
PEDIATRIC-SLEEP	PEDSLEEP@TAUNIVM.BITNET
	Pediatric Sleep List
PERFORM	PERFORM@IUBVM.BITNET
	PERFORM – Medieval Performing Arts
PETS-L	PETS-L@ITESMVF1.BITNET
	Domestic animal care and education list.
PHIL-LIT	PHIL-LIT@TAMVM1.TAMU.EDU
	Electronic Symposium on Philosophy and Literature
PHILCOMM	PHILCOMM@RPITSVM.BITNET
	Philosophy of communication
PHOTOTUJ	PHOTOTUJ@TEMPLEVM.BITNET
	Photojournalism discussion

POET-L	POET-L@GSUVM1.BITNET	Poetry issues
POETRY-W	POETRY-W@PSUVM.BITNET	Poetry Workshops
POWER-PC	POWER-PC@UGA.BITNET	IBM Power PC Discussion
PREVIEW	PREVIEW@RPITSVM.BITNET	Current research in human communication
PRFORUM	PRFORUM@INDYCMS.BITNET	PR and Corp Comm / Academics and Professionals
PRIMENJI	PRIMENJI@UKCC.BITNET	UK's Prime-NJI Emulator
PRINTS-L	PRINTS-L@UKANVM.BITNET	Study of historical & contemporary prints
PROCUR-B	PROCUR-B@OSUVM1.BITNET	Commerce Business Daily – Procurement
PUBRADIO	PUBRADIO@IDBSU.BITNET	Public Radio Discussion Group

Q

QUAKER-P	QUAKER-P@UIUCVMD.BITNET	Quaker peace and social justice issues
QUAKERS	QUAKERS@LISTSERV.ARIZONA.EDU	Crisis Management for Universities
QUEST	QUEST@NDSUVM1.BITNET	Quality, Environment, Safety in Management

R

RA-L	RA-L@TREARN.BITNET	Remote Access BBS Software
RALLY-L	RALLY-L@GUVM.BITNET	The Road Rallyists' Worldwide Discussion/News List
RAT-TALK	RAT-TALK@HEARN.BITNET	Research Animals Topics discussion forum

RC_WORLD	RC_WORLD@INDYCMS.BITNET Respiratory Care Professionals World Forum
RE-FORUM	RE-FORUM@UTARLVM1.BITNET Real Estate Forum
REACH-L	REACH-L@UICVM.BITNET Resident Experts are Convenient Help
RECYCLE	RECYCLE@UMAB.BITNET Recycling in Practice
REED-L	REED-L@UTORONTO.BITNET REED-L: Records of Early English Drama Discussion
RENAIS-L	RENAIS-L@ULKYVM.BITNET Early Modern History – Renaissance
RENDANCE	RENDANCE@MORGAN.UCS.MUN.CA Renaissance Dance Mailing List
RES-COMP	RES-COMP@NKI.BITNET Research Computing Forum
RESADM-L	RESADM-L@ALBNYDH2.BITNET Research Administration Discussion Group
REVENUE	REVENUE@INDYCMS.BITNET Public Discussion: Efficiency and Revenue Enhancement
REVIEWS	REVIEWS@VTVM1.BITNET Forum for Hardware & Software Reviews
RHETNT-L	RHETNT-L@MIZZOU1.BITNET CyberJournal for Rhetoric and Writing
RHETORIC	RHETORIC@RPITSVM.BITNET Rhetoric, social movements, persuasion
RIBO-L	RIBO-L@URIACC.BITNET German/English discussion group
ROCK-ART	ROCK-ART@ASUACAD.BITNET Rock Art Discussion and Information
ROCKLIST	ROCKLIST@KENTVM.BITNET Academic Discussion of Popular Music
RRA-L	RRA-L@KENTVM.BITNET Romance Readers Anonymous

RURSOC-L	RURSOC-L@UKCC.BITNET	Rural Sociology Discussion List
RUSAG-L	RUSAG-L@UMDD.BITNET	Russian Agriculture

S

SANTC-L	SANTC-L@UGA.BITNET	Sustainable Agriculture & Natural Resource Management -
SCCE-L	SCCE-L@PLTUMK11.BITNET	Supercomputing in Central Europe.
SCCIM	SCCIM@SIVM.BITNET	Scientific Computing & Collections Information Management
SCIFRAUD	SCIFRAUD@ALBNYVM1.BITNET	Discussion of Fraud in Science
SCINEWS	SCINEWS@VM.CC.PURDUE.EDU	News Service Science News releases
SCIT-BIB	SCIT-BIB@QUCDN.BITNET	Studies in Communication and Information Technology Bibliography
SCIT-L	SCIT-L@QUCDN.BITNET	Studies in Communication and Information Technology
SCOBA	SCOBA@UMSLVMA.BITNET	School of Business Test List
SCREEN-L	SCREEN-L@UA1VM.UA.EDU	Film and TV Studies Discussion List
SCRG	SCRG@MSU.EDU	Sociocultural Research Group
SCRIB-L	SCRIB-L@HEARN.BITNET	Handwriting Production, Recognition, Reading,Education
SCRNWRIT	SCRNWRIT@TAMVM1.TAMU.EDU	Screen Writing Discussion List
SCUBA-L	SCUBA-L@BROWNVM.BITNET	Scuba diving discussion list
SEARCH	SEARCH@GWUVM.BITNET	World-Wide Discussion of Future Search Technologies

SEASIA-L   SEASIA-L@MSU.EDU
                  Southeast Asia Discussion List

SECURITY   SECURITY@MARIST.BITNET (Peered)
                  Security Digest

SEXTALK   SEXTALK@TAMVM1.TAMU.EDU
                  Intellectual Discussion on Issues Related to Sexuality

SFLOVERS   SFLOVERS@RUTVM1.BITNET
                  SF enthusiasts

SHADOWRN   SHADOWRN@HEARN.BITNET
                  Discussion of the Fantasy game ShadowRun

SHADOWTK   SHADOWTK@HEARN.BITNET
                  Interactive ShadowRun Fiction.

SHAKSPER   SHAKSPER@UTORONTO.BITNET
                  Shakespeare Electronic Conference

SHARP-L   SHARP-L@IUBVM.BITNET
                  Society for the History of Authorship, Reading & Publishing

SIEGE   SIEGE@MORGAN.UCS.MUN.CA
                  Medieval Siege Weaponry List

SIG-QUAL   SIG-QUAL@MIAMIU.BITNET
                  NCTE SIG Qualitative Research in Writing

SIIN-L   SIIN-L@UNBVM1.BITNET
                  Inst. of Island Studies-Small Islands InfoNet

SIUCHELP   SIUCHELP@SIUCVMB.BITNET
                  Information Technology Help Desk Question & Answer List

SOAP-L   SOAP-L@UHCCVM.BITNET
                  Student Opportunities for Academic Publishing Forum

SOCCER-L   SOCCER-L@UKCC.BITNET
                  Soccer Boosters List

SOCNETW2   SOCNETW2@FRMOP11.BITNET
                  2nd European Conference on Social Networks

SOCORG-K   SOCORG-K@UTORONTO.BITNET
                  Social Organization of Knowledge Discussion & Data Exchange

SOCREF-L   SOCREF-L@URIACC.BITNET
                  Discussion of Topics for Soccer Referees

SONGTALK   SONGTALK@PEACH.EASE.LSOFT.COM
             Songwriters Talking About Their Work

SOREHAND   SOREHAND@UCSFVM.BITNET
             Discussion of Carpal Tunnel Syndrome, Tendonitis etc..

SPJ-L   SPJ-L@PSUVM.BITNET
             General Journalism Discussion

SPORTMGT   SPORTMGT@UNBVM1.BITNET
             Sport Management

SPORTPC   SPORTPC@UNBVM1.BITNET
             Use of computers in sport

SPORTPSY   SPORTPSY@TEMPLEVM.BITNET
             Exercise and Sports Psychology

SPORTSOC   SPORTSOC@TEMPLEVM.BITNET
             Sociological aspects of sports discussion

SSREL-L   SSREL-L@UTKVM1.BITNET
             Scientific Study of Religion

STEALNET   STEALNET@MCGILL1.BITNET
             Electronic group to discuss the underground economy

STROKE-L   STROKE-L@UKCC.BITNET
             Stroke Discussion List

STUDEMP   STUDEMP@LISTSERV.ARIZONA.EDU
             Issues related to student employment.

STUTT-X   STUTT-X@ASUACAD.BITNET
             Stuttering – Communication Disorders

SUEARN-L   SUEARN-L@UBVM.BITNET
             Connecting the USSR to Internet digest

SUMINFO   SUMINFO@UNBVM1.BITNET
             Information Summit Discussion

SUPEUR   SUPEUR@FRMOP11.BITNET
             Supercomputing in Europe (user's group)

SWIM-L   SWIM-L@UAFSYSB.BITNET
             Discussion of all aspects of swimming

SWINE-L   SWINE-L@UMINN1.BITNET
             Journal of Swine Health and Production

SWL-L   SWL$L@CUVMB.BITNET
Short Wave Listener's List

T

TALLSHIP   TALLSHIP@VCCSCENT.BITNET
Sailing and Operation of Traditional Sailing Vessels

TBIRDS   TBIRDS@LISTSERV.ARIZONA.EDU
Discussion of International Business

TEC_PART   TEC_PART@SED.BITNET
Technology Partnership Sites – Discussions

TECHWR-L   TECHWR-L@OSUVM1.BITNET
Technical Writers List; for all Technical Communication issues

TESL-L   TESL-L@CUNYVM.BITNET
TESL-L: Teachers of English as a Second Language List

THEATRE   THEATRE@PUCC.BITNET
The Theatre Discussion List

THINK-L   THINK-L@UMSLVMA.BITNET
Critical Thinking Discussion List

THRDWRLD   THRDWRLD@GSUVM1.BITNET
Association of Third World Studies

TOBACTALK   TOBACTALK@LISTSERV.ARIZONA.EDU
A general discussion of tobacco and nicotine topics.

TOLKIEN   TOLKIEN@JHUVM.BITNET
J.R.R.Tolkien's readers

TOM-GILB   TOM-GILB@UCSFVM.BITNET
Discuss Principles of Software Engineering Management

TOW   TOW@NDSUVM1.BITNET
The Online World book information

TPOH-L   TPOH-L@MORGAN.UCS.MUN.CA
The Pursuit of Happiness Mailing List

TQMFSG   TQMFSG@UMAB.BITNET
Total Quality Management – Facilitator Support Group

TRAINING   TRAINING@INDYCMS.BITNET
IT Training Providers List

TRANSNET   TRANSNET@SJUVM.BITNET
TRANSNET Transportation Access Network

TRAVABLE   TRAVABLE@SJUVM.BITNET
TravAble Travel for the Disabled

TRAVEL-L   TRAVEL-L@TREARN.BITNET
Tourism Discussions..

TV-L   TV-L@TREARN.BITNET
TV Discussions

TVDIRECT   TVDIRECT@ARIZVM1.BITNET
Professional TV Directors and Producerss

U

UKERA-L   UKERA-L@UKCC.BITNET
UK's Institute on Educational Reform

UKGEG   UKGEG@UKCC.BITNET
GradCats: Discussion list for UK Graduate Students

V

VAMPYRES   VAMPYRES@GUVM.BITNET
Vampiric lore, fact and fiction.

VEGLIFE   VEGLIFE@VTVM1.BITNET
Vegetarian Lifestyle Discussion List

VETADM-L   VETADM-L@TAMVM1.TAMU.EDU
Veterinary hospital administration issues

VICTORIA   VICTORIA@IUBVM.BITNET
19th-Century British Culture & Society

VIDEOCON   VIDEOCON@ASUACAD.BITNET
Video Conferencing list

VINTAGVW   VINTAGVW@SJSUVM1.BITNET
Air-Cooled Volkswagen Discussion List

VIOLEN-L   VIOLEN-L@BRUSPVM.BITNET
Violence Discussion Forum

VIRUS-L   VIRUS-L@TRITU.BITNET
Open Discussion List About PC Viruses

VISION-L	VISION-L@PSUVM.BITNET Vision Research Group	
VPARTY	VPARTY@DARTCMS1.BITNET A virtual party with real people	
VPIEJ-L	VPIEJ-L@VTVM1.BITNET Electronic Journal Publishing List	
VRINST-L	VRINST-L@UWF.BITNET Virtual Reality – Implications for Instruction	
VTS-L	VTS-L@UOTTAWA.BITNET Virtual Trade Show Project	

W

WCENTR-L	WCENTR-L@MIZZOU1.BITNET Moderated Writing Center forum.	
WCETALL	WCETALL@UNMVMA.BITNET WICHE Western cooperative for educational telecommunications	
WDAMAGE	WDAMAGE@NDSUVM1.BITNET Wildlife Damage Management	
WEB-DEV	WEB-DEV@UMSLVMA.BITNET Web Development Team	
WELSH-L	WELSH-L@IRLEARN.BITNET Welsh Language Bulletin Board	
WEU	WEU@BLEKUL11.BITNET Western European Union (WEU) and Assembly	
WFW-L	WFW-L@UMDD.BITNET Microsoft *Windows* for Workgroups	
WINHLP-L	WINHLP-L@HUMBER.BITNET *Windows* Help Compiler (WINHELP) Discussion List	
WIN3-L	WIN3-L@UICVM.BITNET Microsoft *Windows* Version 3 Forum	
WIOLE-L	WIOLE-L@MIZZOU1.BITNET Writing Intensive Online Learning Environments	
WISE	WISE@UICVM.BITNET Workshop on Information Systems Economics	

WPCORP-L   WPCORP-L@UBVM.BITNET
           WordPerfect Corporation Products Discussion List

WRIT-C   WRIT-C@UMINN1.BITNET
           Discussion List for Writing Center Tutors

WRITE-L   WRITE-L@UALTAVM.BITNET
           WRITE-L is a list for writing groups in cyberspace.

WRITERS   WRITERS@MITVMA.BITNET
           Writers' topics

WRITING   WRITING@PSUVM.BITNET
           Fiction Writers Workshop Writing Discussion List

WS238-L   WS238-L@UBVM.BITNET
           Women, Work and Family in the 20th Century

WVUSTW-L   WVUSTW-L@WVNVM.BITNET
           Scientific and Technical Writing Group

WWII-L   WWII-L@UBVM.BITNET
           World War II Discussion List

WX-TALK   WX-TALK@UIUCVMD.BITNET
           WX-TALK General weather discussions and talk

W231   W231@INDYCMS.BITNET
           Research Methods Study Group

X

XCULT-L   XCULT-L@PSUVM.BITNET
           International Intercultural Newsletter

Y

YACHT-L   YACHT-L@HEARN.BITNET
           The Sailing and Amateur Boat Building List

Numbers

21ST-C-L   21ST-C-L@BRUFPB.BITNET
           Forum about the 21ST century discussions

4CWORK-L   4CWORK-L@INDYCMS.BITNET
           Workshop on Global Networks

Appendix II – Wines Online: a case history

An illustration of the diversity of products now being marketed through cyberspace is Virtual Vineyards, founded by Master Sommelier Peter Granoff.

Granoff was the thirteenth American to be admitted to the British Court of Master Sommeliers and currently serves as an Examiner and Board of Directors member for the Court's American Chapter. He explains how this first online vintner conceived a Web presence.

"I share with customers my experiences with each wine. I answer their wine-related questions and post the most useful questions and answers for all to see. I'm their personal wine steward – I give them the sort of attention they'd expect from a sommelier in a fine restaurant – so they can buy the best wine for that special dinner. With my guidance, they learn about the delights of fine wine, discover their own wine preferences and ultimately get more for their fine wine dollar.

"Wine advice on this level is usually only available to the patrons of a few exclusive wine shops in big cities, but the Internet now lets me offer it to people around the world."

You can see the emphasis on communicating valuable information to online browsers, with a follow-through Web structure to stimulate personal interactive contact with an expert.

Virtual Vineyards features wines from small, well-respected wineries and limited production bottlings from larger, widely-recognised vintners. Granoff personally selects each label in the portfolio, providing clients with a candid description of each wine, its winery and wine-maker.

Anyone can question him on the "Ask the Cork Dork" answer page, or access a tasting chart for each bottle. There are suggested food and wine combinations and recipes, and a glossary of wine terms.

In its first month Virtual Vineyards made most of its shipments by United Parcels Service within the United States, but there were also international orders, including shipments to Japan, Europe and South Africa.

When Web surfers arrive at the Virtual Vineyards home page they see a menu of places to visit. There is a Quick Tour, which covers Internet security and privacy, how to order, shipping details, getting advice, etc. A What's New section is always important here to encourage repeat visits, and this one highlights additions to the wine selection, new food and wine pairing suggestions and developments at Virtual Vineyards.

In the Wine List section., wines are grouped by winery, variety, special offers, sampler packages, choice under $10, and other categories. Granoff gives his personal opinion and supplies a tasting chart that profiles the wine's intensity of flavour, body, acidity, tannin, oak, complexity and level of dryness or sweetness. There are hypertext links to his personal biography, as well as to the hard factual information. The Featured Wineries section provides insight into the idiosyncrasies and personalities behind the wines, with more hypertext links to the owners and wine makers at each winery featured.

Interactivity fostering a sense of involvement is important, and browsers find this in the Opinions and Moderated Forum section. They can print out a recipe and buy the matching bottle of wine, express their views, respond to the opinions of others, or ask Peter Granoff about anything related to wine.

Ordering wine is easy interactive with just a few keystrokes. Customers create a wine shopping list while browsing Virtual Vineyards, then make final decisions when they place an order. The online order form records the kind of wine, number of bottles, the shipping address and type of delivery preferred.

Virtual Vineyards joined with Netscape Communications and Wells Fargo Bank to enable customers to make secure credit card payments over the Internet. The Netscape Commerce Server lets users of *Netscape Navigator* and other Secure Sockets Layer-enable browsers to establish a secure connection for sending payment information. Initially, users of other browsers had to provide credit card information over a toll free phone number, but Virtual Vineyards was also adopting CyberCash Inc.'s Secure Internet Payment Service to permit browser independent secure payment transactions.

You can visit and see how it all comes together at **http://www.virtualvin.com**.

Appendix III – Product protection and order delivery system on the Web

A pioneering way of marketing products on the Web and protecting them until payment has been made has been developed by SoftLock Services and the Web site *Downtown Anywhere*.

The opening page has this excellent example of a simple, effective graphic that will not delay Web browsers by loading slowly on to their systems.

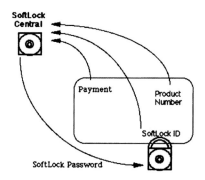

Figure III.1 Softlock system diagram

Once at *Downtown Anywhere* – **http://www.awa.com** on the Web – you can hypertext through to a range of products and services, including the Paperless Publishing Institute, the Marketplace for Ideas, and SoftLock Services for details of its encryption and password protection. The diagram shows how this works. A buyer downloads a locked file, which might typically be an ebook, a software program, or a database of information. He then contacts SoftLock Central by telephone or email with the product number, makes payment by credit card and then receives a unique password that will unlock the contents of that file on his system alone.

There are more details in the following print-out of part of the HTML file used to create this Web site, reproduced here to illustrate how tag codes are added to text to create headings, bold type, paragraphs and hypertext and graphical links.

```
<TITLE>moreonsl.html</TITLE>
<H1>More Info on SoftLock Services</H1>
<P>The business of SoftLock Services rests on three foundations:
<P>SoftLock's (patent pending) technology: product- and machine-
   specific IDs can create a 'lock' which requires a unique and
   unpredictable password available from SoftLock's central
   password 'dispensaries'.
<P>A suite of commercial services, to make life easier for
   consumers and producers of SoftLocked products.
<P>A philosophy: digital products should be virtually free until
   their value to the user is clear. Then, the creator of the
   product should be compensated fairly.
<P>In keeping with this philosophy, our software tools are
   available to potential developers at cost, in order to create
   the market for our reasonably priced Services. By the same
   token, our client's products can be made available at nominal
   cost to Users, who will (hopefully) find them useful when
   locked, and invaluable when unlocked. Users can "try before
   they buy" and then purchase passwords to instantly unlock any
   and all advanced features.
<P>SoftLock's essential Service (and the one for which we take a
   modest commission) is the quick and convenient sale of
   Passwords and other products, round the clock, and around the
   world. Payment can be tendered on-line via credit card, or via
   SoftLock Vouchers through a variety of convenient channels. We
   provide information producers with sales, distribution,
   physical fulfillment and customer registration services and a
   variety of other support services, as well as prompt and
   accurate accounting and payment. We can provide these services
   to our Clients for far less than it would cost them to do them
   it themselves.
<P>SoftLock Services thus creates a whole new venue for the sale
   and distribution of freely copyable information. We do not
   pretend to know how our tools and services will best be
   exploited, but we are confident that we are in a position to
   help our clients and their customers find out.
<P>Browse forward to <a href="fullfill.html">Fulfillment
   Services</a>
<P>Browse back to <a href="copyrigh.html">Copyright Notices</a>
<P>Return to <a href="slhome.html">SoftLock Services Home
   Page</a>
```

Appendix IV – Getting connected in the UK

The range of choices – and prices – to get on to the Internet to do business varies enormously. You may get very little for a comparative lot of money, or receive excellent value and service for a small outlay. Competition between service providers is hotting up, so it pays to shop around for the latest best offers, check out the quality of service with other users, and negotiate hard if you are likely to be a substantial account.

Look out particularly for technical developments and business alliances and strategies that meet your particular needs. For example, one of the most significant developments during 1995 was when PIPEX and Mercury Communications announced they would provide Internet users throughout most of the UK with local dialup access using a network of virtual 'Points of Presence', or POPs. This scheme aims to overcome the perennial problem of traffic jams on the information superhighways, either because the demand from subscibers has outstripped the ability of service providers to connect them at peak times, or because of congestion in the physical capacity of the telecommunications networks.

The PIPEX/Mercury deal aims to offer over 80% of the UK population high speed local call access to the Internet. You use it via either PIPEX resellers or the company's own PIPEX Dial Internet service. There is a commitment to add physical or virtual POPs ahead of expanding demand for local call access to what is claimed to be the biggest and fastest commercial Internet backbone in Europe. Calls are intelligently re-routed if any part of the network is not available in a particular location, but the billing stays at local call rates. You can get more information from the Web pages at **http://worldserver.pipex.com/**

Demon Internet Ltd

Demon Internet claim to be the largest providers of dial up Internet access in Europe. All their connection schemes provide a true direct connection to the Internet, multiple mailboxes and Usenet news. Your computer must run PPP or SLIP software (and a TCP/IP stack). If you do not have these programs, Demon can supply shareware versions. The voice numbers for more information are+44 (0) 181-371 1234 in London, and+44 (0) 131-552 0344 in Edinburgh, with a help line at+44 (0) 181-371 1010. The support email address is **internet@demon.net** and for sales **sales@demon.net**. The latest version of Demon's very comprehensive information document is available by FTP from **ftp.demon.co.uk:/pub/doc/Services.txt**.

The minimum subscription period is one month, with some options requiring an annual commitment. The PoPs are already extensive and being increased steadily, so expect access with a local call in most cities. The typical setup fee is £12.50, and a choice of payment plans includes a fixed price of £120 annually, or £10 per month. (All prices exclude VAT.) Payment for home users can be made monthly in advance by Access or Visa credit cards. Companies are asked to pay annually in advance and receive a formal VAT invoice. There is a refund for any whole months outstanding when an annual subscription is cancelled.

Standard Dial-up users have full email services; while business users have the option of a Mail Forwarding Extension, which is useful in such situations as forwarding messages around an internal network. There is considerable flexibility in chosing your email address, so that you can have the corporate or professional image benefits of your own domain name. If you are looking to set up a busy corporate account, ask for the comprehensive leased line information pack. (A text version is also available from **ftp.demon.co.uk:/pub/doc/Llinfo.txt**.) International travellers should ask about the POP3 service which ensures that you can get your email wherever you can access the Internet. (More details from **ftp.demon.co.uk:/pub/doc/POP3.txt**.)

For World Wide Web activities you can rent space on the Demon server from £25 per 5Mb monthly. Design and conversion services are available – details from **ftp.demon.co.uk:/pub/doc/WWW.txt**. Demon offers extensive technical and consultancy services to create software or perform Internet installations, configuration and training. But they are not cheap, with charges from £500 per day or from £70 per hour (including travelling). In May 1995, Demon claimed over 90% of the then current user base in the UK, resulting from getting into the market early and offering a low cost but powerful service. It is facing more serious competition these days, but as the established market leader is worth checking out first.

EUnet GB

EUnet GB is the UK arm of the EUnet network, with over 13,000 corporate users in 33 countries. It has a complete range of Internet services for businesses, but does not support home users. It has WWW servers from which clients can run their own pages, and provides commercial domain names and Multiple Class C addresses at no charge.

The charges are more complex than for Demon and are billed quarterly in advance. Ensure that you know exactly what you will want to do so that you can compare like with like, particularly for international traffic for which there are various charges passed on. EUnet GB runs the Primary DNS Server for commercial name space in the uk (i.e. **.co.uk** names). There are no charges for registering such domain names, but other organisations needing **.ac.uk** and **.org.uk** names incur a registration charge of £175.

To find out more, contact EUnet GB by voice phone at+44 (0) 1227 266466, fax+44 (0) 1227 266477 or email to **sales@Britain.EU.net**.

EUnet Traveller enables staff on the move to use the Internet from any computer with a modem and appropriate software in twelve European countries: Austria, Belgium, Finland, France, Germany, Hungary, Ireland, Italy, The Netherlands, Norway, Switzerland, and the United Kingdom. More information on this from **traveller@eu.net**

EUnet has four options for organisations wishing to run Web pages' on the Internet. These are a leased line connection to your location, storage space on EUnet's machines located on EUnet's Internet backbone, a server dedicated to your pages located on EUnet's internet backbone, or your own machine housed at EUnet's premises. There are no charges for the volume of traffic generated, but the set-up and ongoing costs need to be balanced carefully against your actual planned usage to evaluate the best deal.

The PC User Group and WinNET

Interesting low-cost options – particularly for email – are available through the The PC User Group, which has 10,000 members and has provided Internet services in the UK since 1988. It has two main options – a BBS style service offering Internet newsgroups and email, and a special WinNET service that automates your computer to call and download your news and mail messages so that you can read and reply to them fully offline.

Details about WinNET can be obtained by emailing to **request@win-uk.net**, by downloading the *Windows* program from the BBS (login winnet,no password) at+44 (0) 181 723 7300 or+44 (0) 181 863 6646, via anonymous FTP from **ftp.ibmpcug.co.uk:/pub/WinNET**, or Web server at **http:// www.ibmpcug.co.uk**.

The WinNET (UK) Mail software is provided free, with access to the Internet and Usenet networks and other usage billed on a connect time basis. There is a monthly minimum of £6.75 plus VAT, including 130 minutes of connect time. Additional connect time is charged at £1.50 per hour.

Because WinNET provides full offline handling of email and news, phone costs can be reduced substantially. Most WinNet users average monthly costs of under £8.75 if they make local off peak calls, or under £10.00 with a mix of peak and off peak local calls. The typical monthly cost if a mix of day and evening long distance calls are required is likely to be around £15.00.

Web home pages start at 512k for £2.00 per month, with additional storage for Web pages and public ftp space starting at £4.00 per month per Mb. One off options include your own domain name for email at £100.00, for the Web (including simple form access with simple scripts) £150.00, and more complex scripts by arrangement.

The standard Web space option can be used for individual or company details and includes a login account on the Group's Web server, your own ftp area for distribution of programs, your name on the local users home page and easy access to uploading your web pages via FTP. For this there is an annual charge based on £48 per Mb per month.

There are annual fees payable in advance which include Site UUCP Mail for £250.00 and mail & news for £400.00, both including domain registration. It pays to join the PC Users Group, as there is a 20% discount for Corporate Members. Membership costs £39.95 (inc VAT) for Personal Membership and £150+ VAT for Corporate Membership.

The fee structure is difficult to compare with other service providers because there are a number of variables, including additional benefits such as insurance schemes and discounts on hardware and software. Best initially to call+44 (0) 181 863 1191 and ask for the latest information pack, including a back issue of the Group's Connectivity magazine.

GreenNet Global computer communications network

GreenNet is a possibility for the environmentally conscious, and it can be practical and low cost for some users. It is part of the only global computer network designed specifically for environmental, peace and human rights groups.

GreenNet belongs to the Association for Progressive Communications. Its users have access to all users and facilities of the other members: NordNet (Sweden), Ecuanex (Ecuador), ComLink (Germany), Chasque (Uruguay), GlasNet (Russia), PeaceNet, EcoNet, HomoeoNet, ConflictNet (USA), Web (Canada), Alternex (Brazil), Pegasus (Australia), Wamani (Argentina), SangoNet (South Africa), Histria (Slovenia) and Nicarao (Nicaragua). There are also very close working relationships with other networks, such as FIDO in Africa, Asia, the Pacific, and Eastern Europe.

The APC serves organisations in over 90 countries, and email can be exchanged with GeoNet, InterNet, Poptel, HomeoNet, the Music Network, Janet, Bitnet, Telecom Gold, FIDO, and most other academic or commercial networks. Telexes and faxes can be sent, but not received. There is a £15 registration fee for individual or non-commercial users (£5 discount rate for low income; £30 for commercial/public sector) and a monthly charge of £5 (£10 commercial) and connect time costs of 4p or 6p per minute plus phone charges (10p per minute commercial.) GreenNet charges can mount up for commercial users, but if your online needs are a good match to its specific services and rates, then membership would be appropriate, perhaps in addition to another service provider.

Over 15,000 groups and individuals are using the APC Networks, includingthe following: Action Aid, ADIU, Aga Kahn Foundation, BASIC, CND, Central America Resources Network, Christic Institute, Climate Research Unit (Norwich), CRIES (Nicaragua), Dept. of Environment (UK), FoR, Findhorn, Finnish Peace Union, FoE, Green Party (UK), Greenpeace, Intermediate Technology Development Group, Int'l Peace Bureau, Int'l Institute for Environment and Development, Inter Press Service, Media Transcription Service, Nat'l Wildlife Fed., NATTA, Nat'l Peace Council, NFIP support groups, Oxfam, Physicians for Social Responsibility, Quaker Peace & Service, Rainforest Info Ctr., SANE/Freeze, Sierra Club, Southscan, Survival Intl., Swedish Peace & Arbitration Soc., UNA, VERTIC, Vlaamse Vredesuniversiteit, War Resisters International, WILPF, WISE, and the Worldwide Fund for Nature.

Call for more information to+44 (0) 171 713 1941, or email to
support@gn.apc.org. CONNECT's main line is +44 (0) 181 863 6646 on
V32bis, V42bis [14400 and below].

A glossary to cyberspace

Most phrases likely to be new to online neophytes are explained as we go along, but here is a quick guide to some of the most useful terms describing online features.

bandwidth is one of the Net's most serious deficiencies – there is not enough of it. Bandwidth measures the volume of information that can be passed along a communications link, and too many of the Information Superhighways are overloaded with traffic because there is insufficient bandwidth.

baud and **bps** (bits per second) are the units of measurement of the speed with which data can be transmitted through a modem. You need a minimum 9,600 bps and preferably a 14,400 bps or faster modem for Internet connections.

BBS is the standard abbreviation for a bulletin board system, a cyberspace entity which may be just a single PC at the end of a telephone line, or a major commercial activity with hundreds of lines, sophisticated features, and access to the Net.

browsers are programs such as *Mosaic* that enable you to move around the World Wide Web by displaying text and graphics, and creating hypertext connections.

DOS stands for Disk Operating System, the software programming that provides the basis for the operation of the vast majority of personal computers.

email describes electronically transmitted messages, the most popular online facility. You type a message and send it by modem to an email address, with automatic programs directing it to its destination over the networks it must traverse to get there. It is one of the wonders of the Internet that this happens so efficiently and without any charge except what you pay as a subscription to your Internet service provider.

encryption is a way of encoding messages and data to try to prevent unauthorised access to them.

FAQ – short for frequently asked questions – describes the questions brought together in a document on the Net that may, for example, summarise the rules and topics discussed in a newsgroup.

firewall describes hardware and software combinations that form a one-way barrier between a private computer or network and the public environment of the Internet. You probably shelter behind a firewall formed by the protective measures adopted by your Internet service provider.

flaming is the sending of insulting messages from others online who feel you have offended them, usually by not following the unwritten rules of Internet etiquette, e.g. inconsiderate junk email or overt commercialism in special interest groups.

hackers are knowledgeable computing enthusiasts. The term is being mis-used to describe cyberspace vandals who disseminate viruses and try to break into other people's systems.

Internet is the global network of networks. It operates largely by informal agree-ment between primary networks which form the Net's backbone, each of them having thousands, or tens of thousands, of smaller networks linking to them.

host is a computer with full Internet access, which may also describe a node or server.

home page is the opening screen or screens at a Web site which welcome you and guide you to the facilities on offer.

HTML is the HyperText Mark-up Language that creates the structure of pages and documents on the Web.

hypertext aescribes one or many documents in which links are created to provide routes to related or supplementary information.

Macintosh describes the proprietary Apple hardware and software systems, the second most popular personal computing format after DOS/*Windows* sys-tems.

PCs are personal computers generally, but the term is often applied to distin-guish the majority of PCs running under the DOS/*Windows* systems from Macintosh systems.

newsgroups are tens of thousands of discussion groups operating on Usenet.

posting is when you send a message – a post – to a public area online.

real-time is when something takes place live, as in a direct communication between two people or a forum discussion.

server describes a computer or program that provides facilities to other computers, which are its clients. A provider of Internet services, such as Delphi, is a server and those who subscribe to it are its clients.

smileys are standard text characters combined and read sideways to express emotions in messages – such as :-) for pleasure, and :-(for sadness.

snail mail requires an envelope and a stamp, and usually costs much more and takes far longer than email.

Telnet is a way to log in to other computers and use their facilities.

URL is an abbreviation for Uniform Resource Locator pointing to a specific resource online, i.e. an address.

VAN is a Value Added Network, like CompuServe. Instead of just being a routing from one place to another, e.g. to get your computer connected to the Web, a VAN is a commercial network providing valuable services within its own environment.

Webmaster is what you may become after reading this – someone who controls a site or collection of pages on the Web.

Windows is a propriety software system produced by the Microsoft company which makes PCs easier to use by providing GUIs – graphical user interfaces – in the form of picture icons which can be clicked on with the mouse pointer instead of having to type in commands. It is the world's most popular way of using personal computers.

World Wide Web – the Web – is the fastest-growing and commercially most important part of the Internet. A giant hypertext system, it is a way of publishing and browsing easily through an immensely complex web of online words and pictures.

T - #0030 - 311024 - C0 - 234/234/13 - PB - 9780851423555 - Gloss Lamination